A SENSE
OF PLACE

A
SENSE
OF
PLACE

Listening to Americans

DAVID LAMB

TIMES BOOKS

RANDOM HOUSE

Grateful acknowledgment is made to the Los Angeles Times for
permission to reprint previously published material, some of which
appears in this book in a slightly different form.

Grateful acknowledgment is made to the following for permission to
reprint previously published material:

Arc Music Corporation: Excerpt from "The Promised Land" by
Chuck Berry. Copyright © 1964 (renewed) by Arc Music
Corporation. All rights reserved. Reprinted by permission.

John C. Dofflemeyer: Excerpt from "'Til I Depart" from Dry Creek
Rhymes by John C. Dofflemeyer, published by Dry Crik Press.
Copyright © 1989 by John C. Dofflemeyer. Reprinted by permission
of John C. Dofflemeyer.

Londontown Music and Edwin H. Morris & Company: Excerpt
from "(Get Your Kicks On) Route 66!" by Bobby Troup. Copyright
© 1946 by Edwin H. Morris & Company. Rights throughout the
world excluding the United States are controlled by Edwin H. Morris
& Company. Reprinted by permission of Londontown Music and
Edwin H. Morris & Company

Library of Congress Cataloging-in-Publication Data
Lamb, David.
A sense of place : listening to Americans / David Lamb.
p.   cm.
ISBN 0-8129-2159-3
1. United States—Civilization—1970–   2. United States—Social
conditions—1980–   3. National characteristics, American.
I. Title.
E169.12.L33 1993
973.92—dc20 92-50554

Designed by Ann Terrell Design.

Manufactured in the United States of America

9 8 7 6 5 4 3 2
First Edition

For Bill Thomas and John Foley
In Memoriam Russell G. Lynch
Without you, I still might be writing obits

Contents

Introduction   3

THE EMPTY QUARTER   9

   Lewis and Clark Revisited   11
   Big Sky, Big Dreams   31
   The Last Frontier   51
   Buffalo Commons   67
   Greyhound Romance   80

THE GOOD LIFE   91

   The World's Best Job   93
   The Gates of Eden   107
   Fifteen Minutes   120
   Without Fear or Favor   140
   Nowhere to Run   152

A VANISHING WORLD   161

   Home on the Range   163
   Over the Rainbow   186
   King Coal   205
   The Road Less Traveled   213

LESSONS OF HISTORY   227

   The Last of the Nez Percé   229
   Fourteen Forgotten Men   241
   Twilight of the Aleuts   253
   Putting People First   263
   Joker in the Deck   275

Acknowledgments   289

A SENSE
OF PLACE

Introduction

Ihave been wandering the country, more often than
not on back roads, since the early 1970s for the *Los
Angeles Times* and still cannot adequately answer,
What is America? or Who are the Americans? Our country
and our people are too diverse to abide easy definition.
America is more about the quality of an idea than it is
about a place. It is, in the ideal, about being young and
confident, finding new frontiers, having the freedom to live
and speak and move as one chooses. "For me, more than
anything else, I guess," Evan Armstrong said the day he
and his wife took the oath of citizenship at the courthouse
in Thief River Falls, Minnesota, "America has meant the
opportunity to grow."

France is a civilization and England is a people, but
what is America? In a geographic sense, America isn't even
a singular place; it's two continents, North and South, yet
unlike, say, Canadians or Mexicans, we call ourselves
Americans as though we had laid claim to everything from
Barrow, Alaska, to Tierra del Fuego, Argentina. But when
you travel abroad and tell inquirers you are an American,
they know exactly what you mean. Your skin could be of
any color, your religion of any persuasion, your financial
means of either extreme, but . . . "Ah, yes, *American,*"

cabdrivers used to say when I lived in Egypt, "America a very good country."

The French traveler Alexis de Tocqueville wrote after his journey through the United States in 1831–32: "The time will therefore come when one hundred and fifty million men will be living in North America, equal in condition, all belonging to one family, owing their origin to the same cause, and preserving the same civilization, the same language, the same religion, the same habits, the same manners, and imbued with the same opinions, propagated under the same forms. The rest is uncertain, but this is certain; and it is a fact new to the world, a fact that the imagination strives in vain to grasp."

Could that be us he was talking about? What Tocqueville didn't foresee was that our commonality would be our differences, not our similarities. Americans would be bound not by language or color or opinions but by sharing a dream and a universal sense of place. America, F. Scott Fitzgerald said, is "a willingness of the heart," and that says it pretty well. Though pop cynics would have us believe such sentiments are antiquated these days, the strength of the American character remains a striking and provable thing. I have seen it on the battlefields of Vietnam and the Middle East, in the prairie towns of the Dakotas and along the long, lonely byways that cut through the heartland of a great nation. From all these places I came away convinced that, however wrenching our problems, the America of the 1990s is an achievement to be celebrated, not lamented.

I may well be out of sync with common sentiment, but the pessimism I hear expressed when learned people gather to discuss our country mystifies me. The self-indulgence of the sixties and the trickle-down indifference of the eighties are behind us, and what the doomsayers tend to ignore are the Americans themselves. I did not find in my travels a defeated people looking backward. Most of the Americans I met had rolled up their sleeves and gotten on with life. They accepted any honorable man as a neighbor and knew that the best social program was a good job. It wasn't very glamorous stuff, and I doubt that Oprah would have booked many of them, but still, they always left me heartened and reminded me that there was a lot to feel good about in America.

Coming home from a trip, I often felt the America I read about and the one I had seen were two different places—the former teetering on the brink, the latter muddling along, as we always do, with hopes of making this a better place. I heard anxiety expressed about our problems but surprisingly little cynicism (except when the subject was political leadership) about our future. An honest day's labor, decency and a faith in tomorrow are no less in vogue than they had been a hundred years ago. Though we may speak many languages—ninety in the Los Angeles Unified School District alone—the American personality remains distinct, shaped by the persuasion of opportunity and, yes, sacrifice. "Work seems to very slowly, but steadily, improve," John Laban, a B-52 pilot during the Vietnam War and now an underemployed Maine forester, wrote me not long ago. "One of the nice things about starting from scratch is that whatever does come along seems like a bonus. Gets you back to basics, and I am silly enough to think that's good."

Laban lives by pride, with his dreams detained, not lost, and I do not find his attitude untypical. We remain a young nation, though we are no longer youthful. Our exuberance has been tempered by caution. In countless conversations from Maine to Alaska, Americans spoke of a bittersweet longing for the past, as though no one knew quite what to make of the social and economic upheavals that have swept across the land. "I'll tell you, this was some town awhile back," a miner said one night at the bar of the Elks Lodge in Sheridan, Wyoming. "You could walk down Main Street and, all in a block and a half, you could buy a saddle, a Pendleton shift, the best fillet you ever tasted. Outside of First Avenue over in Billings [Montana], Main Street in Sheridan was as fine a place as a man'd ever want to go." Yet I don't think the miner or anyone else I met meant they wanted to turn back the clock. They were talking about community and holding on to all that is good and searching for what one New England mill worker calls "the comfort zone" of life.

It had been a long time since I had watched Johnny Carson regularly, but when he left our living rooms in the spring of 1992, I, like millions of Americans, stayed up late for his final shows and found myself saddened that time had claimed another icon. Carson had started on *The Tonight Show* before there was a war in Vietnam and ended after our troops had come home from war in the Persian Gulf. During his nightly visits with us, the Peace Corps had been born and the Soviet Union had disintegrated. John Kennedy had lived and died. The Washington Senators had become the Texas Rangers and Rhodesia had given way to Zimbabwe. Nothing was as it had been—except for Johnny. It was reassuring to know he was there, connecting us to the past, and as we showered him with fond attention before the curtain closed, I wondered whether we were saying good-bye to Johnny Carson, or to ourselves.

Certainly entering the last decade of the twentieth century has given us cause for nostalgia. We went to the polls to choose between two men for President: One likened himself to Harry S Truman (but had voted for Thomas Dewey in 1948); the other had smoked marijuana (but hadn't inhaled). Our prisons are full, our welfare ranks swollen, our budget deficit out of control. If you watch television in almost any major city, you would swear Armageddon is upon us. Life is all 911 calls, and in an era of "infotainment," fact and fiction have become mysteriously intertwined. We talk about "the good old days" without defining what they were. Yes, life was simpler then, but was it better? Do we really want to eat at soda fountains again and travel west at 40 mph on Route 66? Probably not, except in the recesses of our selective memories. Americans are not a people who take their guidance from the past. We push ahead and seldom look back, and our collective national memory is short. We crow in triumph when we prove we are mighty but seem unwilling to take credit for our simple accomplishments in being the most tolerant, generous, prosperous and multicultural society on earth.

From my earliest days as a journalist, I have been drawn not to the cities or to the rich and powerful, but to the towns and ranches and factories where everyday Americans are living everyday lives. I feel at ease with these people. They have taught me about courage and stamina and tradition. From them I have learned the meaning of place—where you belong and not necessarily where you are. When I asked Red Garretson, Wyoming's chief brand inspector, why he wore the working clothes of the range—Stetson, jeans and boots—and kept his .45 revolver tucked out of sight in his Chevy pickup, he explained: "In these parts, you knock on a man's door wearing a uniform and carrying a gun, and, oh, sure, he'll give you respect, but you'll do your talking on his doorstep. You won't get invited in to eat his wife's pie at the kitchen table and you won't really find out what's going on like you have to in this job." In that brief reply Garretson defined, I think, the essence of *place* as eloquently as a poet.

The journeys in the pages that follow span twenty years, though most were made in the late 1980s and early 1990s; two profiles—that of Hurricane Bob Hazle and Route 66—appeared in altered form in a previous book of mine. My intent is not to dwell on political issues or recite a litany of national problems. Rather, I look on *A Sense of Place* as a deliberately selective and personalized portrait of America and some of her people. This is a book about what happens to the pioneer spirit when the last frontier has been settled. If it makes a small contribution toward the continuing examination of who Americans are and what makes us different, if in some out-of-the-way place I have managed to capture the heroism of everyday life, then my reward will be a generous one.

THE EMPTY
QUARTER

✦✦✦

Lewis and Clark Revisited

Flying west out of Denver, on United's nighttime flight to The Coast, I always had the feeling I was back in Arabia. I'd peer out the window and, seven miles down, see only a dark, formless expanse that stretched everywhere and went nowhere. From time to time the blackness would give way to the flicker of clustered lights on the ground, as if from a Bedouin encampment, then the land would slip back into the isolation of the night, and for long distances whatever lay below remained cloaked in ebony, as seemingly featureless and tenantless as a desert. I came to think of this section of America as our Empty Quarter, and whenever I went over it or through it, I was struck by how much room to roam Americans still have. We think of ourselves as a people jammed into cities, beset by unimaginable problems, yet in Montana and Idaho and a good many other places where life still works pretty well, you can drive for hours and encounter not much more than a few sleepy towns and a handful of passing strangers. What brought settlers to these unpeopled lands years ago was opportunity. What keeps them there is quality of life-style—a concept that is uniquely American with its implication of expectation and well-being.

Being a shameless romantic, I have been drawn back to the Empty Quarter time and again, because I find there both the myths and the realities that have fired our imaginations since Lewis and Clark set forth into the West nearly two centuries ago. They made distance irrelevant and space the magnet for a westering, restive people. Even as our cities fill and spill over, we know that somewhere out there, beyond the next ridgeline, is an uncluttered, uncharted place where life is better. When we are betrayed by our dreams, we can simply cut our roots and move on. Space has been our great safety valve. No horizon is out of reach. Our abundance of land and our pursuit of new horizons has made us the most mobile, and probably restless, society on earth. We move with purpose and no purpose. Sometimes we move just to move.

When I was discharged from the army in 1964, I thought nothing of loading up my battered Mercury in Boston with my few possessions and heading west in search of a job and a career. My only destination was an imprecise one—the West—yet spiritually I could imagine no address that was more exact. I knew not a soul beyond Buffalo. It never occurred to me I was taking a risk or might fail. I drove with desperation through the nights, filled with coffee and NoDoz pills, and don't know now why I was hurrying. Nothing and no one awaited me, yet the adventure wasn't in being there; it was in getting there. Torrents of rain pelted the Merc as I sped through the Iowa darkness on a two-lane road. I slowed and strained to make out the shadowy hulks of eighteen-wheelers ahead. Boston lay a hard day's drive behind me. I had bade my parents good-bye, raised a farewell beer with friends. There was no turning back. I was drunk with exhilaration and lonely enough to cry.

My car died in Reno, and I reached Las Vegas on the Greyhound, carrying a pair of suitcases and my last twenty-dollar bill. Within an hour I had hired on as a police reporter at the *Review-Journal* for ninety dollars a week. If I ever hit a hundred, I knew I would have it made. The paper's city editor—a former chorus-line show girl—told me one day I was different from other easterners the paper had hired, sight unseen. "They seem to be always complaining, like they wished they were back in Boston or wherever. But you act like you really like it here." I felt flattered—and bewildered that anyone would grouch about a land where you felt so free, where you could shout your name in a desert canyon and hear the echo come rolling back.

Nevada is a good place to learn about space. Outside of Las Vegas, Reno and Carson City, it is empty. The people who have sunk roots there hear their own drummer's beat and aren't much concerned with what your father does or what school you went to. The yesterdays concern them not at all. "Of course, your normal person doesn't live in Goldfield," the wife of a prospector in the near–ghost town said. "This is a town of 'strange-os,' like myself. We've got brilliant people—poets, mathematicians, inventors—and they look like bums. You see an old scuzzbag on the street and you have to remind yourself that he's smarter than I ever hope to be in my life. It took me awhile to get used to that."

Space. It's where our individualism finds expression. It's what we escape to, and sometimes from. In 1786, nineteen years before Lewis and Clark were dispatched into the unknown West, Thomas Jefferson noted that parts of the United States had already attained·a density of ten persons to the square mile, and "whenever we reach that, the inhabitants become uneasy, as too much compressed, and go off in great numbers to search for vacant country." The population center of the United States was at Chestertown, Maryland, when Jefferson made his observation. Today it's at Steelville, Missouri, pushing southwest, and the density is seventy people per square mile (and 9,883 in Washington, D.C., the nation's "murder capital").

I don't remember studying the Lewis and Clark Expedition as a schoolboy in Boston, though surely I did. But sometime after having helped nudge the population center westward and taking up residency in Nevada, then Colorado and California, I started reading the explorers' journals. I would mark their progress on an old road map, sometimes at an utter loss trying to match description with position. My penciled x's left behind a trail of towns like Three Forks, Montana, and Orofino, Idaho, and The Dalles, Oregon, that sang with the romance of the untraveled road. They became my road map through the Empty Quarter and were the reason why, many years later, I found myself in St. Louis one breathless August day, looking for the footsteps of Lewis and Clark.

Unlike Columbus, who did not know where he was going when he set sail from Spain some three hundred years earlier, Meriwether Lewis and William Clark had a precise target. "The discoverer simply uncovers," said historian Daniel Boorstin, "the explorer opens." Lewis and

Clark did both. They transformed the West from a direction to a destination. Technology put Americans on the moon, but boldness got them to the West. Their expedition came to symbolize all the images of ourselves we hold dear—courage, endurance, self-reliance, the strength of conquest against overwhelming odds—and losing myself for a time along their trail seemed the perfect way to start an American journey.

Although he had spent time in France, President Jefferson had never been west of Staunton, Virginia, when he conceived his plan to find a Northwest Passage that would open trade routes to Asia and lead to an independent Republic of Oregon, populated by Americans. To quiet Federalist objections, he disguised his proposal in a confidential message to Congress in January 1803 as a "literary pursuit" designed to gain geographic and scientific knowledge of a region once ruled by Napoleon. Congress grumbled that the initial expenditure for the expedition—$2,500—was exorbitant. Napoleon's dream of a French North America had been dashed by his army's defeat in Santo Domingo, and for $15 million—or three cents an acre—he sold to Jefferson's government the American West. The Louisiana Purchase comprised all or part of thirteen states and 885,000 square miles of mountains, valleys, prairies, rivers and ports. The Senate ratified the deal in October 1803. "This accession of territory," Napoleon predicted, "strengthens forever the power of the United States and I have just given to England a maritime rival that sooner or later will humble her pride."

Jefferson appointed his personal secretary, twenty-eight-year-old Meriwether Lewis, to lead the Corps of

Discovery. Lewis in turn asked his friend and former commanding officer, William Clark, thirty-two, to be coleader and to assemble a group of outdoorsmen "capable of bearing bodily fatigue in a pretty considerable degree." The discovery of a river route to the Pacific was to be their principal objective; not until they struggled over the Rocky and Bitterroot mountains, descended into Idaho and crossed through what are now eleven states did they learn there wasn't one.

The concept of Manifest Destiny that carried Lewis and Clark to the Pacific was an intoxicating one that still shapes the way we view our worldly role. Just as it was our destiny to forge one country from coast to coast, so was it our destiny to rebuild Europe after the Second World War, to save Vietnam from Communism, to influence the future of the Third World with grants and guns. Ostensibly benevolent and undeniably imperialist, Manifest Destiny holds that Anglo-Saxons are endowed with innate superiority and that they have been chosen to speed up history.

St. Louis, a fur-trading post in Lewis and Clark's time, held no allure for me, and I drove out of town quickly, past Gateway Arch and over the McKinley Bridge. I turned up Route 3, a little-used road in Illinois that leads to the banks of the Missouri River. The campsite where the expedition wintered in 1803–4 is submerged now, claimed by the river's shifting currents, but a granite monument commemorates the site. Clark wrote on May 14, 1804: "I Set out at 4 oClock P.M., in the presence of many of the neighbouring inhabitants, and proceeded on under a jentle brease up the Missouri." Afternoon thunderclouds hung overhead. There was no one else around, and I sat down at a picnic table and unwrapped a Big Mac and a cup of fries I had bought down the road. Nearby, piled against a bench, were stacks of uncollected trash bags, and on the door of the wooden rest room was scrawled, "I'm glad AIDS kills fags!" The monument itself was chipped and scarred, its eleven narrative plaques largely illegible, and across its base someone had painted the words "Trust Jesus." I wondered if a few generations from now historians would examine graffiti as the literature of the twentieth century.

Just south of the monument at Camp Wood, Interstate 270 cuts across the Missouri River and connects with the Mark Twain Expressway, heading west to St. Charles (population 40,000), Missouri's oldest city. The trip took me forty minutes, including a stop at the visitors' center on the Illinois–Missouri border to ask directions. The Corps of Discovery, following the river and having no one to tell them where they were going, needed two days. St. Charles had 450 inhabitants, mostly French and Indians, in 1804, and a number of them turned out to watch the party come ashore. The people, Clark wrote, appeared "poor, polite and harmonious." A few miles away, on Femme Osage Creek, Daniel Boone, then seventy years old, his eyesight failing, was building what was to be his last home.

No sooner had the expedition pulled its three boats onto the shore than two privates, William Werner and Hugh Hall, took off without permission to explore the local taverns. I followed their lead and wandered into Lewis and Clark's Cafe on Main Street for a cold beer. The man next to me was a mechanic from Ohio, and each summer, he said, he spent a week's vacation retracking a section of the Lewis and Clark route. I asked what intrigued him about their journey. "Never could figure that out," he said. "It's just part of America that fascinates me. It's like our whole history is wrapped up on this route, and when I'm on it, I'm part of the history. And, I guess, part of America."

We had nothing in common save someone else's adventure, but we talked for an hour. Road travel does that to strangers. On planes, I fly across the country and spend five hours diligently avoiding whoever is seated next to me, for fear of being trapped in unwanted and endless conversation. On the road there is no such fear. You can always move on when strangers get too close. It is a matter of space, and having it loosens us up, maybe even makes us more trusting.

The currents were strong and the rain heavy as the expedition moved north from St. Charles through plains populated by great buffalo herds grazing on foot-high grass. Clark, the better riverman, usually stayed on the boat, balancing his journal on his knee. Traveling with him was his slave, York, whom one Indian chief insisted on rubbing with a moistened finger, convinced York had been painted black. Lewis walked onshore, making notes on topography, flora and fauna, his Newfoundland dog, Seaman, at his heels. They were, one historian has noted, the "writingest" explorers of all time, and almost everything, from what they ate to what they saw, found its way into their journals.

"This scenery, already rich, pleasing and beautiful,"

Clark wrote at one point, "was still farther heightened by immense herds of buffalo, deer, elk and antelopes, which we saw in every direction feeding on the hills and plains. I do not think I exaggerate when I estimate the number of buffaloes which could be comprehended at one view to amount to 3,000." At what is now Kansas City they found nothing except a rattlesnake sunning itself on the riverbank. Near the empty plains where Sioux City, Iowa, stands today, they paused to bury Sergeant Charles Floyd, the victim of a ruptured appendix. "I am going away," he whispered to Clark just before his death. "I want you to write me a letter." Floyd, the only fatality during the entire expedition, is buried on a hill near a little town named in his honor, Sergeant Bluff.

Lewis and Clark camped on the Missouri's banks a few miles from Bismarck, North Dakota, one night in October 1804, without much of a plan except to proceed on. Ahead lay the true Empty Quarter, the land beyond the sunset. There in the dark corners of a continent dwelled the imagination of a nation. Reality and myth would remain forever scrambled there, yet in generations to come it would be the East to which the nation looked to find its roots, and the West to claim its soul.

I had not seen an Indian anywhere along the trail. It was easy to forget that all this splendid beauty had once been theirs and would be snatched away by those who followed Lewis and Clark. Had it not been, in fact, for the assistance of friendly Native Americans across hundreds of miles of alien expanse, the Corps of Discovery would have failed and been swallowed up by the wilderness, relegated to a minor historical footnote that would have referred to an "ill-fated expedition." History would have left it to someone else to open the West.

Hardly two generations after Lewis and Clark had wintered at Fort Mandan, outside Bismarck, white America was at war with the Sioux on the northern Plains. Near the Corps of Discovery's campsite on the Missouri, Fort Lincoln still stands, a cluster of three hand-hewn timber blockhouses, each with rifle slots. The fort had been one of the most important on the Plains during the Sioux war. Off to one side, on a gentle knoll, is the cemetery. The wind whistles through it in moaning gusts, and in the fields below, waves of alfalfa bend and sway. This is a page of our history to be remembered, but not celebrated. Soldiers who died with General George Custer at Little Bighorn were buried in the Fort Lincoln cemetery in 1876, their bodies having been transported from Montana on the steamboat *Far West.* Other wooden markers bear testimony to the world that would follow Lewis and Clark: Three Indian scouts—Red Bear, Crow Tail and Youngman Chief—killed October 2, 1872; Albert Sharp, shot by a civilian; Michael Donlyn, drowned; Charles Page, frozen to death; Frederic Berowsky, diphtheria; John Steinkes, suicide by opium.

Lewis and Clark spent five months wintering in North Dakota, and during that time the twenty-nine-man unit was transformed from a brawling, boozing group of individuals into a harmonious, well-disciplined unit with a common purpose. When it left Mandan in April 1805— with Sacajawea, the Shoshone woman who carried her infant son, Baptiste (Little Pump), on her back and guided the explorers from North Dakota to the Pacific and back—Lewis wrote in his journal: "We were now about to penetrate a country at least two thousand miles in width, on which the foot of civilized man has never trodden; the good or evil it had in store for us was for experiment yet to determine." No non-Indian had ever scaled the Rockies or set foot in Idaho. Crossing Montana would take four months, and along the way the Corps of Discovery would encounter not a single human, red or white.

"Angela, where's my camera?" The voice startled me. It came from a shirtless man with Wisconsin tags on his car. He had three children in tow, and he barked orders like a drill sergeant. "Get over there with Grandma so I can take a picture. Hurry up, Angela. It's bitchin' hot, ain't it? *Bitchin'* hot!" The child obeyed, squinting in the August sunlight. In the background, where Lewis and Clark had spread their soaked cargo on a grassy bank to dry, complained about the mosquitoes and hunted elk, three rivers—the Jefferson, Madison and Gallatin—quietly join to form the Missouri and begin a 2,466-mile journey to St. Louis. It had taken the Corps of Discovery fourteen months to reach what is now Three Forks, Montana (population 1,400).

Three Forks isn't much of a town anymore, and I sat on the long, wide veranda of the Sacajawea Inn, sipping iced tea with Frances Denning and her friend, Jean Wittmaekers, who had recently moved to Three Forks from Florida and was restoring the 126-year-old inn. "Oh, this town will come back, I'm sure of that," said the seventy-one-year-old Mrs. Denning. "Even when the Milwaukee Road quit in 1980, the town didn't die. Sure, it went down some without the trains, but it didn't die." And, said Ms. Wittmaekers, "I'm going to help make it come alive. This could be a charming little town. The Sacajawea was where everyone always came to drink, to dance, to eat, to just be together. I want that to happen again."

Three Forks had prospered when four trains a day stopped there, carrying passengers to Harlowton via Dot, Bruno, Sixteen and Deep Park. It boomed so fast for a while that newcomers had to sleep in open boxcars and the *Three Forks Herald,* unable to find office space, published its first editions in a tent. Then, sometime after the Korean War, the trains pulled out, the depot at the top of Main Street was shuttered and the Sacajawea Inn closed down.

Wittmaekers, who had traveled from Australia to Mongolia and lived in Europe and Venezuela, discovered the empty Sacajawea when she came to Three Forks to visit relatives over Thanksgiving. She didn't know at the time that her parents had been introduced to each other over dinner at the inn years earlier. "Something just kept drawing me back to the place," she said. She signed the mortgage and spent the winter bundled up in ski clothes, shoveling out debris, painting, mopping—the pail would freeze over each night—and supervising the restoration that was bringing back turn-of-the-century elegance.

"The town used to be this big," Mrs. Denning said, holding a photograph of Three Forks in 1914. "Violet Lilly's was over here. She rented rooms. The Greenhouse was down the street. They didn't sell any flowers; the ladies who worked there at night did something else. The railroad people had their own clubhouse, very nice. But the Sacajawea was always the place to go. I learned to square

dance downstairs here." Ms. Wittmaekers looked at me with a big smile and said, "People in Montana, you know, love to dance."

The open expanses near Three Forks that Lewis described as "one vast plain in which innumerable herds of buffalo were attended by their shepherds, the wolves," are split today by Interstate 90, a single highway that enables you to scurry from Boston to Seattle without seeing a town or having a conversation. But Montana was no easy passage for Lewis and Clark, who had run out of whiskey there. The timberless mountains grew taller, the valleys deeper. Game was scarce and, having abandoned the river to find an overland route across the mountains, they needed desperately to find Indians who would sell them horses. "I fear the successful issue of our voyage will be very doubtful," Lewis wrote. "We are now several hundred miles within the bosom of this wild and mountainous country . . . however, I still hope for the best and intend taking a tramp myself in a few days." They climbed each mountain with the hope of seeing westward valleys leading to the Pacific, but instead all that lay ahead, as far as they could see, were more mountains.

It occurred to me, not without some guilt, that I probably would not have been much good to Lewis and Clark. In my mind's eye I galloped across the Plains alone and struggled up mountains where no man had trod. But the truth is I don't much like horses, and heights scare the dickens out of me. While Lewis and Clark had endured abominable conditions, I had checked into a motel each night and hopscotched to selected spots in rental cars and on planes. The corps would have considered me a wimp.

But perhaps that is part of the reason thousands of Americans take to the road each summer in search of the Lewis and Clark legend: In our imaginations we are participants. We can share the suffering and the daring, and they do not hurt or threaten.

I returned my rental car in Bismarck and flew to Missoula, Montana. Off the interstate and across the state line in Idaho, a sign on Highway 12 warns, WINDING ROAD, 77 MILES. Near there the party was reduced to eating roots, a raven, a slaughtered horse and candles made of bear fat. The campsites they left behind testify to their anguish: Colt Killed Creek, Hungry Creek, Portable Soup Camp, Lonesome Cove. Sick men lay by the side of the trail, waiting to be helped by the next man. Everyone, Lewis said, was "complaining of their bowels," and when a heavy, premature snowstorm struck on September 15, 1805, Sergeant Patrick Gass called the Bitterroots "the most terrible mountains I ever beheld." The mountains are now in Idaho's Clearwater National Forest, and it is there, along with the Missouri Breaks in Montana, that one most senses nothing has changed since Lewis and Clark passed through. Virgin pines tower into the clear, crisp night; the silence is absolute. The nearest Idaho town is a three-day walk away, and the dark, wooded peaks surround their visitors like a fortress. Anyone who has been there will tell you that in the night you can still hear the voices of long-departed men huddled over their campfire.

Cort Conley, who forsook a law career in California to become an Idaho wilderness guide, was cooking dinner over an open fire the night I arrived: salmon and spinach

strawberry shortcake and cowboy-style coffee, with the grounds thrown into a kettle of boiling water. Twenty or so people were scattered about, writing in diaries, thumbing through dog-eared editions about the expedition. Some sat alone on rocks along the Lochsa River, silent with their thoughts. A botanist was pointing out to several students some of the then-unknown species of plants that Lewis and Clark had discovered and recorded in their journals, even as they fought against disaster. "You know, you crawl into a nice, warm sleeping bag at night and you look up at the stars and you wonder how they did it, how they put up with such misery and suffering," said a teacher from New Hampshire.

The group was part of a class the University of Idaho brought every summer into the mountains to trek for a week with a historian along the route of Lewis and Clark. The participants paid $175 each—the equivalent of seven months' salary for the expedition's chief interpreter and hunter, George Drouillard—and received two credits in history toward their degree. "After Lewis and Clark left Fort Mandan, the expedition worked like a well-oiled machine," historian Carlos Schwantes told the group. "In some ways, they made it seem too easy. They only lost one man. They only had one serious encounter with the Indians. Certainly one important element of their success was good leadership and good followership. You can't have good leaders unless you have good people willing to follow."

On October 7, 1805, the Corps of Discovery, having escaped the mountains, pushed their canoes into the Clearwater River and headed toward the Columbia River and the sea, a month's journey away. The Indians there were fishermen who lived in houses made of rushes. Mount Hood was soon visible in the distance (as it now is from Interstate 84, which parallels the route), slicing through Oregon's thick forests and tidy little towns. "The pleasure I now felt," Lewis wrote, "in having triumphed over the Rocky Mountains and descending once more to a level and fertile country where there was every rational hope of finding a comfortable subsistence for myself and party can be no more readily conceived than expressed."

Flushed with anticipation, the Corps of Discovery swept through the Columbia, its canoes sometimes covering thirty miles a day. If the explorers had followed that route today, as I now did on a four-lane highway in my air-conditioned car, they would have passed the stack of the Trojan Nuclear Plant, billowing smoke, and come within shouting distance of the Hanford facility in Washington that made plutonium for the A-bomb dropped on Nagasaki in 1945. Their canoes would have floated under the four-mile-long bridge in Astoria that carries traffic on Highway 101 over the wide Columbia estuary to Washington. They would, I imagine, have looked lost among the gathering of Korean and Japanese freighters in port, exchanging cars and electronic products for grain and timber.

"Great joy in camp," Lewis wrote November 7, 1805. "We are in view of the ocean . . . this great Pacific Ocean which we have been so long anxious to see, and the roaring noise made by the waves breaking on the rocky shores may be heard distinctly." Near the beach where Lewis and Clark finally reached their destination, the waves break

heavily over the hulk of the *Peter Iredale,* a British
freighter that went aground in 1906. A fogbank lingers
just offshore, and the figures on the sand—a few bathers,
a man alone reading, a half-dozen teenagers with bicycles
nearby—appear as apparitions, caught in a veil of mist
and the timeless rhythm of pounding surf.

Lewis and Clark moved a few miles inland, and the
corps built a fifty-square-foot fort with two rows of cabins
facing a small parade ground. It was the first U.S. military
post west of the Rockies, and they named it Fort Clatsop,
for the neighboring Indian tribe. The rain was so constant
on the Oregon coast during the winter of 1805–6 that
everyone's buckskin clothes rotted. The last of the tobacco
was divided up on Christmas Day. The men tired of fish,
and someone shot a "buzzard" with a ten-foot wingspan
(probably a California condor, now an endangered species
last seen in Oregon in 1913).

Fort Clatsop, run by the National Park Service, is a
precise replica of the original post, a sort of living museum
surrounded by tall pines and spirits of the past. Logs
crackle in the fireplace, beef jerky dries on an overhead
beam, and rangers dressed in nineteenth-century buckskin
make candles by hand, using beef fat. More than 175,000
travelers visit the fort each year, and the superintendent,
Franklin Walker, told me he had never seen a single line
of graffiti at the fort. I thought back to the mess at the
campsite outside St. Louis. Is our history more sacred
when it lives not in the cities, but in the same open spaces
in which it has been created? Lewis and Clark gave the fort
to the Clatsops as a hunting camp on March 23, 1806,
and, together with Sacajawea and Baptiste, the Corps of

Discovery left the Pacific coast for the six-month trek back to St. Louis—a trip cars can now make in fifty-seven hours and jetliners in four. "We have lived as well as we had any right to expect," Clark said.

The Lewis and Clark Expedition has inspired an eleven-volume account of the journey published by the University of Nebraska Press, a quarterly magazine, more than three hundred books, and several movies, including one starring Fred MacMurray as Lewis, Charlton Heston as Clark and Donna Reed as Sacajawea. ("It was a wonderful movie," said historian James Ronda. "Everything in it was wrong.")

And what of the corps itself? After a heroes' welcome in St. Louis—the Corps of Discovery had long since been given up for dead—Lewis and Clark were awarded 1,600 acres of public land each; each enlisted man received 320 acres. Everyone got double pay. Captain Meriwether Lewis, appointed governor of Louisiana, died three years after the expedition of an apparently self-inflicted gunshot wound in a squalid Tennessee cabin while traveling to Washington, D.C. He believed he was under suspicion of mismanaging public funds. Lewis is buried near Hohenwald, Tennessee, and his tombstone bears an inscription written by Jefferson: "I died young; but thou, o good republic, live out my years for me with better fortune." Captain William Clark was promoted to brigadier general and appointed superintendent of Indian affairs. He died at the age of sixty-eight in 1838 and is buried in the family plot in St. Louis. York, the slave, was freed in 1811, failed in several businesses and was last reported to be living among the Crow Indians with four wives. The youngest member of the party, Private George Shannon, who was nineteen when the corps wintered at Camp Wood, became a circuit judge in Missouri. George Drouillard returned to the wilderness and was killed by Indians near Three Forks, Montana, in 1810. Sergeant Patrick Gass married at age fifty-eight, fathered seven children and died in 1870, at the age of ninety-nine. Sacajawea is believed to have died in North Dakota in 1812, when she was twenty-three. Her son, Baptiste, went to St. Louis, was educated by Clark, traveled in Europe and later returned to Missouri to become a widely known trapper and guide. The Clatsop Indians gradually disappeared as a full-blooded people.

Lewis and Clark's journals—volumes of scientific notes on the unknown animals, plants and Indians of the West—lay in the American Philosophical Society in Philadelphia for nearly a century before being published. By then the West had been settled and the Indians had been moved onto reservations. Our destiny was manifest, though for a good many years after Lewis and Clark's return, we didn't know what to do with the foreboding land they had uncovered. Washington Irving expressed the fear in 1836 that a great part of it "will form a lawless interval between the abodes of civilized men. . . . Here may spring up new and mongrel races, like new formations in geology, the amalgamation of the 'debris' and 'abrasions' of former races." And Daniel Webster vowed he would spend not a cent from public funds for postal service "to place the Pacific Coast one inch nearer to Boston than it now is." Ironically, though, now that the tyranny of distance no longer rules America, it is the people of the Empty Quarter who look at the crowded East and the troubled cities everywhere and worry about protecting our last great chunk of law-abiding civilization.

Big Sky, Big Dreams

Ll summer the weather had teased and taunted with its promise of rain. Swirling clouds as blue and deep as an angry ocean built to the south, dancing over the fields of withered wheat. Lightning crackled, and in the night sky there was thunder and a restless wind. Sometimes the wind awakened Duane Weigel before dawn, and he would go downstairs and stand by an open window of his North Dakota farmhouse to watch the storm approach. But the clouds always broke apart just as they seemed within reach, leaving not a dew-drop of moisture, and with the morning, day after broiling day, came clear, dry skies and heat that baked his land and rattled his composure.

"There's not much a man can do to prepare for drought, not much he can learn from it when it does happen," Weigel said. "You just have to take things as they come." He kicked at the earth in disgust. The spindly stalks of wheat barely reached his ankles, and it was difficult to believe he would ever again wade through the fields of chest-high golden waves he had known as a child. "Funny thing is," he mused, "the southeast wind always brings rain, except this year. The ants are busy and the flies are big and that usually means rain, too. I remember last spring my buddy Randy saying, 'It's going to be a dry year.' I asked him how he knew, and he said because the Catholic church was putting in a sprinkler system."

Over the last decade more than one million Americans have been forced off their farms by drought, falling commodity prices and bad management, and year by year the number of farm-dwelling Americans has dwindled: from 30 percent of the population in 1920 to 15 percent in 1950 to 1.6 percent in 1990. The Empty Quarter that Lewis and Clark had traipsed through—North Dakota, Montana and Idaho—is getting emptier. Duane Weigel feared he was about to become its next victim.

I left Weigel on his doorstep, looking at the sky, and drove into Napoleon (population 1,104, including a recent birth). The Pepsi thermometer on the general store read a steady 107 degrees. The Soo Line to Minneapolis ran straight through town, but the tracks were empty, and the towering grain elevator at the top of Napoleon's only street was deserted. With no hay to harvest and time to spare, farmers were gathering in such large numbers to talk weather over coffee and fresh apple pie at the Downtowner Cafe that the proprietor had had to open a side room.

It took me only an hour to cross the Missouri and find my way to Dick and Teresa Tokach's 4,500-acre farm near Mandan. Tokach's father had lost the property to a federal land bank back in the bone-dry thirties, then struggled most of his life to buy it back. Tokach was out behind his barn, digging a well. He had gone down 440 feet, spent $4,000 and found not a drop of water. "To hell with it," he said, wiping his brow, "let's get some coffee." We went inside and sat at his kitchen table. I am always surprised how briefly one remains a stranger in the rural West. Teresa put a piece of homemade pie in front of me and said that every time she went over the accounting books, she would suggest they cut back their expenditures for fertilizer and seed. No, Tokach unfailingly responded, they had to prepare for the return of the prairie rains. They would scrimp on groceries before they did on seed.

"I always thought when we got to be fifty years old, we'd have things made," Teresa said. "Oh, you know the dreams women have—the kids are gone and now you can do this and that. Then all of a sudden you find out you can't do that, and you're afraid of losing what you have." Her husband fidgeted in his chair. "The toughest part is not knowing what'll happen day to day," he said. "You can't plan. You see the savings drying up. But then you remember how you feel seeing calves born in the spring and knowing the crops are coming up hearty and thick and you understand why you don't quit."

Outside the southeast wind blew and the cottonwoods groaned and swayed. The sky was hazy blue, the temperature was climbing and the Tokach Angus Ranch baked in the heavy morning heat, its earth parched and full of grasshoppers skittering among frail stalks of grain. The forecast for tomorrow and the day after that was the same as yesterday's: hot and dry. When Teresa had awakened that morning, she had turned to her husband and said, "Dick, are we going to make it?"

The vast underpopulated reaches of the West have much in common with other Empty Quarters I have encountered in my travels: Alaska, upstate Maine, parts of the southwestern desert. The young flee toward city lights at first opportunity, and those who remain fear social change, believing the lesson of the city is that nothing ever gets better. They had staked their roots in an unforgiving land and did not dream of distant shores. What they wanted was what they had. Their challenge was to keep others from exploiting it. Or, as Teresa Tokach put it, to keep from losing what was theirs. Ironically the very characteristics that had enabled them to preserve their compelling life-styles—slow economic growth and small rural populations—were precisely what threatened their well-being when the economy went sour, jobs became scarce and fourth-grade kids, nationally, spent four hours a day tuned in to television. Wolves howled at the door, and they hunkered down, waiting for the rains or the return of prosperous times or just assurances that they could keep what they had built. They didn't want newcomers moving in, for fear "they won't contribute the way we have." They weren't keen on large businesses coming in either, because they tend to be bossy and set their own rules. Tourists were okay as long as they didn't get notions about settling. Montana even came up with a word for out-of-state transplants who cannot claim lineage to the frontier settlers— honyockers.

"We're victims of the old mind-set, that any corporation heading for Montana must be bent on rape," Michael Malone, president of Montana State University in Bozeman, told me. "Montana is the last of the Old West and we're in crisis and we're not doing the most obvious things that have to be done. First, the state seems to look on higher education as just another expense. Second, we're trying to preserve a unique life-style and trying to put our feet into the future at the same time. So far we really haven't come to terms with the conflict this creates."

Like Montana itself, the American outback has always been exploited: by timber companies that ravaged the forests, by mining companies that tore up the earth, by developers who turned deserts into unsightly collections of cheap houses and tacky malls, by the federal government, which was the West's biggest landlord, by railroads and insurance companies and corporate easterners who sent their profits back home.

For years the Anaconda Company operated Montana as a colony. The Company—as everyone called it—owned all the daily newspapers but one in the state until 1959 and was so defensive about opposition voices that letters to the editor were banned. It ran a boozy, twenty-four-hour-a-day hospitality suite in Helena when the legislature was in session, and no one contested an Anaconda official's boast in the 1940s that The Company had lost only one governorship since statehood. Anaconda's fortunes began declining in the 1960s, at the same time America's cities were being consumed by decay, racial riots and antiwar protests. Suddenly all that Montanans had considered a curse—fierce winters, great distances to their commercial markets, geographic isolation—seemed a blessing. The tyranny of distance had become the therapy of distance. Montanans sensed that things were changing forever, and they reached out to save what was special to them. A new populist constitution, emphasizing environmental and consumer-protection values, was passed in 1972 (the only copy of the first proposed constitution had been lost en route to the printer in St. Louis in 1866), and an antibusiness attitude flourished.

With copper prices sagging, Atlantic Richfield Company, which had bought Anaconda in 1977, announced after a four-month strike in 1980 that it was closing its smelter in Butte, claiming that modernizing the facility to meet federal and state pollution and safety standards would cost $400 million. The mine at Butte—which produced "the richest hill on earth" and one of the West's wildest towns—became a dormant wound on the Montana landscape. Other energy companies rushed to exploit the state's riches, including the largest coal reserves in the nation, but Montana refused to relax its environmental standards in favor of quick cash. "All we're saying to industries that want to come in," said James Murry, executive secretary of the Montana AFL-CIO, "is, Don't treat us like South Africa does its blacks. We're just saying, If you come in, you have to be responsible, you have to be willing to contribute the way the rest of us have."

Montana is not a state to hurry through. Everywhere I turned, hidden in valleys and tucked on the shoulders of wooded hills, were the remnants of the West's Golden Age, each a reminder of how fragile and temporary frontier life had always been. These places are ghost towns now, their boardwalks crumbling, their miners long since departed, and only in the stirrings of the imagination does one hear a piano's notes drift out from behind the doors of boarded-up saloons.

Bannack, Montana's first territorial capital, appeared to have been abandoned only yesterday. There is a sadness in the dead towns of the West that comes back to haunt me at unsuspecting moments, and I walked the deserted main street, as alone as the last man on earth. Bannack's buildings were still upright. I looked up at the bedrooms above the storefronts and would not have been surprised to see the curtains part and the faces of some old couple staring at me, as though asking what right I had to disturb the final days they had chosen to spend together and in isolation. After a year in Bannack, the seat of government was moved, in 1865, to Virginia City; that, too, is a town of the past now, kept alive by tourists. In Nevada City, three wooden passenger cars from the Butte, Anaconda & Pacific stood idle on a siding, but the town had no residents, and the rail line had ceased operations years ago.

Butte, which John Gunther described as "the toughest, bawdiest town in America," was eerily still when I pulled off the interstate at 10:00 A.M. Its population, over 100,000 at the turn of the century, is 36,000. I took a seat at the bar of the M and M Saloon and asked for a cup of coffee. The miner to my right shot me a disrespectful glance. Jack Kerouac had been particularly fond of the M and M, and of Butte, and after stopping there in the sixties had written, "I walked the sloping streets . . . and saw that everybody in Butte was drunk." Isolation had extracted its price.

Novelist Thomas McGuane, one of Montana's better-known honyockers, had pondered that price and asked himself on many occasions what he had had to sacrifice professionally by living in Montana. The balance sheet always came up in favor of staying. McGuane had left California more than twenty years earlier and lives in the middle of nowhere, on his Raw Deal Ranch, seventeen miles from the nearest store, five hundred miles from the nearest major league baseball team. The day I met him he was waiting impatiently for the FedEx driver who would bring him his quarterly supply of cigars. McGuane's rancher-neighbors didn't know quite what to make of a man who earned his livelihood writing. "But what do you *do?*" they would ask. The mention of *Ninety-two in the Shade* or *The Bushwhacked Piano* would draw a blank, though there would be approving nods if he specified his screenplay for *Missouri Breaks,* a Western starring Marlon Brando and Jack Nicholson. McGuane also raised cutting horses, had tried rodeoing and actually felt a sense of relief sometime back when he broke his thumb in a roping contest. At least his hands finally looked like those of a working man, not a writer.

"I'll tell you what I miss the most," he said. "It's to walk down a crowded street or sit on a park bench and just watch the stuff that goes on. Rubbing elbows, I miss that. I get back to New York for a book party or whatever and it's exciting to catch up on the literary world, but after an hour or two, that's all you need. You've heard it all. You realize so many people back there have created their own little empires around 'the me' and they have to work hard to protect them. That sort of thing just doesn't happen here. So familiarly, I haven't sacrificed much. If you think about it, how many friends can you really attend to—two or three at a time? Sure, we don't have films, theaters or all the things of the city. But people who have those things don't have the time to read thirty books a month, which

Laurie and I both do. That seems a pretty close call to me."

From their living-room window, they could see their youngest child, Annie, at play each noon outside the little white-stucco school across the dirt road. The West Boulder River runs through their property, a few yards from the house, and I left McGuane splashing through the water in his hip boots, engaged in his daily ritual of matching wits with the wily trout. There is a saying in Montana that God doesn't subtract from a man's life the hours spent fishing. If that is really the case, I suspect McGuane will be around a long time.

Montana's appeal is an unspoken, unseen thing, an awareness that the "unique life-style" people talk about is a state of mind as well as of being. There are only 800,000 Montanans, roaming around a state a little larger than Japan, and each has a fifth of a square mile all to himself. Montana is a place where you still drink beer out of the bottle, say good morning to strangers and drive halfway across the universe to visit a neighbor. Montana has but a single congressman (fifty-one fewer than California) to represent its interests in Washington, and everyone calls him by his first name. Even when economic times are tough, Montanans don't do much grousing, except about the boneheads in Washington. They have their big, clear sky, and their land is still wide and handsome. They figure their frontier heritage gives them the right to live as they choose, even to create myths that need to be lived up to, for in every true Montanan there is something that says, "I am a last holdout."

The Dakota Territory's most famous cattleman, Teddy Roosevelt, wrote wistfully in 1888, "The best days of ranching are over." So he left the Badlands and went east to be a politician. A hundred or so years later, I went the other way, from east to west, to see if he had been right. My impressions of the cattle industry had come straight from television: the Cartwrights on the Ponderosa, wide vistas, corrals and coffee drunk out of tin mugs around the campfire. A friend of a friend had given me the name of a Montana rancher, and when I called to invite myself out for a few days, he said, " 'Bout all we're doing this time of year is hayin', but you want to visit, we'll take care of you. It'd be good to have you." I'm not sure I would have been as accommodating if a stranger from the country had called and asked for my spare bedroom so he could see how city folks lived. I drove out of Helena in the early-morning darkness and followed the Boulder River along Route 69, with the theme song from *Bonanza* rattling in my head.

Dawn crept across the land, and frost clung to the high-country meadows. The autumn breeze was sweet with the smell of new-cut hay, and from the road the ranch houses that reached through the Boulder Valley appeared to be not much more than silhouettes lost in the shadows of cottonwoods and rolling hills. Then, as if on prearranged signal, bedroom lights flickered on one after another, and soon men in sharp-toed boots ambled onto their porches, coffee cups in hand, collars of sheepskin jackets pulled high. Their faces were turned toward the west, toward the snow-dusted Bull Mountains, and they knew they had to hurry to cut and stack the hay and drive the cattle to lower ground before nature sealed both men and animals in a capsule of winter isolation. The ranchers who stood there in the half-light of dawn, who roamed the valley in pickup trucks, tending their cattle as mindfully as parents do their young, sleeping for weeks on end in sheds with newborn calves before the first thaw of spring, were the guardians of a vanishing world. Progress should have done them in, or at least made them obsolete, like some old horse-drawn mower rusting in an overgrown pasture, but it hadn't. A lot of them had college educations. Some had a computer for their office that shared a corner of the kitchen. But they were still as tough as chunks of over-cooked beef, and they remained both masters of and hostage to the homesteads their ancestors carved out of raw wilderness in Boulder Valley a century ago.

Jack Dawson, the rancher who had invited me to visit, was forty-six years old and a former professional rodeo rider. He was of average height and trim as a fence pole. His legs were bowed, his hands coarse like sandpaper. "Time to get to work," he said. It was 7:00 A.M. He set down his coffee cup and tucked a pinch of chewing to-bacco alongside his gum. He climbed into his Dodge pickup and drove slowly out onto the range, across a stream, past tightly wrapped, round bales of wild hay as tall as a man. His dog stood in the back, with the roll of barbed wire and a bunch of digging tools, yelping unmer-cifully. "Badger," Dawson yelled, rolling down his win-dow, "keep still!" The dog ignored him. "He minds 'bout as well as my wife," Dawson noted.

Dawson slipped the Dodge into four-wheel drive. In the meadow ahead, his eighty-three-year-old father,

George, was in the cabin of a stalled cutting tractor, and Jack's brother, Dave, was laboring over the machine, pulling clods of dirt and clumps of hay from its bladed mouth. Jack's inclination was to bang the $30,000 machine with a hammer and cuss a bit, a technique he found remarkably successful with expensive equipment, which has never been quite as reliable as a good team of horses.

"I'm plugged up good," his father announced, glancing at the sky and fearing rain or, worse, snow. "Damned gopher mound. Can't see 'em too good out here, and now I'm plugged up."

"Okeydoke," Jack said. "We'll get you fixed."

George Dawson's Quebec-born father, John, had left Deadwood, South Dakota, after years of prospecting and moved to Boulder Valley in 1882, when Montana was still a territory and the valley, according to a door-to-door census by Assistant Marshal Harim Cook, had a population of "forty-eight white males, forty-two white females, no colored males, no colored females, no blind, no deaf, no idiots, no insane." John Dawson carried with him tales of his friend, Wild Bill Hickok, and a scar in his shoulder from a poisoned Indian arrow, which George remembers as "a homely looking thing." Land was cheap then—160 acres cost only a registration fee of thirty-four dollars if you stayed five years—and John Dawson laid claim to a homestead, the same one that was now the 8,000-acre Dawson ranch. There he met and married another settler's daughter, Alice Porter from Virginia, and they had thirteen children. The youngest was born when John was seventy-nine. As the Dawson family grew, so did Boulder Valley. Irish Catholic settlers, many direct from Ireland, poured in, and a whole deer would be consumed at a wedding or wake. A stagecoach line to Helena opened, and a post office was built not far from Dawson's log home, in Coldsprings, though Coldsprings is no longer on any map. In the fir-covered mountains just up the road, the mining town of Elkhorn boomed with a population of 2,500, boasting its own rail line to Boulder, a grand fraternal lodge and nine saloons. "They was evidently drinkin' people," George Dawson now noted.

Even though signs of failure are everywhere in the valley—Elkhorn is a ghost town; Coldsprings has disappeared; abandoned homesteader cabins are scattered among the juniper and aspens—the thirty-mile-long valley is a peaceful place that exerts a powerful grip on the soul. With the love these ranchers have for the valley comes the belief that hard work on the land is still a noble endeavor and that honest labor is the first step toward a secure future. Ranches are passed from generation to generation, and the same neighbors have been in place for a lifetime. "Now, right here is where our spread ends," Jack Dawson said as his pickup bounced up the country road toward Elkhorn. "The Carey ranch starts at the property line. They're real good people. They'd go out of their way to help you, and they sure wouldn't let you pay them anything for it. Their daughter got married Saturday. Let me tell you, that was a party. Anybody left the ranch sober that day, it was their own fault."

The leaden clouds that hung over the mountains smelled of snow, and the unmowed hay reaching out on both sides of the road rippled gently like the ocean on a calm day. Sitting alone in the meadow, as though misplaced, was a small, white Catholic church built with hand-hewn lumber by the first settlers in 1880. It was open for mass only on special occasions now, but the ranchers donated their time and money to maintain it, and St. John's looked cared for and fresh enough to have been set there only yesterday. Dawson pulled off the road, unlatched the gate and walked around back to the cemetery. Many of the homesteaders and their families were buried in the tidy little graveyard. The McCauleys. The Murphys. The Flahertys. John Dawson (1837–1922) rests next to his wife, Alice, who died when a gas lamp exploded in the ranch house where Jack Dawson now lives. Jack's great-uncle is here, as are four of his uncles. "And my mother's over here," Jack said, pausing in front of a headstone that bore the inscription "Edna, 1977."

The wind had picked up, and it swung out of the west with a cold sting. Dawson thrust his hands into the pockets of his denim jacket. He said, "What we'd like to do is have the ranch here for the children, if they'd like it. That's what Dad and my mother did for us. They never made you stay or leave. It was your choice. But if you stayed, you helped make decisions. You were never treated like a hired hand. I figured last year we could probably sell out and live pretty good. Figure our folks could have done the same thing, but I'm sure glad they didn't. You couldn't ever afford to get a start now, and you couldn't ever find another place like this valley. Even though it's getting scary how much money you need to stay in business these days, I'd like our kids to have the same choice Dave and I did. For a while, every paper you picked up, someone was figuring beef caused this and beef caused that. You wondered if people were going to plumb stop eating beef. There seemed a time sometime back when I could see myself getting out of debt. Now I'm not so sure I can. It's getting so the prices we're getting just aren't enough to meet expenses."

Last season, Dawson said, had been spooky. The hay ran out in the dead of winter, and he and his brother and father had to truck in feed at eighty-two dollars a ton to save the herd. His banker told Dawson he had lost $10,000 on the year. His accountant figured Dawson's taxes and said he owed the government $5,000 and with beef prices down, Dawson doubted that he'd ever get comfortably ahead. But at least this year the summer rains had been generous across Montana, producing good crops of alfalfa and wild hay for winter feed, and there was hope that the farm crisis creeping west across the Great Plains could be held at bay a bit longer.

The problems he and other western ranchers faced were not unlike those of midwestern farmers: Costs were going up and commodity prices down. The price of their land was inflated, making it difficult either to sell or to buy more, and high interest rates and the need for expensive equipment—tractors, balers, cutters, irrigation systems— had sent indebtedness soaring. The secondhand tractor George Dawson purchased thirty years ago cost less than the lawn mower he had just bought from Sears. On top of all that, Americans were eating less beef, cutting their annual per capita consumption to less than fifty-nine pounds from seventy pounds in 1976. Montana ranchers, who received no government commodity support, still dreamed about the days their beef earned them, briefly, a dollar a pound—once during the Truman administration and again under President Carter. The result was that ranches were getting smaller in number and larger in acreage; Montana, which had 58,000 farms and ranches in 1920, now has 24,000.

Even in tough times, ranchers were under pressure to acquire more land in the belief that they had to run more cattle to be profitable. They were, in fact, spiritually obsessed with the acquisition of land; it was their legacy to their children and the only real yardstick of success and wealth. Land and the size of one's herd are to the Montanan what a stock portfolio and a healthy checking account are to the city professional. "I don't want to own all of Montana," a rancher would say. "Just what's next to my property."

The sentiment was about as old as America. "The pride and delight of Americans is the quantity of land," Harriet Martineau wrote in her book *Society in America* in 1837.

> ✍ I do not remember meeting with one to whom it had occurred that they had too much. . . . The possession of land is the aim of all action, generally speaking, and the cure for all social evils, among men in the United States. If a man is disappointed in politics or love, he goes and buys land. If he disgraces himself he betakes himself to a lot in the West. If the demand for any article of manufacture slackens, the operatives drop into unsettled lands. If a citizen's neighbors rise above him in the

towns, he takes himself where he can be monarch of all he surveys. ✎

Jack Dawson's workweek ran Monday through Sunday, sunup to sunset. Badger had quieted down by the time dusk came, and Dawson headed back toward the ranch. Though his backyard was as big as a national park, reaching all the way out to the Bull Mountains, the house itself was modest and would not have looked out of place in a suburban development. I asked Dawson how many head of cattle he had. He pretended to be occupied dodging ruts in the track and didn't answer. When I asked again, he said he didn't have an exact count. "Well, *about* how many do you have?" I pressed, so lamebrained I was missing the message. Finally he said, "That's a question you don't ask in Montana. Just like I wouldn't come into your home in the city and ask you how much money you had in your bank account, you don't ask a man in Montana how many head he runs."

It was nearly dark when George Dawson and Dave shut down the cutter and baler. Dave headed out into the hills to drain the irrigation pipes so they wouldn't freeze, and George drove across the meadows to Jack's, where I sat at the kitchen table with five-year-old Matt and seven-year-old Trudy, the fourth generation of Dawsons to call the ranch home. The kids were fascinated to find someone from the city as a houseguest and asked if they could bring me to school the next day for show-and-tell. Since George Dawson had been widowed nine years earlier, he had taken his meals with his sons' families—lunch at Dave and

Ann Marie's, supper at Jack and RaeCille's. RaeCille, back from substitute teaching for the day, had put together a feast right off the ranch: vegetables from the garden; the roast from a recently slaughtered cow; the butter, bread and pecan pie homemade.

"Well, there's George now," RaeCille said as the front door opened. "How'd it go today with the haying, George? Jack says you plugged up. You want a short snort before dinner—Walker and 7UP?"

"Yup, that'd be good, bourbon and 7, and don't forget the bourbon. I didn't go too good today. I plugged up a few times on those damn gopher holes. Wasn't for them, I'd've finished up easy."

With some encouragement from me, George Dawson got to reminiscing about his eight decades on the land his father had homesteaded and he himself had labored on to build into a successful ranch. (It turned out the Dawsons had five hundred head of cattle.) George was proud that the Dawson cattle still carried the same brand—a JD pushed together to form a single character on each cow's right rib—that his father had registered at a time when owning all this land was but a dream. He believed that hard work was a panacea for all ailments.

"I remember back in the winter of 'nineteen and 'twenty, there was lots of snow and it was cold, too," he said. "At that time, by God, some of the homesteaders— they called 'em dryland farmers—were losing their milk cows and homes. We bought some hay from one of the Dakotas, but the damn stuff wasn't any good. Had cat-o'-nine-tails in it. That broke a lot of people. Some of 'em never did come out of it. There were some pretty rich people in the valley in those days. I can remember talking about someone and saying, 'By God, I bet he could get *ten thousand dollars* together.' Today, I do believe, it's getting tougher to make money with all that expensive equipment you need. The first mower I bought cost forty-five dollars and you pulled it with a horse.

"You asked if this was ever the Wild West. Hell, no. This was just always honest ranchers here. Just damn good people. They got along and they were good neighbors, and they still are that way, I think. I never forced the boys to stay around, though. I just tried to point out the good parts of ranching to them. The best part is knowing you're your own boss and there's plenty of work to do. You can't ever get bored."

"We stuck around," Jack said, "and that's why you're still working so damn hard to support us, isn't that right, Dad?"

RaeCille cleared away the dessert plates, and George pushed back his chair. "Best be going," he said. "We got a lot to do tomorrow." His grandchildren, sitting in the next room, by a roaring fire, came into the kitchen to say good night.

"You know," RaeCille said, "I read in *Reader's Digest* about how a lot of teenagers took over an area of China in 1977 and killed all the educated people or made them clean out pigpens. Then China went in and killed off the teenagers, and I tell my kids, 'You don't know how lucky you are until you make comparisons.' Most kids come home and turn on the VCR. Matt and Trudy come home and climb on their horses.

"Of course, they complain some. They say they'd like

to have a VCR. But I think they understand what a good life we have here. We may not have a lot of money—there are lots of things I'd like to have that I can't—but if you look at our life, at this ranch George built up, at our friends in the valley, then I'd have to say in that respect we are rich, very rich.

"That's what being rich really means, doesn't it?"

The Last Frontier

Six years before Japan's attack on Pearl Harbor and seven years before its invasion and occupation of Alaska's Aleutian Islands, Brigadier General Billy Mitchell told the House Military Affairs Committee that Alaska was the "key point to the whole Pacific. . . . He who holds Alaska holds the world." Few took him seriously, and when Alaska's nonvoting delegate to Congress, Antony Dimond, introduced a bill for $10 million to build air bases, the House dismissed his request as pork-barrel politics. Asked one congressman: "What would anyone want with Alaska?"

Everyone in Anchorage told me to get out of town if I really wanted to find the heartbeat of Alaska. So I took the ninety-minute flight on a Markair turboprop to Bethel, the biggest and most important commercial hub of western Alaska, a region as big as Oregon. The Alaska state troopers kept the peace there in planes, not cars, though they did patrol the forty-eight-mile network of ice roads on the Kuskokwim River in the winter. Bethel is Alaska's eighth largest city. It has a population of 4,200. The September skies already held the breath of winter. I waited at the Bethel airport for a taxi. None showed up. I collected my bag and started walking into town to find a woman named Rosie Porter. She had grown up in a New Jersey cold-water flat, I had been told, and now ran a bed and breakfast above the office of her weekly newspaper, *The Tundra Drums.*

The gravel road was rutted and muddied, and I was forced to share it with four-wheel-drive vehicles that splashed by, the town being without sidewalks, curbs or gutters. Bethel sits on a windswept desert, its buildings perched on pilings driven into the permanently frozen earth. Like most small towns in Alaska, Bethel was one of those places you took one look at and said, "Oh, my God!" It had no sewerage system, but twice a month workers emptied the septic tanks and "honey buckets" and dumped the waste into the fresh waters of the lagoon. Outside of almost every home were piled crippled cars, broken machinery and discarded housewares: blenders, sewing machines, toaster ovens, busted TVs, old mattresses—a reminder that in the Arctic, where spare parts are difficult to come by, junk is tantamount to an insurance policy.

I managed to wave down a taxi after a while. The driver, Frank Mustafa, had escaped from communist Albania some years earlier, and he and his four passengers were engaged in a lively discussion about a recent crime in town. "I'll get off over there, Frank," one of the passengers interrupted. "Just take the fare off what you owe me." I asked Mustafa about the crime. What had happened, he said, was this:

Three months earlier, a man had walked into the Alaska Company Store, stuck a dozen cassette tapes—

including Jethro Tull's *Thick as a Brick*—into his backpack and left without paying. He was spotted by employees, arrested and charged with shoplifting. The incident caused quite a stir along the Kuskokwim River because the suspect was Bethel's thirty-two-year-old district attorney, Bryan Schuler, and almost everyone started speculating why a man earning eighty thousand dollars a year would swipe sixty-six dollars' worth of cassettes. What made the case even stranger, police said, was that Schuler returned to the store with his hot tapes just after he had left, as though he wanted to get caught. The police chief, Kevin Clayton, described Schuler as "a personable enough fellow" who didn't socialize a lot. "With him," the chief told me, "it was work, work, work. He didn't have much of an outside life, and that makes it difficult to survive in Bethel. Something just clicked." Within hours, a new district attorney was on his way to Bethel, and Schuler was headed back to Anchorage. The former Russian fishing outpost was left to reflect on the fact that its remoteness and trying conditions had claimed another victim.

Mustafa dropped me off at *The Tundra Drums*. The office was deserted. I walked upstairs and found Rosie Porter in the kitchen of her inn. A sign tacked to the wall said: ONLY SOCIAL DRINKING PLEASE. NO CONTROLLED SUBSTANCES IN THIS BUILDING PLEASE. Rosie was a good-sized woman, about fifty, with a hearty laugh, and I liked her immediately. She was brewing a pot of coffee—Bethel, I would learn, ran on coffee, whiskey and reindeer sausage—and had two lit cigarettes going in the ashtray. She had once flown all the way to Paris to take a quit-smoking medical cure but had recently started again. "Smoking's my friend," she said. "It never deserts me."

I asked her about the district attorney. "I've seen people do ghastly things to get banished from here, like shooting moose out of season. It's obvious the guy was burned out. It was just his way of saying, 'Get me outta here.' A shrink might give you other reasons, but that's my analysis.

"I'll tell you how it is. Bethel's got an old, old reputation of being a terrible place. Well, that reputation comes mostly from snot-nosed people who are new to the state or from those hotsy-totsy people in Anchorage, who are getting so pretentious they think Anchorage is Seattle. As far as I'm concerned, Bethel is a secret, a great place to raise kids, to live. It's also a dynamite place for news. There's never a week you're sitting around with a finger up your nose, saying, 'Oh my God. What am I going to put in the paper this week?' The issues we get are real hot. The little guy versus the big guy. This town's taken on the entire nation of Japan for Christsakes on the issue of fishing rights when they were out there scooping up our salmon.

"You gotta remember, we're animals here. We store up nuts for the winter and huddle in little caves trying to stay warm. There's more drinking in the winter. Course, that's not to say there isn't a lot in the summer, too, but I mean, who the hell wants to go outside when it's minus seventy? Then the summer comes. Hibernation is over and we live outside. You should see our birds. We've got them galore—ducks, geese, everything. This is a prime area for bird-watchers, most of whom are real cheap and don't like

spending a dime. But I'll tell you, I put on Bach and I watch a swallow sitting on the wire outside, and what I know is that the meanness of spirit you find in urban people isn't here. People come up here and spend any length of time and the country bends them and they adapt some of the ways of the Eskimo, just as the Eskimo has had to adapt some of our *gussak* [white] ways."

Bethel reminded me more of the Third World than it did the United States. Its population was about evenly divided between Yupik Eskimos and nonnatives, an inordinately high number of whom had college degrees and had come to Bethel from "away"—Greece, Vietnam, Iran, Great Britain, Eastern Europe, Korea, the "Lower Forty-eight." Like Alaska itself, the town had become a collection point for an odd assortment of misfits, outcasts, adventurers, escapists, opportunists, wanderers, malcontents and rootless folks just plain weary of civilization's restraints and predictability. They had come to the frontier, as often as not, because their recent lives or past endeavors had been scarred by failure. What kept them on the frontier was the challenge of standing up to a harsh, spartan world and knowing they had not yielded or been conquered. The frontier built character and toughness and was a place where the weak and fainthearted seldom lingered long. The survivors did not expect to be victors against their environment. All they asked for was a standoff.

"People come up to the frontier from ordinary societies, and they're not knowledgeable enough about themselves to adapt," said Bill Biven, general manager of a native corporation whose investments ranged from real

estate to a car wash. "I know flexibility is an overused term today, but you need psychological and intellectual maturity to survive here. You can't take a person who's spent thirty years in an urban environment and expect him to make it in Bethel."

Everywhere I went in Alaska, the prime topic of conversation was Alaska. Alaskans wrote book after book about Alaskan sourdoughs, lost patrols and Klondike gold miners. Alaskans talked endlessly about the toughness of the Alaskan spirit (even though half the population lived in charmless Anchorage, where helicopters provided rush-hour traffic reports). Alaskans harped constantly that the federal government (which owned 98 percent of the state) didn't understand Alaskans. Alaskans published a magazine called *Alaska Men* that noted the state had "an abundance of interesting and exciting men whose rugged individualism, spirit and vitality makes them unique among men of the world." Among those profiled in the first edition were a fireman, a salesman, a magician and a bagpipe player. It was as if the people wanted confirmation that they weren't nuts to live in a land whose character is shaped by weather and isolation. They warded off their doubts by wrapping myths around their Last Frontier, and they delighted in referring to far-off "America" (never "the United States") as a foreign country, which in many ways it is.

Alaska is the nation's largest (four times the size of California), most sparsely populated (less than one person per square mile), youngest (median age twenty-six) and richest (average annual salary nearly $30,000) state, and

certainly the only one that ever had a Russian governor. It has fewer miles of road than Vermont, and the capital, Juneau, isn't reachable by car; you can only get there on a plane or boat. Thirteen percent of Alaska's households lack flush toilets. Alaska is so far from anywhere that American tourists often inquire at their hotels what kind of postage to affix to their postcards. "You use *U.S. stamps?*" one said. "How odd." If prestige is equated with money in Los Angeles, with political power in Washington, D.C., and with family heritage in Boston, what counts in Alaska is longevity. It is what separates the *cheechako*— Chinook jargon for someone who is dumb, greedy and, as one third the population has been since 1980, newly arrived—from the old-timers who had tried to push through the legislature a bill imposing an income tax exclusively on newcomers. The old-timers had toughed out a decade or two of horrible winters, lived through the boom and bust of the oil bonanza and accepted the fact that if Alaska were in Africa or Latin America, it would be considered part of the developing world.

Joe Vogler, a craggy-faced old man I met in Fairbanks, had moved north years ago, the son of a farmer who had been born in a sod dugout in Marshall County, Kansas. The farmer had told his children there were only two kinds of people: "Poor people and very poor people. We're the latter." Vogler set out to prove his father wrong. He had gotten a law degree; worked as a miner, logger, merchant and developer; and learned the value of things you can hold on to. "Only three things really matter," he said. "Real estate, gold and equipment." We were in his logged hilltop home, talking about the state's future now that the hysterical optimism of the oil boom era had faded, having made Alaskans humbler. No longer poor, he put down his coffee cup, looked me squarely in the eye and said, "I want America out of here."

Out of here? Yes, he said, pushing back his visored cap. Just write the statehood vote of 1958 off as a tragic error. Alaska's future is as an independent nation, not a colony over three thousand miles and four time zones from the federal capital. "America's gutting this country," he said, "and when the oil's gone, the copper's gone, the gold's gone, what are they going to leave us? What have they done for us—build the Dalton Highway? Well, that's a disgrace to civilization that'll tear hell out of your truck."

Vogler, head of the Alaskans for Independence party, had won nearly 6 percent of the vote in his 1986 run for the governorship. Alaskans admired his rebellious spirit more than they did his platform, but the separateness he preached did find sympathetic ears in a state where, at the closest point, the former Soviet Union is only three miles away and you can catch daily nonstop flights to London and Tokyo but not to Washington or New York. Alaskans, in fact, found the federal government such a heavy-handed interloper that they voted in 1980 to set up a commission to probe the state's relationship with the United States and consider, among other options, independence. It was the first time since the Civil War a state had questioned, by vote, the wisdom of the federal union. The Alaska Statehood Commission reported three years later that it had examined the alternatives and found "none preferable to statehood." Still, Alaskans weren't so sure. They were a cocksure, exuberant bunch in those days, riding the crest of the energy windfall, and there was no reason to believe good times wouldn't roll on forever.

I first spent time in Alaska during the frenzy of the pipeline construction in 1975. I had just beaten a hasty retreat from Saigon, a day or two before North Vietnamese tanks rumbled into the city, and my nerves were still jagged when I stepped off the plane in Fairbanks. The friend who met me there was drunk, in full stride on a round-the-clock bender, and insisted I needed a boilermaker to steady my legs. *My* legs? The saloon he took me to was raucous. Every stool at the bar was taken. It was 10:00 A.M. I quickly caught the spirit of the place and in no time had joined the roomful of strangers, who, with raised glasses, were singing salutations to Dan McGrew:

> *A bunch of the boys were whooping*
> *it up in the Malamute saloon;*
> *The kid that handles the music-box was*
> *hitting a jagtime tune;*
> *Back of the bar, in a solo game, sat Dangerous*
> *Dan McGrew,*
> *And watching his luck was his light-o'-love,*
> *the lady that's known as Lou.*

In Saigon, I had witnessed the end of an American era. In Alaska, I was seeing the beginning of one. Eight thousand people a month were pouring into the state, drawn not by the promise of long-term opportunity or the thought of contributing anything. What enticed the new wave of Alaskans was money. The jobless became bartenders, bartenders became bar owners, bar owners became real estate developers, and no one remembered how to mix a dry martini. Prostitutes cruised Cushman Street in Cadillacs, and one woman Teamster pulled in $29,000 in eighteen weeks' work. Her hourly rates: $11.30 for truck driving; $500 for time with a white man, $250 with an Indian or Eskimo. Old-timers cringed and put bumper stickers on their cars that said: HAPPINESS IS 10,000 TEXANS HEADING SOUTH WITH AN OKIE UNDER EACH ARM. But they knew they could not slow the inevitable. America had found a new frontier. We had slunk out of Vietnam and were now strutting across Alaska.

"People want to make money," realtor Mick Killion told me, "and there's plenty of it to be made even though everything's gone nuts—the prices, the pace, everything. To get that money, we're sacrificing a lot, like our sanity." The opening of the pipeline would shower Alaska with a $24 billion godsend over ten years' time and kick off a spending spree that would have done justice to King Fahd of Saudi Arabia.

One state representative, Pappy Moss, proposed bailing out Chrysler, Cleveland and almost everyone else with financial difficulties south of the sixtieth parallel. Dade County, Florida, officials wrote in, asking for a $200 million grant to build a sports complex. Alaska spent $100 million to study the construction of two dams on the Susitna River (they weren't built) and $4 million for a grain export terminal in Seward (it was abandoned). Fairbanks paid its city engineers $75,000 a year, its grade-school teachers $42,000, and hired a full-time employee to name streets.

State income taxes were repealed in 1981, and to keep

retirees in the state, Alaska gave all persons over sixty-five a monthly bonus of $250, paid their property taxes and gave them free bus passes and fishing licenses. On top of that, it mailed out royalty dividends each year to every resident. The independent-minded Alaskans hated the idea of socialism and loved the perks it provided. "My wife goes out to the mailbox one day and comes back with checks for five thousand dollars—one thousand for each member of the family," recalled airline executive Lou Cancelmi. "Not only wasn't the state taxing you, it was paying you to live in Alaska. It was bizarre. Really wild."

The history of bonanzas in the Empty Quarter is a simple one: What goes boom will soon go bust. And by the 1990s Alaska had sobered up. Oil prices had collapsed. Their legacy had been a huge state debt, massive unplanned development, a plethora of government regulations and moneyed values that seemed to belong more to Los Angeles than to the Last Frontier. No longer did one see bumper stickers about Texans and Okies heading south. Now the banners pleaded: PLEASE GOD, GIVE US ONE MORE BOOM. WE PROMISE NOT TO PISS THIS ONE AWAY. The boom and its consequences had made Alaska more humble and less introverted and had taken some of the rough edge off the Alaskan character. The people became softer and whinier. Everyone complained that the Alaskan fiber had been tested—and weakened—by the greed of the seventies. Things, they said, just weren't the same. Which they never are.

Three days before Christmas, I found myself in Barrow, North America's northernmost town. The southern tip of the earth's axis was inclined twenty-three degrees toward the sun. It was the winter solstice. The sun had abandoned Barrow, casting it into twenty-four hours of utter darkness, and not for sixty-five more days would the godforsaken town on the Arctic Ocean see the glimmer of another sunrise. The endless nights play tricks with the biological rhythms of the body, manipulating moods and behavior patterns, and remind Alaskans across the state that winter is their master, as uncompromising as a dictator. Jars of vitamin C were piled high on the shelves of drugstores. Bars and tanning parlors overflowed. Flights to Hawaii—a destination one in fifteen Alaskans visits in an average year—had been sold out for six months. In Fairbanks, social worker Marsha Schneider found herself walking through her home at midday, turning on the lights. (Her husband followed behind, turning them off.) At Prudhoe Bay, Don Haverkamp would walk into his Arco office each morning and close the window curtains, as though to shut out a world that reflected nothing of itself in the first place. In Anchorage, which shares roughly the sixtieth latitude with Oslo and Stockholm, night after night some gathering required guests to wear tuxedos and gowns.

"That's an attempt to deal with these winter problems," Dr. Aron Wolf said. "It's a way of saying, 'You have something to look forward to, something to dress up for.' Yet if you try to hold a professional meeting in the summer, forget it. You simply can't get ten people together. They're all out in the midnight sun, on the river." Dr. Wolf is a specialist in a debilitating affliction known as SAD (seasonal affective disorder), and I had called to ask if we could meet for lunch to talk about it. He brought along one of his patients, Martha Roderick. Energetic and articulate, Mrs. Roderick was walking proof of the role the absence or presence of light plays in behavior and mood swings. For her and thousands of other victims in the Far North, SAD struck in the long, dark days of winter, turning the brightest holiday moods into a nightmare of depression, irritability, lethargy, carbohydrate craving and impaired concentration. The Swedes call these midwinter blues Lapp sickness; the Finns refer to them as *kaamos.*

Martha Roderick first noticed the symptoms when she and her husband, Jack, moved to Juneau in the winter of 1975. The thick mist clung to the city, and trees bent low under their burden of snow. The world closed in like a windowless cabin until the spirit seemed to die. Gradually she found herself unable to get up in time to give tutoring lessons at the school across the street. She gave up (indoor) tennis because she couldn't keep track of the score or who had won the last point. If friends called to invite her out, she made up excuses to avoid them. "Once when Jack was out of town, I realized I had stayed in bed an entire day and part of the next one," she recalled. "I wondered if I was losing my abilities forever." Then spring came, and finally summer, with its late-night sunsets, and Mrs. Roderick recovered and was again full of energy. But each autumn brought a sense of foreboding, and in the darkness of winter she would slip back into her state of depressed hibernation.

Mrs. Roderick had been free from SAD for four winters when we met, because Aron Wolf and another doctor at the Langdon Clinic in Anchorage had tricked her body into thinking it was spring with phototherapy, an antidepressant light treatment whose benefits are often apparent within a few days. Each morning she spent an hour reading or listening to the radio at her desk, located a precisely measured distance from a full-spectrum light that emitted the infrared and ultraviolet rays of the sun at an intensity of 2,500 lumens, about the same as the first stage of twilight. No one can adequately explain the effectiveness of phototherapy on SAD, but one theory holds that bright light hitting the retina blocks the release of the hormone melatonin, which is secreted at night in the brain and is associated with depression. There is, though, general agreement that SAD affects women more than men, adults more than children and whites more than native Eskimos or Indians, and that it becomes more common the farther north of the Equator one lives.

Alaska's harsh environment and its two major seasons—light and dark—do more than make people SAD. They influence the state's character and antisocial behavior and help explain why the registrar of vital statistics lists the leading cause of death in Alaska as "accidents and adverse effects." Suicide is the fourth most common cause. On a per capita basis, Alaska leads the nation in forcible rapes, ranks second in divorce and third in alcohol consumption. Alaskans die younger than other Americans and have an incidence of aggravated assault that is among the highest in the country. I called the University of Alaska's Health Center and asked the director, Dr. James Cole, if there was an explanation for such abnormal statistics. "A lot of the social factors you see in Alaska are those of the frontier," he said. "People who come to a frontier tend not to have been doing well where they were. They have a higher degree of emotional problems."

In many ways Alaska is our forgotten corner, a region of noble beauty, strategic value and bountiful minerals that would seem to belong more fittingly to Canada than to the United States. Except when we have needed its resources or worried over the possibility of an enemy attack by air or sea, we have treated Alaska as irrelevant. Americans settled it only as a last resort, after the Great Plains and the West began filling up late in the nineteenth century. President Eisenhower, who favored statehood for Hawaii, long held to the belief that Alaska should remain a territory. The ceremony, on October 18, 1867, in which Russia formally transferred the territory to the United States—we had bought the whole chunk of wilderness for three cents an acre in the greatest real estate swindle since the colonialists hoodwinked the Indians into giving up Manhattan for some beads attracted no more than a handful of frozen spectators in Sitka. The Russian flag jammed as it was being lowered, and a sailor had to be hoisted up the flagpole to cut it free. The young wife of the retiring Russian governor, Maria Maksutova, fell over in a dead faint, the minor delay in getting the hell out of Alaska apparently being more than she could bear.

Unlike the homesteaders of the West, the Americans attracted to Alaska were not farmers or ranchers, and, their souls less rooted in the land, they came with the idea that one day they would leave. In Nome—whose eight bars do considerably more business than its thirteen churches—the entire population still turns over every nine years. Even Wyatt Earp had a tough time with Nome. Fresh from Dodge City and Tombstone, he moved there for the gold rush in 1898 and ran the Dexter Saloon. Other than getting arrested for drunkenness one night, he remained on good behavior but could endure only three howling winters before heading south to take up residency in the gentler climes of California. My friend who had picked me up drunk at the Fairbanks airport left too. He went on the wagon and moved back to New England. I asked him why. "After twenty years, Alaska wasn't a challenge anymore," he said. "Something inside just told me it was time to go, that if I didn't go soon, it would be tough to ever get out."

Buffalo Commons

It struck me on Christmas Eve, 1991, while I was in Saudi Arabia waiting for the Persian Gulf War to happen, that what makes me feel comfortable in small-town America is exactly what had always made me feel at home with foot soldiers. I was among people who cared for and needed one another and spoke with unguarded words. You started a conversation from a position of trust, and you seldom left their presence wondering what they meant or felt. They had nothing to sell and nothing to protect, and they took responsibility for their individual actions but understood they did not have ultimate control over their common future.

Christmas Eve was a lousy time to be in Saudi Arabia and a good time to get life in perspective. I had gone north to a forward marine base, and, just after dusk, I followed Gig and Smiling Jack and Camel Killer and Pedro and a bunch of other young navy corpsmen through the sand and into a tent identified by a handwritten sign as the CAMEL'S ASS ENLISTED MAN'S CLUB. There were two picnic tables inside, and Spike, who had gotten there early, had already staked out one of them for a game of Monopoly. A note on the wall advertised iced tea, Pepsi, and Saudi slammers (water mixed with various artificial fruit flavors offered in combat rations packages), and near it stood an artificial eighteen-inch-high Christmas tree someone had received from home. The mood was surprisingly festive, as though no one dared reveal a heart that ached.

"I call these guys my desert family," said corpsman Shane Cadlolo, his tall paper party hat set at a jaunty angle. "Gig, Don, Dave, Doc—if I can't be with my real family back home, these are the guys I'd want to spend Christmas with." Two of Cadlolo's colleagues, Peter Holten of Beloit, Wisconsin, and Paul Lacombe of Yakima, Washington, had formed a musical group of sorts known as the Fried Brains. They took up position by the dart board and sang about white Christmases and sleigh bells ringing, then tried some jokes and retreated as good-natured hoots and boos filled the tent. Cadlolo asked me if I had received any Christmas presents. I told him my wife in the States had sent me a long fax and that it was as special a gift as I had ever gotten. "I know what you mean," he said.

Outside the stars seemed close enough to touch. "The brightest one there," said Terry Aragoni, a surgeon, "that's Mars. Did you know Mars is the god of war? Ironic, isn't it?" The night felt peaceful and had fallen quiet, and from somewhere in the shadows I heard a voice call out, "Merry Christmas, Sarge." And the reply came back, "Merry Christmas."

Four months later, the war and my exotic wanderings over, I was back in a more familiar setting. I sped across the Great Plains of eastern Colorado, a land as flat and often barren as Kuwait, and was filled with a sense of exhilarating freedom. There were no checkpoints, no dangers or uncertainties in the road ahead. Every turn was of my choosing, and no uniformed gunmen stood guard to tell me whether I could head north or south. All this, and so many other freedoms, Americans take for granted. Yet they are privileges, not rights, to many peoples of the world, and I wondered if our national spirit would not perhaps have been healthier had we not been given so much that demanded so little of us.

The Center for the New West in Denver defines the Great Plains as the dry, timberless expanse bordered on the east by Interstate 35, which runs from Minneapolis to Laredo, Texas, and on the west by Interstate 25, from Buffalo, Wyoming, to El Paso, Texas. (What would Lewis and Clark have said had they been told that one day highways, and not mountains or rivers, would shape our regions?) Between these two great interstates are twelve states, an area larger than Western Europe. Had the Great Plains been a nation, its gross domestic product (more than $650 billion) would rank behind only those of the United States, Japan and Germany. The 3 percent of the Americans who live there account for one third of the nation's agricultural products.

But since the 1890s, the population of many Plains' counties has been dwindling and towns abandoned, and now a new thesis has come into vogue: The Great Plains are dying. Among the remedies offered was one from a Montana group that wanted to turn moribund regions of the Plains into a giant hunting preserve and dude ranch known as the Big Open. A University of Oklahoma geographer said the Forest Service should start buying out marginal farmers. And, after announcing that more than a third of the Plains' counties were "beyond redemption," Frank Popper, a Rutgers University urban studies professor, proposed letting the region revert to its natural, depopulated state, as a sort of national park he would call Buffalo Commons.

I was on Highway 34 in Colorado, headed for Wray. Among the eulogies one heard for the small towns of the Great Plains, one might have expected to find the name of Wray. "I wonder why this place died," a passerby would ask, and the answer would come in the wind and the dust and the silence of the prairies. The wind is the lifeblood of these towns that stand like sentries, almost always fifteen miles apart, at each country crossroad. It guides the storm clouds, creates the dust bowls, heralds the bone-chilling cold of winter and the withering heat of summer, and because of it and the vicissitudes of life in the American outback, the longevity of places like Wray has always been measured in generations, and sometimes even in seasons.

Wray had been flattened by a tornado in 1971. The next day Dale and Eunice Wisdom opened the doors of their lumberyard and told people, "Just take what you need. You can figure out what you owe us later." The Red Cross showed up to provide disaster relief, and the mayor said, "Thanks, but we can handle this ourselves." School was canceled in the neighboring communities, and the kids were bused into Wray to sweep up the streets. In six months Wray had been rebuilt. The Wisdoms took inventory and found only two sheets of plywood unaccounted for. "Somebody'll be along to pay for them," Dale Wisdom said.

When I had called the Center for the New West to ask if the death of the Great Plains was imminent, Philip Burgess, the president, replied, "All that stuff is pure bull." He maintained the pundits had mistaken change for catastrophe, and he offered a long list of towns that were prospering because their community leaders understood that brains, not brawn, would determine the future of Main Street, USA. Among the towns he mentioned was Wray, Colorado. "What's going on out there on the Plains is a lot of economic churning and change, just like in the rest of the world," Burgess said. "The Soviet Union called it *perestroika* and we celebrated it. The same thing happens in our country and we say it's a problem."

Burgess believes we are seeing on the Great Plains the emergence of an "archipelago society"—urban islands, linked by interstate highways and airports, in a sea of wheat. Within the area, economic units will consolidate, some fragile towns will die, economies will become more diverse and the relationship between heartland and city will become more national than regional. Sioux Falls, South Dakota, for instance, has become the site of a major credit card clearinghouse and now finds itself linked more to New York City than to Bismarck, North Dakota, or Billings, Montana. Marriott put its worldwide hotel reservations center in Omaha, and Kansas City has become the largest assembler of automobiles outside Detroit. Nearly one quarter of North Dakotans are employed in businesses that did not exist in 1980, and less than 4 percent of those businesses are in agriculture.

Wray is but a speck on the map. It has a forty-eight-page phone book that covers ten communities, one main street, a couple thousand residents and a motel, all anchored by a cluster of grain elevators at the doorstep of town. If I hadn't been there with a purpose, Wray would have blurred in my mind's eye as indistinguishable from scores of other outpost towns except for one thing: It had a movie theater that was open seven evenings a week, a telltale symbol of a town's viability in an era when movie houses have largely disappeared from the main streets of America. I stopped in the coffee shop—which in small towns substitutes for the courthouse as the place where the affairs of community are discussed and decided—and fell into conversation with Gene Cranwell, who owned the local motel. Times in Wray, he said, were pretty decent. I mentioned that the nation as a whole seemed obsessed with the notion that society was in decline and asked what made Wray different. "Caring's the difference, I guess," he said. "We never stopped caring about ourselves, about each other, about our community. People need each other on the Plains."

Hearing a familiar ring, I went back to my notes to see what Shane Cadlolo had said on Christmas Eve in Saudi Arabia and realized both Cranwell and Cadlolo were talking about the same thing. Like a lot of farming towns on the Plains, from Broken Bow, Nebraska, to Linton, North Dakota, Wray had left the intensive-care ward because it had a cadre of dreamers—a group of unpaid community leaders who thought there was a good deal worth saving in their rural environment and who were willing to take action independently of federal and state government. And that's where Mike Wisdom, the son of the lumberyard owners, fitted in.

Wisdom had left Wray in 1969, two years before the tornado, to attend college on a wrestling scholarship. When he returned a decade or so later, the town was in decline and old friends were still sitting around wondering what had happened to the carefree, prosperous fifties. What Wray had to do, he decided with several friends over a beer one night, was find a way to hold the young and comfort the elderly. The idea they hit upon was a rehabilitation and recreation center, something that might sound pretty ordinary to those of us who live in cities but that to Wray would become the showcase of a community's faith in itself. The only catch was that the new center would cost $2.3 million—a thousand dollars for every man, woman and child in Wray.

I waited in the trailer at the top of Main Street that served as Wisdom's office. He was already thirty minutes late. His desk was a cluttered mess, and above it was tacked a quotation attributed to Einstein: "Great spirits have always encountered violent opposition from mediocre minds." Wisdom finally appeared, a broad-shouldered man of forty, rubbing soot smudges from his face. He had been with the volunteer fire department fighting a brushfire at the edge of town, and his tardiness was unavoidable, he said. Wisdom worked full-time raising funds and overseeing the rehab and rec center that was nearing completion outside his trailer door. Unbeknownst to his fellow townspeople, he turned his modest salary back to the center each month and lived on savings. "We're paying for this a square foot at a time, and when the doors open, it's going to be clear and paid for," he said.

It had taken six years, but the money was nearly in

hand, and Wray had raised every penny itself. Private people, Wisdom liked to say, had assumed responsibility for a public project. They held bake sales and countless little fund-raisers and sold lifetime lockers at the center for a thousand dollars. Thousands of people around the country responded to one brainy promotion and paid twenty dollars to be Wray's honorary mayor for a day. Gene Kramer donated a semitrailer, Max and Mark Shively a can crusher and Larry Allen a conveyor, and soon there wasn't an aluminum can in town that didn't get recycled; that netted a steady thirty-six dollars a month. To celebrate the end of harvest each year, Wisdom and his colleagues sold a thousand rubber ducks for five dollars apiece and dropped them into the nearby Republican River for a six-block race. Disc jockey Bruce Palmrose followed in a rubber tube to confirm the winner of the five-hundred-dollar first prize (which was donated by a Wray businessman). The local judge got into the act too, and instead of fining youths for minor infractions of the law sentenced them to forty hours' community service, helping build the center. Then there was the local seamstress, Ollie Wood, who every month, year after year, managed to set aside forty dollars. She died before the center opened, but her $429,000 estate went to the local hospital and that helped Wray attract three young doctors from the city.

Wisdom packed me into his pickup truck and took me out to a cluster of hidden bushes where kids drank beer on summery Saturday nights and up to a hill that overlooks the town. I imagined that people had stood on the bluff, carrying dreams for themselves and their community, ever since Wray was founded in 1886. Wisdom said he believed a man shouldn't take more out of his community than he was prepared to put back into it. I told him I thought that attitude had probably helped snatch Wray from the death rolls of the Great Plains but doubted it was applicable to the problems of urban America, and he replied, "Why not?"

Francis Parkman, a historian from Boston, crossed the Plains in 1846 and wrote: "No living thing was moving throughout that vast landscape, except the lizards that darted over the sand and through the rank grass and prickly pears at our feet. . . . Before and behind us, the level monotony of the plain was unbroken as far as the eye could reach. Sometimes it glared in the sun, an expanse of hot, bare sand; sometimes it was veiled by coarse grass. Skulls and whitening bones of buffalo were scattered everywhere." When Parkman made his journey, the Great Plains was identified on maps—and engraved in the minds of easterners—as the Great American Desert. Rainfall averaged no more than twenty inches a year, and the land, covered with rocky clay soil and clusters of cottonwoods and hackberries, appeared decidedly unsuitable for agriculture or habitation. Until the Civil War, travelers viewed the arid expanse as a hostile wasteland that was memorable only because it slowed their trek to California or Oregon.

But the rangeland of the Plains had once sustained 75 million buffalo, and what it did have was grass that was remarkably nutritious and resistant to drought. With the slaughter of the buffalo for their hides after the Civil War, the grass lay unused, and that brought the longhorn cattle. More than 5 million of them were driven north from Texas over the Plains between 1867 and 1887 to be shipped from Kansas railheads to eastern markets. Merchants and money and commerce followed the cattle, and rowdy settlements took hold. At the same time railroad builders and land speculators worked to capitalize on the Homestead Act of 1862 and erase the image of the Great American Desert. They put journalists and scientists on their payrolls and launched a propaganda campaign to settle the Plains under the slogan "Rains follow the plow." It was a lie, of course, but by the end of the nineteenth century, hundreds of towns like Wray were scattered across the Plains, and with the advent of barbed wire, windmills, new farm machines and farming techniques, improved irrigation and drought-resistant plants, the term Great American Desert was heard no more.

No comparable area of the world today produces more beef and wheat than the Great Plains. In terms of infant mortality, teenage births and deaths, it is healthier than the rest of America, though per capita health-care costs are below the national average. The Center for the New West also reports that the Plains spends less for education than most other regions but turn out more high-school graduates. They in turn have helped entrepreneurship thrive: Every state on the Great Plains except New Mexico exceeds the national average of small business per one thousand residents.

Across the Plains I found many towns like Wray, towns that would have died in the farm recession had it not been for grass-roots leadership and entrepreneurial spirit. Ellsworth, Nebraska (population 27), had been saved by one family that started a mail-order business and had a payroll of sixty-five workers. In Cheney, Kansas, a farmer's wife set up a day-care center for ninety-one children, enabling their parents to commute to jobs in Wichita. Residents in Strasburg, North Dakota, started a thriving tourist industry by restoring the farmhouse Ludwig and Christina Welk had built and raised their son, Lawrence, in after reaching the town in an ox-drawn wagon in 1893. After the restoration was under way, Strasburg applied for and won a $500,000 federal grant to build a museum honoring the German-Russian immigrants who, like the Welks, had settled the region. It was, everyone agreed, a perfect way to attract more visitors and tell a largely unknown story about the Great Plains.

Lawrence Welk, the multimillionaire "King of Champagne Music," held a special place in North Dakota's heart. The state has produced its fair share of celebrities, among them Angie Dickinson, Eric Sevareid, Roger Maris, Peggy Lee and Louis L'Amour, but most of them had fled North Dakota at first opportunity and didn't seem to give two hoots about coming back. Welk was different. He had left his windswept prairie town on his twenty-first birthday, in 1924, carrying a suitcase and his accordion, and even after he became rich and famous, he kept coming back. He would sit in the cafe on Main Street, drinking coffee and greeting many of Strasburg's six hundred residents by name. He sent thousands of dollars a year to support the local Catholic church, the high school, the nursing home where his sister lived and the community swimming pool (which was built with funds from a concert he gave in Minot).

But no sooner had the grant to build the museum been announced than Strasburg found itself being denounced as a recipient of government waste and pork-barrel politics. "What will they do for an encore?" a congressman from Massachusetts asked in attacking his colleagues' largess. "Earmark funds to renovate Guy Lombardo's speedboat? Or restore Artie Shaw's wedding tuxedo?" A few months later the Farmers Home Administration responded to the flap by announcing it wouldn't give Strasburg the funds after all. Strasburg cringed that its good intentions had become the brunt of jokes on late-night TV talk shows. The Welk homesite had been restored with private funds, and after all, everyone asked, weren't a lot of museums supported by federal monies? The town's Pioneer Heritage committee nailed a sign on the faded red Welk barn that said: NO FEDERAL FUNDS HAVE BEEN USED TO RESTORE THE BIRTHPLACE OF LAWRENCE WELK. WE STILL NEED TO RAISE $60,000. PLEASE HELP. And it set out to find money to build the museum.

"I think we could have won and kept the grant if we'd caused a big stink," Evelyn Schwab, Lawrence Welk's niece, said over a cup of coffee in the town's cafe. "But that takes money and it takes attorneys to fight the case for you and where are you going to get that kind of money out here on the Plains? So we'll do it ourselves. We've already planned some fund-raising events." The first was to be an ethnic dinner on Lawrence Welk's eighty-ninth birthday— just down the street from the cafe, in Horner's pool hall.

"It's a start, not a big one but a start," said Evelyn Schwab. "You'll see. We'll have our museum yet."

The irony in the brouhaha over the Buffalo Commons proposal is that alarmists have spent a century writing epitaphs for the Great Plains. Yet the Plains survived the terrible depression of 1876 (when the nation's banking system collapsed and three states scarred by the Civil War—Florida, Louisiana and South Carolina—were under martial law), the grasshopper plagues of the 1880s, the Dust Bowl of the 1930s, the drought of the 1950s, the rioting blizzards of a hundred winters. The prairies endure, at least in part, because there is something wonderfully square and old-fashioned about people who find optimism—or perhaps patience is a more appropriate word—in adversity and who have a sense of history to draw on when the day seems unbearably gloomy. In the cities we are apt to throw up our hands when times turn troubled and exclaim, "Things have never been worse." On the Great Plains, people know better.

Greyhound Romance

I left my home in Norfolk, Virginia—
California on my mind.
I straddled that Greyhound and rode
it into Raleigh and on across Caroline . . .
CHUCK BERRY, "The Promised Land," 1964

Before there were Greyhound buses, western railroads or even much in the way of roads except rutted trails, an army captain named Randolph B. Marcy wrote, in 1859, a book titled *The Prairie Traveler*. Published with the authorization of the War Department, it offered practical advice on how to travel from the Mississippi to the Pacific. Marcy detailed twenty-five western routes, noting among other things that as one approached the city of Los Angeles on the trail from Albuquerque, "The road passes the Mission of San Gabriel, then enters a ravine among hills and broken ground; it then descends and crosses the river which waters the valley, and enters the city. There is a good camp upon the point of a ridge on the left bank of the river."

For journeys of more than fifteen hundred miles, Marcy preferred oxen to mules to pull the wagons (better endurance, cheaper to buy and, in a crisis, tastier to eat) and suggested that each person's bedroll should consist of two blankets, a comforter, a pillow and a painted canvas cloth to spread on the ground. One large kettle would accommodate the needs of six people, he said, and medicine chests should include quinine, opium and a cathartic. Every man needed a rifle and a revolver—which "he should never, either in camp or out of it, lose sight of"— and each wagon should contain an ample supply of buckskin—"one of the most indispensable articles to the outfit of the prairie traveler"—to repair harnesses, saddle and bridles. Marcy went on to note that

> the scarcity of water upon some of the routes across the plains occasionally exposes the traveler to intense suffering, and renders it a matter of much importance for him to learn the best methods of guarding against the disasters liable to occur to man and animals in the absence of this most necessary element. . . . Water taken from stagnant pools, charged with putrid vegetable matter and animalculae, would be very likely to generate fevers and dysenteries if taken into the stomach without purification. It should therefore be thoroughly boiled, and all the scum removed from the surface as it rises; this clarifies it, and by mixing powdered charcoal with it the disinfecting process is perfected. Water may also be purified by placing a piece of alum in the end of a stick that has been split, and stirring it around in a bucket of water. Charcoal and the leaves of the prickly pear

are also used for the same purpose. I have recently
seen a compact and portable filter, made of char-
coal, which clarifies the water very effectually, and
draws it off the siphon principle. It can be obtained
at 85 West Street, New York, for one dollar and a
half. ✍

Traveling west had gotten easier, but only a little, by
the 1860s, when Mark Twain and his brother (who had
just been appointed secretary of Nevada Territory) spent
$150 each for a ticket on the stage from St. Joseph, Mis-
souri, to Carson City, Nevada. Twain was armed with a
Smith & Wesson seven-shooter, and his brother carried an
unabridged dictionary, for fear one could not buy books
in the territory. Passengers were allowed twenty-five
pounds baggage. Twain wrote of the "great swinging and
swaying coach" flying over the land, pulled by six handsome horses, which went flat out and were changed every
few hours. The brothers and another passenger sat surrounded by 2,700 pounds of mailbags. As they were crossing the Rockies, rain came down so heavily that the driver
sent the conductor ahead on foot to search for the road
with a lantern. "I never saw anything like it [the rain]—
indeed, I did not even see this, for it was too dark," Twain
said.

✍ We fastened down the curtains and even
caulked them with clothing, but the rain streamed
in in twenty places, notwithstanding. There was no
escape. If one moved his feet out of a stream, he
brought his body under one; and if he moved his

body he caught one somewhere else. If he struggled out of the drenched blankets and sat up, he
was bound to get one down the back of his neck.
Meantime the stage was wandering about a plain
with gaping gullies in it, for the driver could not
see an inch before his face nor keep the road, and
the storm pelted so pitilessly that there was no
keeping the horses still.

Less than seventy years after Twain's journey to the
Far West—"The idea of coming to a standstill and settling
down to a humdrum existence in a village was not agree-
able," he said as Carson City came into view on the twentieth day—the hardships of traveling by road were
changed by a significant event: The Pioneer Yelloway Bus
Line introduced, in 1927, transcontinental bus service—
New York to San Francisco (for seventy-two dollars) in
five days and fourteen hours. The bus opened up the
United States, as the railroads had earlier, ending the
isolation of countless small towns and giving Americans,
for the first time, easy access to America itself.

I don't remember exactly when I became smitten with
Greyhounds, though by the time I was a teenager I had
ridden them all over the place and could recite the schedule from, say, Boston to Denver as readily as I could the
starting lineup of my favorite baseball team. My friends
considered this obsession a character flaw. But I knew
better. For to those whose souls are captive to the restless
energy of the open road, the long-haul buses that criss-
cross the nation are no ordinary thing. They speak of
small towns wrapped in darkness, of the loneliness of

passing as strangers through the night, of a sweetheart left behind in the dusty-hamlet shadows of another era, where the bus moves slowly away at dusk, its destination sign bearing the name of some far-off place. Airline terminals exude a sense of expectation, bus terminals, resignation. They make the miles between here and home seem great, and I don't think I've ever been in a bus depot that didn't smell of sadness. They are where, in my mind's eye, it is always early Christmas morning and a solitary sailor sits, half dozing, on a wooden bench, hands thrust in the pockets of his pea jacket, duffel bag at his feet, waiting for the bus that will take him home, too late for family dinner, or perhaps head him off in some direction far from home. I look at my watch. It is midnight. I feel like the sailor and want to be somewhere else.

The Greyhound station in Billings, Montana, was a drab room with a closed cafe. Half a dozen people waited with me there, some for the transcontinental express, others for connecting buses to Thermopolis and Shoshone, Roundup and Great Falls, Casper and Cheyenne. A cowboy shoveled quarters into a video machine in the corner, but everyone else seemed dazed with sleeplessness. Billings was as quiet as the prairie, its streets dark and deserted. Everything in town appeared closed except for Cattin's Cafe ("We gladly accept local checks") on First Avenue, just across from the terminal.

Promptly on schedule, at twenty-five minutes past midnight, the eastbound Greyhound from Seattle hissed to a stop outside, destination Chicago, two days and a lifetime of highway miles away. "You got time for a quick breakfast over at Cattin's," the driver said as his bleary-eyed passengers filed off the bus. "But don't linger too long. You aren't where you're going yet." A new driver, Francis Sullivan, took over the bus in Billings. He wore a freshly pressed uniform with a seventeen-year safe-driving patch on the sleeve and had one of those chiseled western faces that stare you down in Marlboro ads. When Mark Twain traveled west by stagecoach, the men who ran the way stations where the horses were changed and the passengers fed were mostly desperadoes and thugs. But the bunch along the route now were as honorable as a county sheriff, and after a while Sullivan called out, "Anyone heading east, we're boarding. Line up on Platform One, please." He checked his tires, adjusted his seat, tucked his folded jacket in the overhead rack and at 1:35 A.M. eased out of town and turned his forty-three-seat bus onto Interstate 94, toward Huntley, Worden, Custer, Hysham and the other little ranching communities scattered across the plains of eastern Montana and North Dakota.

The bus was half full. "I could've flown to Cleveland and it'd be cheaper," the man across the aisle from me said, "but airplanes scare hell out of me." A retired couple, with time to spare and things to see, had staked out the front-row seats to the right of Sullivan and said they had no real destination at all; they just got on and off the bus whenever they liked the look of a place. There was also a nurse who had flown to Billings from a fling in Las Vegas and was trying to get back to Glendive in time for her morning shift; a cowboy traveling to Bismarck, with a connection on to Minot, "to do some fishin' and drinkin'—and not necessarily in that order—with my brother"; and a man about forty who boarded without a suitcase and said his last meal had been five days ago. His only possession was a bus ticket to Chicago. "There's work there, I heard," he said.

The murmur of conversation quickly faded. The rain beat down, and the $200,000 coach sped through the night, our journey as effortless as Twain's had been perilous. In the freight compartment of the bus's belly were bundles of the morning newspaper, *The Billings Gazette,* a shipment of blood and medical supplies for several country hospitals, a new saddle and spare parts for a rancher's broken tractor in Medora, where cattle rustlers once were hanged from a tree that still stands in the town of ninety-four inhabitants. The rancher would be waiting for us at the gas station when our bus pulled into Medora at 6:30 A.M.

While urban Americans by the millions, lured by cheap airfares and the demands of time, have turned away from intercity buses in the past decade, out in the open spaces of the West, where people have been abandoned by trains and scheduled airlines, the Greyhound is still the heart line, much as the stagecoach was in the days before the railroad. Without backtracking through Denver or Minneapolis, you cannot fly from Billings to Fargo, North Dakota, the largest cities in neighboring states. Nor can you fly between the capitals of Helena, Montana, and Bismarck, North Dakota, without making a double connection. Just one passenger train, the Empire Builder, rolls across the two states once a day in each direction on the far-northern High Line that links Chicago and Seattle. So, in the Empty Quarter, if you want to travel, if you need machine parts, medicine or a set of tires in a hurry, if you have to get to a funeral or a wedding or bring your son home from college for Christmas vacation, you have two choices: your car or the bus.

Most Americans, of course, share neither a dependency on nor a romance with the nation's intercity bus system, which serves 15,000 communities (compared with 625 cities served by scheduled airlines and 525 by Amtrak, the federally subsidized passenger rail service). The bus is their choice of last resort, and in less than a generation the number of Americans who ride the Greyhound each year has fallen from 60 million to 16 million.

A few months before I sped east with driver Sullivan on that rainy Montana night, a Dallas investor, Fred G. Currey, had bought Greyhound—including its 3,100 buses and sprinting dog trademark, one of the nation's most recognizable logos—for $350 million. Currey was trying to convince Americans to get back on the bus and "leave the driving to us," and he used to startle employees by showing up unannounced on buses to question passengers and by taking off his jacket on the docks, rolling up his sleeves and pitching in to help baggage handlers load and unload freight.

"If you tell me bus transportation is dead, I'll tell you you're wrong," Currey told me one day. "Our market is alive and well. It's a matter of focusing on what the traveler's needs are and responding to changes in the marketplace. We tried to ape the rail industry and what we forgot was that we have the flexibility to go anywhere the highway goes. Population shifted from the rural to urban areas and subcities grew around the cities, and bus industry people still talked about nonstop runs from Los Angeles to San Francisco. But hell, our passengers didn't live there anymore. They lived in between, in Glendale and Santa Ana and the San Fernando Valley, and we weren't picking them up."

On the bus, I nodded off and didn't awake until North Dakota, a night's ride out of Billings. The dawn sun was a ball of burning coals on the horizon. A new driver, Monte Schneider, was at the wheel, rolling east through the Badlands, a stark, foreboding region that once lay beneath an ancient inland sea. Huge columns of unsupported rock soared skyward, like the pillars of some collapsed temple. Ahead the landscape was etched with steep cliffs over which the Sioux used to stampede great herds of bison. The little one-street towns slipped by as a blurred portrait of America—bib overalls drying on a backyard clothesline, a weathered American Legion hall, a sod lookout used by General George A. Custer, Gerry's Bar & Groceries with its Copenhagen snuff poster, combines and tractors for sale in an open lot next to city hall, Dairy Queens, crumbling drive-in movie screens, barbershops bearing the first names of the proprietors.

I had moved into the row behind the driver's seat and needed a wake-up cup of coffee. "The towns out here are slowly dying off," said Schneider, who was born and raised in Hebron, North Dakota (through which the bus would pass at 9:23 A.M.). His retired parents still lived there on their twelve-hundred-acre ranch, but the land was leased out now. "Towns like Antelope and Eagles Nest are gone, and now you're talking about places like Hebron, Richardton and Glen Ullin losing the young, too, because there's no jobs. Maybe it's a cycle. Maybe they'll come back sooner or later, when they find out you can only take so much of the big city. I'll tell you, though, it kind of makes me feel good to come through Hebron and these towns with medicine and whatever else they need. I feel like I'm paying back my debt to the people, for educating me, for giving me the chance not to have to work at the brick plant. It gives me a chance to say thank you."

Schneider, a bachelor, earned $24,000 a year. He had been driving the same route for eight years and said he loved every mile of it. Late in the afternoon, on schedule at 4:35 P.M., Schneider pulled into the docks at the Fargo terminal, just as another driver was arriving from Winnipeg with a load of connecting eastbound passengers. Schneider called the dispatcher in Minneapolis on an 800 number, then headed for the cafe across the street for soup and coffee, his day's work done. We sat there for an hour, talking about this and that. Schneider bought a newspaper to check the baseball scores and the latest price of Greyhound stock. "Well, better get back and do my paperwork," he finally said, and we walked back to the terminal. The dock he had pulled into was empty.

The bus had been serviced and taken on 180 gallons of diesel fuel, and a new driver was somewhere out on the road, his Greyhound rumbling through the afternoon shadows for Moorhead, Dilworth, Glyndon, Hawley, Lake Park, Detroit Lakes, Frazee, Perham, New York Mills, Wadena, Verndale, Aldrich, Staples, Motley, Brainerd, Little Falls, Royalton, Rice, St. Cloud, Minneapolis, Eau Claire, Black River Falls, Tomah, Wisconsin Dells,

Portage, Lake Delton, Baraboo, Sauk City, Middleton, Madison, Goerke's Corner, Milwaukee, Northbrook and Chicago, with connections on to Cleveland, Pittsburgh, Washington, New York and Boston.

THE
GOOD LIFE

The World's Best Job

I t would have been hard to miss the sense of discontent across the land in the summer of '92. We distrusted our elected leaders, worried about our crime-plagued cities, felt guilt over race relations and feared the growing federal deficit. Our self-confidence had been shaken, and our faith that each generation would live better than the one before it had been challenged. We had swelled our chests for one giddy moment after the Persian Gulf War, then, no sooner had the welcome home parades subsided and the streets been swept clean of confetti, we felt penitent again. "What's so great about whipping some inept Third World army anyway?" we asked ourselves.

If we dared feel good about ourselves for even a moment, we needed only turn to the media to hear otherwise: Polls told us what we thought (and 85 percent of us thought the country needed fundamental change), and television defined who we were. (Judging by the afternoon talk shows, most of us were cross-dressers, serial killers, incest survivors or infidels.) There weren't any normal people left, television kept reminding us, and all those god-awful things we kept seeing happen on our screens, well, we had to be careful: Any one of us could be the next victim. The self-indulgent eighties had given way to the cautious nineties. Belonging to a twelve-step program was considered a prerequisite for being well-adjusted. Nothing was safe anymore except oat bran. Cigarettes killed us, so we gave up smoking. Alcohol destroyed us, so getting drunk wasn't any fun. Sex was out because of AIDS, and office flirtations were clearly risky because everyone was in a litigious mood. Red meat, eggs, cheese and most other things that tasted good plugged our hearts, so we started paying fifty dollars at restaurants for mysterious ingredients whose colors matched but which weren't particularly filling. Indeed, what everyone was telling us was that we did have cause for fear: It was life itself. If hamburgers didn't kill us, muggers would.

At the root of our national anxieties was a longing for the remembered past. Our presidents with oratory skills, from Franklin Roosevelt to Ronald Reagan, often tied themselves to the past to remind us where we were capable of going. And we, too, found strength in looking back, because there lay the confirmation of the possibility of our dreams. The more the future scared us, the more appealing became the innocence, real or imagined, of yesterday. Remember the Eisenhower years? We put pennies in our loafers, necked at the drive-in, watched Ed Sullivan Sunday evenings and listened to songs about the lazy, hazy days of summer. Nothing seemed very threatening or complicated. Attaining the "good life" was an American right.

But there was a rub in all this. The Boston where I grew up in the fifties was part of a segregated world. My favorite baseball team, the Boston Braves, had one black, a center fielder named Sam Jethroe, but he was an oddity and could not join his teammates in the dining cars of trains. My neighborhood had no minorities, except one "Chinaman," who stood in the window of his little shop ironing shirts long into the night. Shamefully, my friends and I made fun of him. The country club (to which I did not belong) near my house did not admit Jews or Catholics. Homosexuals were "queers," and words like *nigger, spic* and *wop* didn't even draw a blush or an apology. However we choose to remember them, the fifties were a bad time to be "different."

We are, today, a healthier nation than we were in the fifties, and closer to being *one* nation, because, no matter how desperately we cry out for creative solutions, we no longer dare ignore any segment of society. We have confronted our problems—or more to the point, they have confronted us—and we hear many voices now instead of just the echo of our own. Anthony Trollope wrote in 1862 that "the traveler who desires to tell his experience of North America must write of people rather than of things." And that's why I was never quite comfortable with what television and the pollsters were telling us about ourselves. Television entertained us with the 2 percent of the population whose behavior was aberrant, and the polls seemed fixated on the demise of the American dream (though a good part of the world still wanted to move here). What these opinion-shapers needed to do was go out and kick tires and talk to people. If they had, they would have found that most people were not leading lives of quiet desperation but were, in fact, muddling through in relatively good spirit. They put in an honest day's labor, raised decent kids, obeyed the law, paid their taxes and weren't falling off the edge.

Because of an earlier book I had written, I had gotten
to know a good many people who earned their livelihood
in baseball, and in their lives, I found qualities of the
quintessential American. Unlike the disgruntled major
league players whose salaries were as large as their egos,
the underpaid, unrecognized people I had spent time
with—scouts, grounds keepers, bus drivers, coaches and
managers toiling in the minors—all seemed to understand
their own level of containment. They were ordinary people
who had found a niche. In their fraternal world, people
protected one another, and men believed a career in baseball was a veritable expression of patriotism. "I'd *pay* to
do this job," scouts and low-level executives told me over
and over with missionary zeal, as though the lower the
compensation, the greater the act of faith.

Tommy Ferguson, a scout with the Philadelphia Phillies, had ignored Eddie Stanky's advice—"Kid, never let
'em get you out of the majors, even if you have to be an
usher"—and now Fergie, pushing sixty and far from the
bright lights of the big leagues, was speeding south
through the late-afternoon dusk in pursuit of someone
else's dream, his miniature poodle and constant companion, Albert, asleep on the backseat. He reached for a cigar
and, having second thoughts, stuck a piece of spearmint
gum in his mouth instead. His white Chevy swung off
Interstate 5 in San Diego, and Ferguson checked his watch
as he pulled into the parking lot at Smith Field, ready for
work. It was 5:30 P.M., still ninety minutes to game time,
and the admission gate was padlocked, the stands were
empty and everything was quiet except for the hollow echo
of an aluminum bat hitting baseballs with rhythmic regu-

larity. "Hey," he called to a custodian in a Boston accent as thick as Irish stew, "when you gonna let us in? I wanna see batting practice."

Ferguson, the son of a policeman, had started in baseball as a teenager, shining shoes in the visiting clubhouse of Boston's Fenway Park in 1945. He fought in the Korean War, then worked his way up through the Milwaukee Braves organization and later accepted an offer from Gene Autry's Los Angeles Angels, even though his father gave him hell for going to work for a movie actor in California, of all damn places. When Autry asked him what kind of a traveling secretary he thought he'd make, Ferguson replied, "Gene, I'm going to spend your money just like it was my own." They got along wonderfully.

Ten years later he returned to Milwaukee as a vice president for the Brewers, but a lifetime on the road was taking its toll. He quit drinking—"That's the dark side of baseball," he said. "You drink when you win and you drink when you lose"—and after the Brewers lost the last game of the 1982 World Series, he quit baseball too. "The magic had left me," he said. "When Cleveland looks like New York and New York looks like Cleveland and the lunches in every press box taste the same, you know you've run out of gas. All those hotel suites with apples and booze were nice, but you get to thinking, thinking about your wife putting up with you during all those traveling years, about the kids, and you realize that fancy stuff doesn't mean nothing. I had a great life but I knew there had to be a little bit more." Ferguson went home to Massachusetts and spent a season on the beach at Cape Cod. He was fifty years old and had to figure out what to do with the rest of his life. Then the Phillies called offering a scouting job in Southern California, and in a flash he and his wife, Petey, were gone. The miles were easy now, and every night he slept in his own bed.

The custodian finally unlocked the gate, and Ferguson was the first in, carrying a fold-up padded seat and a stopwatch. Ray Boone, a sixty-five-year-old former major leaguer, followed and set up his picnic chair behind the screen, to the right of home plate. Then came Dick Wiensek, whose business card said, "An acre of performance is worth a whole world of promise." Finally, by the first pitch of the San Diego State–Washington State game, a dozen men—each a harbinger of potential fame and fortune—had taken their places among a handful of fans in the wooden stands. All except Ferguson had a radar gun. "I don't need one of those silly things to tell me if a pitcher is throwing fast or not," he said, quietly enough so his colleagues could not hear.

It was early spring, and all across the country hundreds of scouts like Ferguson were scouring high-school and college diamonds for raw talent to supply an industry that had room for only 624 performers and paid each an average annual salary in excess of one million dollars. The scouts are the unheralded architects on which pennants are built. They labor in obscurity and in the heartless world of corporate baseball are treated by many clubs as not much more than janitors. Most earn less than thirty thousand dollars a year, and one club owner—I believe it was the eccentric Marge Schott of the Cincinnati Reds—dismissed the whole profession with a wave of the hand. "All they do is watch games," she said.

I asked Ferguson if he remembered the first player he had signed to a major league contract. "Oh yeah, absolutely," he said. "I go into his home and all the family's there. The father's a high-school principal. They're all lovely, educated people. The grandfather's sitting there, too, and he's maybe eighty-five or eighty-six, a real fan, and I'm thinking, What a thrill this must be for him. That was the first time I really realized what I'd been doing. Here I'm taking a young man and giving him an opportunity to play professional baseball, and maybe if I hadn't seen something in him, and nobody else had either, he would have gone on to some other career. It gave me goose bumps. So that's what you're looking for out here, not finished products but treasures in the rough." I thought his voice was going to break.

The games Ferguson and his peers scouted from noon until well into the night were the ones reported only in agate in the back sports pages. Like racetrack handicappers, they looked for speed and strength and winning instincts, studied past performances, the quality of competition, breeding lines, work habits. But unlike handicappers, what interested them was the potential to develop; success was measured not by today's event but by what would happen in four or five years.

"I'll tell you what it takes to be a successful scout," said former Cleveland Indian third baseman Ray Boone, the top end of baseball's first three-generation family—his son had spent nineteen years in the majors, and his grandson had debuted in 1992. Boone, now a scout for Boston, traveled to games in his mobile home, towing a sports car. The other scouts around listened up because an elder statesman was imparting knowledge. "Number one, it takes just going to work, just showing up at the games, being here for batting practice. If you go to enough games, it doesn't take long to get the hang of it."

"If you guess right more than you guess wrong, then you're a success, right, Boonie? And if you're not a success, you're fired 'cause you're spending the other guy's [the owner's] money," said Dick Wiensek, the Detroit Tigers western scouting supervisor. One hundred twenty-eight of the players Wiensek had signed over a thirty-five-year career had made it to the majors. "The average fan can probably tell you who the best player is out there tonight," Wiensek went on, "but he doesn't know who's going to be the best player three years from now. That's where our professional guess comes in. Now, take the kid up at the plate: He can throw, but he can't hit a lick, and he's got no chance to play pro ball. Course, I went to Omaha in the sixties to scout Don Kessinger, and I said the same thing about him, and he played in the majors for sixteen years."

They carried on their conversation without looking at each other, their eyes never leaving the field. They scribbled notes on their scorecards but never revealed what player they had come to bird-dog and seldom commented favorably on an athlete's performance, for fear of titillating another scout's interest. I never heard them refer to a player by name; everyone was "kid," a term that in baseball is used to describe anyone under the age of forty. "Did you see that kid dog it down to first?" Ferguson muttered, making a note on his scorecard. "An NP [no prospect] if I ever saw one." I didn't know if the young man had had major league aspirations or not, but if he had, one lazy run to first had probably ended his career before it had even started.

By 11:00 P.M. the game was only in the seventh inning and looked as though it might go on forever. Ferguson stuck his scorecard in his pants pocket, folded up his lawn chair and was soon back on Interstate 5, homeward bound. He had abandoned the gum and was smoking a cigar. His dog Albert, who was blind, had fallen asleep again on the backseat. We pulled into a restaurant after a few miles for dinner. "You gotta try the split pea soup," he said. "You've never had anything like it. I have it every night." As with others whose livelihood was the pastime of youth, to Ferguson the summer game was no less complex than life itself. The magic had returned, and after a thoughtful puff he said, "You know, in forty years, I don't think I ever met a bad guy in baseball." So, his pea soup finished, Ferguson motored north, toward Petey and home in Santa Ana. He told me that one of his prospects had performed well last season in Utica—"Hey, I'm not oh-for-oh!"—but we made most of the return trip in silence. Ferguson already was thinking about the three games he had to scout tomorrow, and he knew that in the morning he would leave his house excited, aware that another Willie Mays or Eddie Mathews might be waiting, undiscovered, in some little ballpark, just over the next hill.

President Herbert Hoover said, "Next to religion, baseball has furnished a greater impact on American life than any other institution." That may not be as true today as it was sixty years ago, but to many of us the sport still harks back to what Americans love to call "the good old days," which, given our short memories, are often the yesterdays of only a year or two ago. In a world that seems to go faster and faster, baseball plods along at its own leisurely pace, its traditions and rituals oblivious to the world beyond the outfield fence.

One baseball tradition had mystified me for years. I had been brought up to believe that the shiny whiteness of a new baseball was a thing of beauty to be preserved, but before every game, professional umpires stacked up a pile of the finest looking new balls you've ever seen and rubbed them all with mud. They did it, I was told, because new baseballs are slick and have to be "deglossed" so they don't slip out of a pitcher's grip. None of the umpires could tell me why this process wasn't done by the manufacturer or where the mud came from or who supplied it, although one said he had heard it was dug out of a cave in the Colorado Rockies.

With the help of a friend, I tracked down a company in Seminole, Florida, with a marvelous name—the Lena Blackburne Rubbing Mud Company. Burns Bintliff, the seventy-year-old proprietor, answered the phone and seemed none too pleased to find a journalist on the other end. His mud, he said, was a deeply held family secret— sort of like the formula for Coca-Cola—but he did finally consent: If I wanted to fly down to Florida, we could go to a spring-training game together in Dunedin as long as I didn't ask too many nosy questions. "Don't come thinking I'm going to talk about how the mud's made, because I'm not," he warned before hanging up.

Bintliff, it turned out, was a retired carpenter with the New Jersey Turnpike Authority, and not at all the gruff ogre he had sounded on the phone. Although practically no one in professional baseball even knew his name, everyone agreed that his mud was really wonderful stuff—smooth as melted chocolate, light enough not to discolor the ball—and as the sole purveyor of mud to major league baseball, Bintliff had what might have been the world's smallest monopoly. There was a large untapped market out there that went well beyond the major leagues, and Bintliff wanted none of it.

He didn't give a hoot about publicity and usually declined interview requests. Once he tossed away a letter from a Tokyo firm wanting to promote Lena Blackburne mud in Japan. He didn't even like the idea of shipping mud to Canada, although he had to because there were two major league teams there. Admittedly, he said, he would starve to death if he had to depend solely on his income from mud, but expand? What in the world for? "I'm really happy and satisfied with things the way they are," he said. "As far as trying to improve the product goes, I wouldn't even consider it. This mud is perfect. It's magical. One umpire, Tom Gorman—poor soul, he's dead now—told me a number of times that if I stopped supplying mud, umpires would be out of business. Course, he was exaggerating a bit."

It was two hours before game time, and we walked into the umpires' room. Dan Morrison was in his underwear, dusting lint off his jacket, and the home plate umpire, Larry Young, was sitting by his locker, working his way through a dozen new balls. He would put a dab of

Lena Blackburne mud in his left palm, spit into it, and work his hands over each ball as though he were shaping a chunk of clay. I told the umpires who Bintliff was, and they were fascinated, knowing that one of the little mysteries of their own lives was about to be solved. "Well, this is an honor," Morrison said. "I've heard so many stories about the mud and I never knew what to believe. I'll tell you what the main question I want answered is, Mr. Buntliff. How much does a container of this mud cost?" Bintliff hemmed and hawed and allowed that it probably didn't cost as much as Morrison thought and let the matter drop. Well, then, Morrison asked, how did he get the mud? And for that, the one-man cottage industry had some answers.

Once every summer he and one of his sons rowed out into a creek in New Jersey's Burlington County at low tide, to the precise (and secret) location where major league mud has been harvested for more than fifty years. Wallowing waist-deep, they skimmed off the top half-inch layer of mud and shoveled five hundred pounds of it into their boat. Later it was mixed with another (secret) substance. The mud was packed into three-pound plastic containers in his son-in-law's basement in Delran, New Jersey, and his own garage in Seminole, and shipped out to the major league clubs in March. One container (which he neglected to mention cost twenty-four dollars) was enough to last a team for an entire season, although occasionally an uninformed janitor or construction worker had been known to discard the container—"Whaddya mean it's important? It's just mud"—and the team's traveling secretary would have to contact Bintliff for an emergency shipment.

"Damn, that's interesting," Young said. "You know, in the minor leagues, we had to scrounge for our own mud. Getting good mud like this was a big deal. Coming into a big league umpires' room was a real plus in those days. I'd show up holding a Styrofoam coffee cup. I didn't want the umps' shoes or hats or anything like that. I wanted their mud."

In baseball's early days, players took the shine off new baseballs with shoe polish, dirt, tobacco juice or by making fingernail scars. Then in the mid-1930s, a coach with the Philadelphia A's, Russell Aubrey (Lena) Blackburne, found the perfect rubbing substance in the waters near his Palmyra, New Jersey, home. The mud has been used exclusively by major league baseball since 1955 and is on display at the Hall of Fame in Cooperstown, New York. Blackburne died in 1968 and left the little business to his boyhood chum, John Haas, who ran a bakery and had helped Blackburne in the annual harvesting and processing when both men were in their eighties and would teeter off together into the mud flats at low tide. Haas taught the secrets of mud making to his son-in-law, Burns Bintliff.

Driving back to Seminole that afternoon, Bintliff said, "That was a great day. I really enjoyed it, talking to Morrison and Young and all. You heard what they said when I asked if I should make changes in the mud? They said it was already perfect! That's what everyone says." He slapped his leg with glee. Burns Bintliff and Tommy Ferguson didn't know each other—indeed, had never heard of each other—but they shared something you find in many baseball people once you escape the clique of millionaire players: an enthusiasm that is both childlike and infectious. They believed the significance of their lives was what they did, not who they were. Money was a result of work, not the reason to work. Their reward was simply getting up in the morning and mixing some good mud or extending an opportunity to some starry-eyed young athlete, and that, I think, is an admirable way to spend a day.

The Gates of Eden

Coming into Rumford, Maine, on Route 108, the starless night icy black and very silent, soft rain glistening in the reach of headlights, the traveler feels that he alone survives in a world of tall pines and sleeping villages and eternal isolation. The road dips and climbs through the wooded foothills, following the meandering course of the Androscoggin River, moving on through emptiness, and it was not until the last bend before the bridge that I became aware of the terrible odor, saw the sudden explosion of light and sensed that I had stumbled onto an alien planet.

In the valley below, the mill loomed out of nowhere like a giant armada on a deserted ocean. Lights ablaze, chimneys firing wood smoke and steam into the night, its form was discernible but vague, almost shapeless, a creation of brick and aluminum and sawdust piles and log heaps towering ten stories high, stretching over several dozen city blocks to the edge of town, where the darkness and the wilderness began again. For more than eighty years the mill had dominated Rumford like an emperor, controlling the beat of life and holding the young as surely as a magnet. Many of the workers' fathers and grandfathers had labored at the pulp and paper mill, and now their sons went off to the University of Maine in Portland or Orono to get educated, but they, too, returned to find their places in the mill and in the town, where they would marry, raise children and be buried. For them there was no sweeter smell than the dreadful stench of sulfur dioxide, oozing from the smoking stacks and hanging over everything like the smell of rotting cabbage. It was a reminder that Rumford and its eight thousand residents were producing paper for the world and that on Thursdays—when the banks open an hour early to catch the graveyard shift heading home—one fifth of the town's population would leave the mill with a paycheck from Boise Cascade.

Jimmy Kinney, whose mother, father, brother and aunt had spent, as a group, over 130 years in the mill, remembered how, back in the autumn of '49, he came this close—and he held his thumb and forefinger just a hair apart—to taking his leave of Rumford. "I was all set for college, packed up and everything and ready to head off to Orono," said Kinney, shouting to be heard over the din of "Mighty Andy," a single papermaking machine that filled a building eight times larger than a football field. "So that morning, everyone says, 'Come on, Jimmy. Get up. Time to go.' And I say, 'Nope, I changed my mind. I'm staying here at the mill.' I just couldn't imagine myself in some classroom on a fine, snowy day when I'd rather be deer hunting."

Ask Tony Koris, a mill superintendent and University of Maine graduate, why he stayed in Rumford, a dark, stone-faced town whose main street starts at the American Legion Post and ends at the Ed Muskie Development Center, and he will talk about what he calls "the comfort level" of Maine—knowing not just his neighbor but every-one in town, sharing camaraderie at the Elks Lodge, not having to lock his front door or worry when his wife, Billie, is out after dark. "Oh, I had a decent offer once in Lisbon, and I almost moved there," Koris said, referring to a town forty miles down the road. "But the fact is, I never really intended to leave Rumford. One night I came home drunk and I says to Billie, 'Load up the kids. We're moving to Alaska.' The next morning, though, my wan-derlust was gone, and I went back to the mill. Sure, some-times you feel the mill controls you, but it's given us a good life. It's our existence."

Koris was lucky. He found his "comfort level" with-out having to really look. For most of us, the journey is tougher. When Brigham Young, an ailing Vermonter lead-ing his Mormon flock westward in 1847 in search of Zion, first gazed down on the empty oblong plain where Salt Lake City stands today, he declared, "This is the place." I've always envied people who are so certain of where they belong. How could Young—or Kinney and Koris for that matter—be so sure that Salt Lake or Rumford was *the* place and not just a place? Given the fact that the average American changes his address eleven times during his life-time, do they know something I don't? We are an urban people, but two thirds of our 20,000 towns and cities still have populations under 2,500, and I wonder if what H. L. Mencken had written in 1925 is still true of Maine and the rest of rural America: "Maine is as dead, intellec-tually, as Abyssinia. Nothing is ever heard from it." In Mencken's time, I suppose, most of America outside the Boston–New York–Philadelphia triangle was silent. But the hardships that then made rural America insular and unappealing to many have been tamed by modernity. Mud roads have been paved, CNN and *USA Today* have ended the information gap between city and village, commuter airlines and fax machines have made distance irrelevant. Spiritually the heartland is no longer remote.

The opening up of the country resulted in dramatic demographic shifts, and for the first time in more than a hundred years, more people were moving into Maine than out of Maine. A few of the newcomers were gentleman farmers who had one hand on a pitchfork and the other on a phone to their broker, but the great majority, said University of Maine sociologist Louis Ploch, were professionals under forty with small families and a lot of education. "What we're seeing, really for the first time," said Ploch, "is a brain inflow." Maine—whose population reached half a million in 1840, then took another 150 years to double—was now growing at a rate faster than the national average. The state's new residents, Ploch determined after a five-year study, came from counties with populations of over 500,000, and their motivation for moving was more pull than push: That is, what Maine offered them was more important than what they were escaping. The median cost of a house in Maine in 1992 was less than $38,000; the median rent was $173 a month. Sixty-three percent of the households were occupied by married couples (compared with 34 percent in Los Angeles). Only one state (North Dakota) had a lower homicide rate; only three (Delaware, South Dakota and West Virginia) had fewer resident millionaires. Eighty percent of the land was forested, and 99 percent of the people were white. Simply put, life was cheaper and relationships were less complex in Maine than they were in Boston or New York.

"The difference for me between living in Los Angeles or Sacramento or Houston and living here in Bangor is the concept of community," said Dick Cattelle, a realtor who moved to Maine after a career with McDonnell Douglas's manned space program. "In a place like Los Angeles, sure, I had a life, a profession. Other than that, you're just kind of there. In a place like Bangor, you have people believing that communities operate well as a function of those who participate in their operation."

I was no stranger to Maine. Like Tony Koris, I had attended the university in Orono, but unlike Koris, I arrived there in 1958 as something of a city snob, thinking that the street smarts I had learned growing up in Boston were somehow more valuable than what the sons and daughters of potato farmers and fishermen knew. That missed the mark by a wide margin, and when I last returned to the Beta House for a homecoming weekend, it struck me that the friends I had made in Maine are the ones I hold closest. But I don't remember having any great affection for the state when I lived there or having any intense ambition other than to get out of college and on with my life. The day I graduated and was commissioned a second lieutenant in the United States Army, I was in an alcoholic haze and led a celebratory procession of cars straight across campus without using a single road. Only by the grace of the university's sole campus policeman was I saved from having to leave Orono in censure, or worse.

Coming back after so many years, I was surprised how little of Maine I had bothered to see or learn about when I'd had the opportunity. Maine is New England's poorest state and the mostly sparsely populated state east of the Mississippi. Maine, I was told, was where, in 1607, the first seagoing vessel in the New World, a pinnace named *Virginia of Sagadohoc* was built and where a king of England, James I, had masts cut for his navy. Maine was where ships from distant continents once steamed up the Penobscot River to Bangor to load up on spruce and balsam fir, and where, until the drives ended in 1976 for economic and environmental reasons, rivers were jammed each spring with tons of logs floated to the waiting mill towns downstream. The state's fortunes were still closely entwined with lumber (only nine *nations* produce more paper than Maine), and like other resource-dependent regions, the decade had not been kind to Maine: Over forty thousand jobs had disappeared, and to make ends meet, countless professionals had become handymen; in the inland areas the cash economy had reverted to a barter economy, with, say, dentists and woodsmen swapping products—a root canal for a couple of cords of winter firewood. The taciturn, dry-witted and frugal "Downeast Yankees" of Maine said conditions hadn't been so desperate since the Great Depression, yet they seemed more resigned than despondent, resigned to the notion that somehow, on a wing and a prayer, they would muddle through, survive, struggle on.

I stopped in Cherryfield on the Narraguagus River. The former schoolhouse there had been turned into a city hall, and in it was a small library, where I met an elderly lady named Virginia Grant, the volunteer librarian. She said her Washington County community used to be an important shipbuilding and timber center. "Now," she added, "it's just our two blueberry factories that keep us going." She turned to a man who was perusing the paperback books in the war section and said, "Wouldn't you say that's right, Buddy, about the blueberry factories?"

Buddy Parker, a retired fisherman, did not answer.

"We've got so many people on welfare now, more than I can ever remember," Mrs. Grant said, "and we'll probably see more before the winter's out. Am I right on that, Buddy?"

"Yup, you hit the nail on the head," Parker said, settling on *The Story of Wake Island.*

"Of course, people also get money digging clams down on the flats, but I don't think all the flats have clams anymore, do they, Buddy?"

"Some do, some don't," he replied.

Then Parker offered: "They say Washington's the poorest county in Maine, but you got to remember some of these women in the factory, they don't plan to work the winters. They figure on going unemployed come December. That's just a way of life here."

"That's exactly how it is," Virginia Grant said.

Winter waited in the dark forests that afternoon as I left Cherryfield. The trees had been stripped bare of leaves, and the smell of wood smoke hung in the frosty air. Maine was closing down for the season. The moneyed summer colony had boarded up its coastal homes, and oil drums blocked the driveways of motels and restaurants, whose owners had headed for Florida.

I found a pay phone and called John Laban, a friend from college days, to ask if I could drop by for the night. He said finding his farm once I got to Bethel was tricky and suggested I ask directions at the post office. I drove through town and, not finding much of interest, doubled back to the little post office. It was empty except for the woman at the clerk's window.

"Excuse me," I said. "Do you know where John and Suzanne Laban live?"

"I do," she replied. I waited, but she offered nothing more.

"Um, well, exactly how do I get there?"

"What's your business with the Labans?" she asked, fixing me firmly with a hard stare.

"No business. I'm a friend."

"Are they expecting you?"

It took me a minute to figure out that she was merely protecting the Labans from a possible intruder, and I had no doubt that she would have directed me straight out of town had my response not satisfied her. As it was, she said I should take a left at the bridge and follow the dirt road for a few miles until I came to an old farmhouse at the foot of a pasture. "It's the original farmhouse," she said. "You'll see sheep out back. John's the only one around with sheep. You can't miss them."

John, who had grown up in the Boston suburbs, was a professional forester. He had lost his job as the development manager for the Bethel Inn & Country Club a year earlier, when a cash-strapped bank called in the inn's loan, killing a $7 million expansion project. John, Suzanne and

I sat around the kitchen table, warmed by the wood stove and glasses of whiskey. Their income had dried up, except for the hand-spun skeins of wool Suzanne sold, and prospects for work did not look good. John took out a small ad in the local paper each week, offering his services as a forester, but there was no work in Maine and the ad drew few responses. On the lawn outside stood a 1938 John Deere tractor, in perfect working order, with a hand-lettered for sale sign ($1,800). "What's frightening," Suzanne said, "is that for the first time we don't have a plan. You live day to day, hoping things will turn around. But there's no safety net."

I asked John if he would consider taking an out-of-state job. No, he said, he didn't think so. Tough times tested your mettle. They were only temporary. They brought you, in the country, back to the basics, and there was something reassuring about that. "The dentist, the guy who delivers my hay, the car mechanic, they all know what happened," he said. "They're not knocking on my door to collect bills. They say, 'Can you pay a few dollars this month?' or 'Don't worry about paying anything till you get back to work.' Friends and neighbors help you like you'd never see in the city. They give you a cushion and that makes the difference. I don't think I could ever leave Maine."

John was a lot calmer than I would have been had our situations been reversed. True, with his garden and his sheep he was largely self-sufficient, but more important, I remember an offhand remark he made the next morning while we sat on the riverbank at the edge of his property.

"I've never been afraid in my life and I'm not afraid now."
I believed him. And I wished I could have said the same
thing about myself and meant it.

Despite all the memories and friends I have in the
state, Maine always seems to me to be a lonely place. The
woods close in on you, and the winters are unbearably
long and forlorn. Old friends who live twenty miles apart
never see each other because there are always excuses for
staying home. Lives become self-centered because survival
is a personal battle that takes great energy. In many ways
Maine seems to be two states: The rocky coastal region is
cosmopolitan and attracts money, artists and city es-
capees; but in the vast, isolated interior north of Portland,
the outside world doesn't count for much and conformity
is an essential ingredient of "fitting in."

If people aren't "like-minded," small towns can be
cruel. That was the lesson I took from Jay, another mill
town on the Androscoggin, where twelve hundred mill
workers had been on strike for 481 days against the International Paper Company, the world's biggest paper
company and the nation's largest private landholder. It
was a David and Goliath battle, a fight not just for jobs
but for the soul of an old town and the value a hired hand
placed on his own worth. The workers who walked the
picket line were proud men; papermaking, they said, was
an art form mastered over a lifetime of experience. Convinced that the mill couldn't operate without their exper-
tise, the men had walked off their jobs to protest the
company's attempts to cut costs, gain concessions and
reduce union featherbedding. Jesse Jackson came to Jay to

salute the workers' courage. Support poured into Local 14 of the Paperworkers International Union from other locals around the country. The union president came to Jay too, and drove to the mill, waving his clenched fist from the backseat of a convertible. The strike was Jay's first in sixty-one years, and what stunned everyone was how quickly the town's neighborliness was pulled asunder and how easily decent men accepted violence as a natural expression of their frustrations.

Strikebreakers' homes were defaced with ugly words, windows were broken, car tires slashed. Those who did not support the strikers were taunted with curses, and men whose closest brush with the law had been no more than a parking ticket started carrying guns and baseball bats in their vehicles. For the first time, the people of Jay began locking their doors at night. A divorced mother of two became the first striker to resign from the union and return to work; a relative threatened to blow her head off, and on her home were scrawled in orange paint the words *scab* and *slut*. Men dropped out of their fraternal organizations, which were torn between strikers and nonstrikers, and started driving up to Farmington for a beer to avoid the cold stares of neighbors. The Little League coach quit because his young players were as divided as their parents, and when Peter Fredericks, a salaried mill supervisor, went with his wife to a graduation party for their godson, the room fell deadly silent the moment they walked in. "This was a crowd we'd socialized with for years," Fredericks said. "I tried to initiate conversation, but it was a very forced situation. I never felt so out of place in my life. We left early."

The old Chinese restaurant that had been turned into a union hall was abuzz the morning I arrived in Jay. With no warning the international's leadership had just called to say that its strike fund was running low, the union was in danger of being decertified at several mills in the East and other locals were no longer willing to strike in support of their "brothers" in Maine. The Jay papermakers, abandoned and betrayed, had no choice but to surrender. They wandered about the hall, numb with confusion, while a local representative cradled a phone on his shoulder, trying to explain to a caller what had happened. "Yeah," he said, "it's true. The strike's over. . . . No, we didn't lose it. They lost it for us. The international did. It's an unconditional offer to return to work. Sixteen months down the tube. . . . What'd we get? Nothing. We don't know the details, but it looks like we lost it all."

I felt sorry for the workers because honorable lives were about to be destroyed. They had been done in by their own union and their isolation-induced ignorance. History had outwitted them. In recent years, air traffic controllers, professional football players, interstate bus drivers, newspaper printers, loggers in the Pacific Northwest had all learned that once the picket line went up, management increasingly was able to hire replacement workers and sustain production. And long before the strike collapsed, the Androscoggin mill had hired strikebreakers; most had never seen the inside of a paper mill before, but they quickly mastered their jobs. They became permanent employees, and soon the plant was again operating at near-capacity production. The strikers' offer to return to work without conditions was irrelevant; there were no vacancies left to fill. Nor were there any jobs in Maine that paid as well as the ones they had walked away from.

The men gathered in small groups in the union hall, and they talked not so much about money and perks as they did about the pride and dignity of honest work. Their wives brought homemade pastries and passed out coffee in paper cups. "My IRA's gone," one man said. "That's what it cost me to stay out and support the strike—my entire IRA, eleven thousand dollars. I'll tell you this: I'm fifty-one years old and you don't get a job in Maine at fifty-one." Someone asked, quietly, almost as though talking to himself, "When all is said and done, what's the bottom line in all this? What's the lesson to be learned?" A man in a plaid shirt, his collar turned up against the autumn chill, thought for a moment, took a sip of coffee and said: "We're all replaceable."

Fifteen Minutes

Whether by design or accident, my life on the road has not been spent rubbing shoulders with famous people. Perhaps this reflects my own insecurities, but unsettling things happen to journalists who spend a career writing about Hollywood or Washington or professional athletes: They take on the trappings of those they cover. Too often they appear important merely because they are around those who are important, or at least recognizable. They become part of the power structure they are meant to confront, and eventually it gets harder and harder to get out of, say, Washington, and find out what ordinary people are doing, thinking and talking about. At political conventions, I get uncomfortable watching a group of highly paid insiders from Washington (where journalists and politicians are interchangeable) sit around a studio conference table and pontificate and ponder how "Middle America" will react to this speech or that policy. Why don't they just put an articulate Nebraska farmer or a New Hampshire business-man on the panel and ask?

The answer, I suppose, is that the anchors and talk-show regulars we watch have become celebrities, and in an age when the Madonnas and Trumps of the land are embraced as icons, ordinary folks are not perceived as having anything very significant to say. For most of us, the distinction between hero and celebrity has become fuzzy; the line separating fame from notoriety has blurred. We can't hold television wholly responsible: Fans used to applaud Al Capone when he took his seat at Chicago's Comiskey Park for a ball game in the twenties. But before *People* magazine and Larry King, men were made famous by deeds, not the media, and greatness was judged by achievement more than image. It is no wonder America welcomed General H. Norman Schwarzkopf home from the Gulf War as a sort of grand marshal of heroes. Yet ironically his fame was a product of television too; had there been no TV cameras to record his masterfully conducted briefings, we would have known little of him and no multimillion-dollar contract for an autobiography would have awaited his return to the United States.

Many Americans winced when Schwarzkopf stepped off the plane in Florida and seemed to show up in a million places at once—posing at parades with Mickey Mouse in Tampa and the Ziegfeld girls in New York—and then in a West Point speech referred to post–Vietnam bureaucratic peaceniks as "military fairies." Uh-oh. Would Americans soon be saying, "I'll never forget what's-his-name?" Would Schwarzkopf next be promoting Jell-O or modeling Jockey shorts? Fortunately Schwarzkopf had both dignity and common sense. He knew the public has a short attention span—"Being a hero," Will Rogers once said, "is about the shortest-lived profession on earth" (a sentiment Andy Warhol would later echo with his crack about modern fame lasting only fifteen minutes). And he understood that his journey to stardom was a perilous one. For every Dwight Eisenhower, who became a beloved two-term president, there were a hundred Charles Lindberghs, shunned by the public once their exploits faded or their views fell out of favor.

Lindbergh returned to New York City in June 1927 from his solo flight across the Atlantic and found more than three million letters, fourteen thousand parcels and a hundred thousand telegrams waiting for him. *The New York Times* devoted its first sixteen pages to him. One manufacturing company offered him its presidency, and a cigarette company put up $50,000 for him to promote its brand. (Charles Curtis of the U.S. Senate was endorsing Lucky Strike at the time.) Lindbergh wrote back that he didn't smoke, and the manufacturer "offered me a package so I could speak truthfully and from experience." Lindbergh wrote a quick autobiography, titled *We,* that shot to the top of the best-seller list and went through twenty-eight printings in six months. But he became politically controversial after traveling to Nazi Germany and accepting a medal from Hitler and was driven into seclusion by the press after the kidnapping and murder of his son. In 1957 the movie *Spirit of St. Louis,* starring Jimmy Stewart, did poorly at the box office; an audience poll revealed that few viewers under age forty knew or cared much about Lindbergh.

At different times on trips spread a good many years apart, I met three people who, in varying degrees, had encountered fame: Glenn Yarbrough, a folk singer; Anne Matthews, the radio voice of Stella Dallas for many years; and Bob Hazle, an outfielder with the Milwaukee Braves.

What interested me was not so much their accomplishments as the way they handled their success and the meaning they attached to it.

Glenn Yarbrough, in the early seventies, lived in the Hollywood Hills, in a million-dollar home that, as I recall, was protected by a large fence and included a sound studio and a swimming pool outside his bedroom. He had made a lot of money with a group called the Limeliters, then as a solo singing Rod McKuen songs about San Francisco and love and loneliness. He had no idea how many records he had sold over the years—fewer than Bing Crosby, more than Tony Randall, he said—but whatever the number, it was enough to make him rich, famous, secure and not particularly content. Yarbrough was forty-one years old when I met him and was having what most of us would call a midlife crisis. He was giving away everything he owned to charity and laying plans to abandon his career and sail off for South America.

I hadn't lived in Los Angeles long at that point, but I was wise enough to be suspicious of gimmicks that smack of press agentry. My guard was up. I looked in his garage to see what kind of car he was driving. It was a Volkswagen. He had sold the Rolls-Royce, the Porsche, the Bentley and the two Ferraris. Also the Beverly Hills apartment building, the house in New Zealand and the banana plantation in Jamaica. Most of the money, as well as the royalties from a recent album, had gone to support a school he had founded near Palm Springs for underprivileged children, most of whom were black.

My suspicions ebbed. The son of social workers, Yarbrough had majored in Classical Greek and pre-Socratic

philosophy and spent more time thinking about the meaning of life than was probably healthy. He had found that
affluence and fulfillment are not likely companions and
believed that when a man reaches forty, he should ask
himself if he is really content with what he is doing. If not,
he should move on before it is too late. And Yarbrough
was about to move on. He was bored with singing, bored
with the symbols of success. Music, he said, was only
music—a reflection, not a vanguard, of the times, and he
chuckled when he recalled how some of his colleagues
thought they were going to change the world with their
songs.

"It's just miserable for me to play for thirty-year-olds
who want to hear the same stuff I did five years ago,"
Yarbrough told me. "I did a show last year at the Fair-
mont in San Francisco and there was a big cover charge.
The only people who could afford it were people already
so embroiled in money that they're already dead inside. I
looked out at them and they're just sitting there and
they're not even living people anymore. It just doesn't give
me a good feeling working for those people. It's like television. I do a show and then I say, Now what the hell did I
do? There's no feeling there, no warmth, nothing's happening."

A few days later I went up to San Francisco to hear
Yarbrough perform at Basin Street West, a club tucked
among the topless joints of North Beach. I had been back
from Vietnam for less than a year. The war was winding
down toward its tragic conclusion, and the hippie movement was fading away. The whole country was in a reflec-
tive, melancholy mood. Basin Street was only a third filled

for the 2:30 A.M. breakfast show. Yarbrough's words floated across the darkened room and seemed intended more for himself than for his audience:

> *I wish I could get all that I'm*
> *longing to get.*
> *I wish I could live like I'm longing to live.*
> *I wish I could know what it means to be me.*
> *Then you'd see, then you'd agree, each man*
> *should be free.*

Yarbrough was out the back door before the applause had ended from his last song, walking alone down Broadway. Eleven months later he headed off with his wife and daughter on his forty-six-foot sailboat, *Jubilee,* to travel for five years, and maybe forever if the seas were smooth.

I did not hear of Glenn Yarbrough again until 1992, twenty-one years later, when I read that he was giving a concert at a hilltop amphitheater in Front Royal, Virginia. Only a couple hundred of us showed up for what was the final performance of the season sponsored by the Blue Ridge Arts Council. The night was cold, and all around us were dark woods, the town nowhere in sight. "I realize," Yarbrough said, "that a lot of you are wondering who in hell I am." By then he had crossed five oceans, gone through three wives, exhausted his fortune and seen the school he had founded fail for lack of financial backing. He was living on the Washington coast with a girlfriend and was sixty-two years old with snowy white hair and a Santa Claus–like body packed in a five-foot eight-inch frame. He was going to sail again, but he would never be just a sailor. He had come to learn that aimless wandering was self-indulgent and riding the currents to remote islands for more than a decade had no worthy purpose. A doctor or social worker or teacher could have left behind something of value; Yarbrough left only his footprints.

"What I did, I guess, was take retirement in the middle of my life instead of at the end, and it changed my attitudes about lots of things," he said. "First, I really found that I was far more happy with nothing than I was when I had everything. For me having money was work. You had to take care of it, do things with it. It was on your mind." He had walked out of a partnership with Rod McKuen that cost him about $15 million, surrendered a mint in divorce settlements and turned down a name-your-price record contract at the height of his popularity. "I told RCA it was a matter of principle, not money. Well, *zip* my lip." He laughed. (Yarbrough's father now works as a caretaker on a farm in Hawaii that Yarbrough used to own.) What he did manage to hold on to, he gave away. "There must be something wrong here," the IRS man had said, auditing Yarbrough's returns, which showed most of his possessions being turned over to the school for underprivileged kids. "Nobody does anything for nothing."

The ironic, and perhaps sad, thing was that Yarbrough had a wonderful talent he had considered frivolous. In searching for a purpose to his life, he had tossed aside the one gift he could share with others. His songs weren't going to change the world, but if he had gotten to know his audience he would have understood that they could soften a scowl or lighten a burdened heart or coax a smile. The more he sailed the more he realized time was wasting. And one day, in some far-off place, having discarded a career that would never quite go away, he said to himself, "To hell with it. Let's go back to work." So Yarbrough came home and was performing again. It wasn't the money that brought him home or the longing for applause. Rather it was the realization that fulfillment grows from a man's relationship with others, not himself, and although he could no longer fill a five-thousand-seat auditorium or get a record contract, there were people who remembered him and his music and embraced them. They told him about their own restlessness and how his songs had carried them, in the recesses of the imagination, home from the jungles of Vietnam or helped them through a lonely night. Glenn Yarbrough wondered why for so long he had not understood that through his music he had touched some lives and imparted something of value, and for the old fans, and the new ones he hoped one day would fill the auditoriums, he sang:

I could have been a sailor,
I could have sailed the seven seas with the wind
in my face all day.
Can't you taste the salty breeze?
I could have been a dreamer, but dreams
just fall apart.
So I settled for the safer harbors of my heart.

Glenn Yarbrough was putting the finishing touches on a new thirty-four-foot sailboat when we last talked and was slowly reviving his singing career, with a score of engagements lined up. Unable to get a record contract, he had produced his own album and sold it through sailing magazines and personal appearances at boat shows. "You have to be crazy to give away a million dollars," he said, "but let's face it, this is America. No matter what happens, we live. It's not like Africa, where people are starving to death."

Anne Matthews poured a glass of homemade root beer and put a package of oatmeal cookies on the kitchen table of her country estate in Stockton, New Jersey. "Take two," she said, "they're good." I did, relieved that life had been kind to Stella Dallas since she'd left her roomin' house and sewin' shop. In the next room, Mrs. Matthews's husband of fifty years, recovering from a heart attack, sat smoking his pipe and reading the afternoon paper. And as Mrs. Matthews—the radio voice of Stella Dallas for all nineteen years of the popular soap opera—opened her scrapbook, I almost expected to hear the husky, plaintive words: "Lolly Baby, I got no time for nuthin' but trouble." (Cut to mood music and announcer for Haley's M-O: "Here's great news for anyone who finds it at all unpleasant to take a laxative . . ." Then theme music muted and Stella: "Oh, Doctor Foster, can you imagine her doin' a thing like this to Dick Grosvenor and my Lolly Baby?")

For millions of Americans, including my mother, who sat solemnly by the radio each afternoon, Stella Dallas—the beautiful daughter of an impoverished farmhand—was part of the family. No matter how terrible their problems, hers were always worse. And from 1937 to 1956 the faithful legions tuned in to NBC at 4:15 P.M. to follow the

semi-literate Boston seamstress whose daily fifteen-minute
misadventures with love and life were sandwiched between
Backstage Wife and *Lorenzo Jones.* "When Stella went off
the air," Mrs. Matthews, a vivacious, gracious woman in
her seventies, said, "a part of me died. After all those years
of being, really *being,* Stella Dallas, I felt lost. Yes, I
coped. Just as Stella would have coped. Stella was such a
warm, wonderful person. She did have such terrible times
but she was always so brave, and no matter what happened to the people who listened, they could always say to
themselves, 'Poor Stella, she's so much worse off.'"

Poor Stella indeed. She was the consummate humorless downer, sacrificing her own happiness for her daughter Laurel (Lolly Baby), who had married into wealth and
society. Her love for Laurel took her from the Himalayas
to the North Pole—not to mention the Sahara, where she
was lost in a sandstorm for three days before freeing her
kidnapped daughter from a sheik's harem. But happiness
for Stella was never to be. "Two men, multimillionaires,
wanted to marry me," said Mrs. Matthews, who often
spoke of herself and Stella as one person. "Well, I finally
accepted one of the proposals and he died at the church
while we were being married, before I could say, 'I do.'"

Mrs. Matthews laughed and recalled that sometimes it
was a challenge to make the scripts believable. She picked
up a letter she had just received. "Stella Dallas," it said,
"you were part of my life and I am grateful to you for
brightening a young mother's dull life." Dozens like it
trickled into the two-hundred-year-old stone farmhouse in
the rolling hills of New Jersey, where the Matthewses led
a quiet life. Although Mrs. Matthews and Stella went off

the air when Eisenhower was still president, most people in Stockton (population 650) greeted her as "Stella," and the restaurant she and her husband, Jack, owned for many years in nearby Lambertville received as many orders for her autograph as it did for stuffed trout.

Mrs. Matthews, the youngest of eight children of a prominent Lake Charles, Louisiana, cattleman and insurance executive, was an accomplished actress when she won the NBC audition for the role of Stella—primarily, she believed, because she sounded most like Barbara Stanwyck, the last of the Stella Dallases in four movies based on the book by Olive Higgins Prouty. The banal serial immediately became a mainstay of radio's golden age. "The main reason we lasted so long," said Mrs. Matthews, "was because the show was based on motherly love and the Golden Rule, two things we don't have enough of today. You see all this immorality on TV today and it makes you wonder why they can't be more tasteful. You'd think they could do more interesting things without making everything sex. It just gets rather boring. I'd love to get a good commercial but it couldn't be anything that was detrimental to Stella, nothing that was distasteful. Why, they talk about things you'd never believe on TV today just to sell something."

Mrs. Matthews hadn't acted since Stella went off the air. She spent her time gardening on her twenty-six-acre property, volunteering in community affairs, answering correspondence and, until her husband's illness, trap-shooting and big-game fishing (she once caught a 475-pound tuna) around the world. Her warmth and wit would not have disappointed fans who remembered the divorced

Stella Dallas always finding a good word, if not a laugh, in the most terrible of situations.

I had first met Glenn Yarbrough a few years earlier, and the contrast seemed striking. Anne Matthews had welcomed fame, or whatever it was she had, and found that it sustained her for a lifetime. Yarbrough had grappled with it, found it empty on its own merits and run from it. Mrs. Matthews and I chatted for a couple of hours at the kitchen table. I got up to leave, but she motioned me back into my chair. "Now," she said, "I don't think Stella ever took a drink, but I do believe I'll have a glass of sherry."

Anne Matthews died of a stroke in 1981 at the age of eighty-two. Her obituary mentioned a comment she had made when Stella Dallas went off the air: "Sometimes I've found myself caught up in Stella's problems. Now I won't have to take them home with me." But despite her own privileged upbringing, she never did forget the ache the Boston seamstress carried, and that was part of her eternal charm.

Somewhere between Newberry and Joanna, South Carolina, out where the road winds north through tired mill towns and hills of honeysuckle and kudzu, Bob Hazle starts to sing softly to himself, accompanying the instrumental on station WEZY on his car radio: "The wind and the willow play, love's sweet melodeeee . . ." He reaches down to the floorboard and takes a sip from his mug of coffee, grown cold in the miles between Newberry and the home he left early that morning in Columbia. "This beats the dickens out of sitting behind a desk, I'll tell you that," he says. His '82 Buick Regal, air conditioner purring, windows rolled up to keep out the heavy, damp noontime heat, speeds on toward the one-room whiskey stores ahead, carrying a man in pursuit of his livelihood, if not his dreams.

Hazle, a whiskey salesman on the back roads of South Carolina at the age of fifty-six, wondered sometimes where life would have led him had he finished college like his three older brothers, who, he said, "have moved far ahead of me now." But he had been to the extremes. Back in the fifties, he had flirted with fame in a brief, spectacular major league baseball career. For one shining moment he was the Hemingway of his profession; the dream ended as suddenly as it had begun, and he had to learn how to be ordinary again. Then, a few years before the summer days we spent together rolling through the Carolina hills, he had been struck by a massive heart attack. Medics repeatedly "shocked" him back to life. "I woke up when I was having the attack and I couldn't see any heartbeat on that machine I'm hooked up to," Hazle said. "I thought, This is crazy, but I said, 'Lord, here I am. Here's Mr. Hazle.' They called in Mary Webb, a chaplain. 'Mary,' I said, 'don't worry about me. I believe.'" What Bob Hazle had learned from his journey was this: Know what you are prepared to give to, and expect from, your work, and life will offer the reward of contentment, or at least acceptance. Hazle lived with his blessings instead of his regrets.

I had been a diehard Milwaukee Braves fan in 1957, when I was seventeen, and the slugger known as Hurricane Hazle had been a hero I ranked right alongside Randolph Scott. Thirty years later, while I was working on a series titled "Americans at Work," his name came to mind, and I called to introduce myself and ask what he had been doing since he left baseball. "Aw shucks," he said, "there's nothing about this job that'd interest you at all." He was reluctant to let me tag along with him for a few days, but I persisted and he finally relented. Hazle's manner was country-boy gentle. He had a square jaw, gray hair and big, powerful hands. He said he didn't miss baseball, though I later learned his Braves uniform, with No. 12 on the back, hung in his closet, still carefully wrapped in plastic. We talked about baseball and work. "This isn't a glorified job," he said. "It's just a living. Don't get me wrong. I like my work, even though you tell some people you're a whiskey salesman and they frown. It keeps me active and that I've got to be. I like selling. I like being around people. The money's not great, but if your brands get hot, you can make a decent living. Pat and I don't really need much to live on anyway. You know what's hot now? Peach schnapps. I never saw so many sweet drinks around in my life. In my day, we drank for the feel. Now I guess the younger generation wants taste."

Most of the privately owned liquor stores that stretched through the seven hundred miles Hazle traveled every week were hardly bigger than rabbits' dens. Outside on each was painted a huge red dot—an identifying mark that goes back to the days when many people in the back hills of Carolina were illiterate. Hazle knew every owner along the way. He knew their ailments, their spouses' names, their favorite fishing holes, their golf handicaps. No matter what burdens he might be carrying that day, the moment he set foot inside their stores he was a man on stage—smiling, relaxed, attentive, a friend of southern charm come to visit. "Why, Miss Marilyn," he said, entering a shop, his eyes instinctively sweeping the shelves to check the placement of his brands, "you look better than you did last Tuesday, and I feel good about that because you had me downright worried after that cooking grease went and splattered your eyes."

Marilyn Axson, a very large woman in a pink dress, is known around Simpsonville as Big Mama. She had been engrossed in a conversation about strawberry pies with two other liquor salesmen. "Well, I do feel better and thank you, Bob," she said. "How's the folks?"

Hazle took Big Mama's weekly order on a hand-held computer. He scribbled reminders to himself, noting what she may be running low on by next week. He reminded her of his discount on R&R, a Canadian whiskey that was getting hot, and suggested she may need some more Red Rooster, the sweet, forty-two-proof "Wine for the 21st Century."

On every brand he had a quota—a quota that the distilleries set for the distributors and the distributors demand of the salesmen. Meeting quotas translates into pressure, and pressure means living with the constant threat of losing a brand if the salesman doesn't produce.

Farther down the road, coming out of another store, Hazle got back into his car, put his hands to his forehead and closed his eyes. "Come on, Hazle," he muttered to himself, "use your brain. Think this out." I asked if he had a headache. "No," he said, "I'm just thinking and relaxing. I've got to get an order from Benny in there, and he's out tending to golf instead of tending to business. His clerk can't order for him. Next Tuesday when I come through, I'm going to have to get here earlier, and that's going to mean missing a couple of stops in Greenwood and picking them up later so I can get in to see Benny before he gets on the course."

Hazle drove slowly through Woodruff, the little town at the junction of Routes 101 and 221 where he was reared. On the road expenses came out of his own pocket, and he had canceled his credit cards as a foolish temptation to spend unnecessarily. He shunned motels in favor of spending nights with relatives and friends, particularly his pal Don Buddin, who had played shortstop for the Boston Red Sox for five years and ran a whiskey store in Fountain Inn. "If you look through the trees there," Hazle said, "that's my old high school. The practice field was just over the bank." Nearby, the little weathered house on North Main Street that had belonged to his parents was in need of painting and was for sale. Hazle wished he could afford to buy it and fix it up, if only for old times' sake. "And over there, that's where my mother and dad are buried," he said, pointing to a small cemetery. "They raised six of us and, you know, I think they did a pretty good job."

Back in the forties, when Hazle was growing up in the Carolina hills, all the textile mills had baseball teams. If you could hit or pitch, the mills would give you a summer job and ask you to do not much more than stroke liners or throw strikes. Robert Sidney Hazle—six feet tall, 190 pounds—could bang the ball clear to Greenville, and from the mill leagues he went on to play professionally in the minors. He was with the Wichita Braves that summer in 1957, an unknown journeyman with a bat and glove, when the Milwaukee Braves unexpectedly called him up in July, at an annual salary of six thousand dollars, to spell Andy Pafko in right field. "I promised myself one thing—that if I failed, it wasn't going to be for not trying," Hazle recalled.

Well, what Bob Hazle did to National League pitchers was roughly equivalent to what the tropical storm Hurricane Hazel had done to his South Carolina coastline in 1954; he destroyed what stood in his path. For eight fairytale weeks, the Hurricane was the mightiest hitter in baseball, and for a fleeting moment he became what most men never achieve in an entire lifetime—he became an instant American hero of the first order. "I suppose he'll cool off, but right now this kid is Musial, Mantle and Williams all wrapped up in one," the Braves' second baseman, Red Schoendienst, said as the team drew close to the pennant.

Although his minor league credentials had been ordinary enough, Hazle came through in game after game with winning clutch hits for the Braves. He sprayed home runs and doubles all over Milwaukee County Stadium. He helped the Braves hold off the Dodgers and the Reds in the stretch drive with his bat—a bat he had borrowed from Chuck Tanner—and he carried the Braves to the only world championship they would ever win in Milwaukee. His batting average for that partial season he played was .403. "I wasn't doing anything different; it was just that everything was working for me. I didn't want to wake up. Gosh, that was a good life."

Hazle smiled faintly at the memory and pulled into another whiskey store, his twenty-third stop of the day. "But I tell you the truth," he said, "once I left the game,

I never thought of going back managing, coaching or whatever. What's done is done. Besides, the way it ended, I left with kind of a bad taste in my mouth for baseball." The Braves' general manager, John Quinn, had promised to reward Hazle with a bonus after the season, but when the bonus came it was what Hazle considered a miserly thousand dollars. The Hurricane mailed the check back, saying he needed the money, but not at the cost of his pride.

In 1958 Hazle was hit twice by beanballs—spending two weeks in a St. Louis hospital on one occasion—and then was traded to Detroit. He had differences with the manager, Bill Norman, and was exiled to the minors, where he spent two undistinguished seasons. At the age of thirty-one, though convinced he was still a major league ballplayer, he retired and went home to South Carolina. "Everything went wrong and that was the end of it," he said. "I told the wife it was time to wrap it up. Please appreciate, I'm not griping. I had my shot. It's just that in the majors you have that vinegar, that intensity, that gives you strength, and in the minors I couldn't get that pep back. Oh, well . . ."

Back home, Hazle sold granite for tombstones and monuments, then switched to selling whiskey. His wife died of cancer in 1970, and two years later he married Pat, an accountant. He called her Mama, and the two of them spoke often of the fun they'd had together over twenty years. Their ranch-style house, on a cul-de-sac in Columbia, was full of laughter and friends either theirs or those of their four grown children. There were always drinks available on the bar and, as often as not, a barbecue being fired up on the porch near the swimming pool. When it rained, Hazle did his grilling with an umbrella over his head.

Hazle plopped into a chair in his living room, the two-day selling trip over. "You know, people'll come by and say, 'You played ball. You ought to be retired,'" he said. "And I say, 'Do you know what you're talking about, fella? We didn't make enough money to amount to anything then. I got to work to pay the bills like anyone else.' I'll tell you what changed my values, though; it was the heart attack. The first thing it taught me was the value of money, which is nothing. If you don't have your health, what good is all the money in the world? All of a sudden Pat and me found we didn't need all those things you're always buying and saving for—isn't that right, Mama? And I must say, I'm not the go-getter I was. I mean, I ask myself, what is this? You push yourself, all the time trying to meet quotas and get ahead, and you push yourself right into a heart attack. Well, I figure now, go ahead, do the best job you can. Take pride in what you're doing. But don't die for something that doesn't really matter."

Hazle stretched out his legs, a glass of R&R in hand, trying to get whiskey stores and quotas and brand names off his mind. His two daughters dropped by, and his granddaughter jumped into his lap and gave him a kiss. Pat took rib-eye steaks out of the refrigerator. They freshened up their drinks, and Hurricane Bob Hazle poked the coals on the grill and said that this—coming home, being home, staying home—was the grandest reward that work could offer. "The Hurricane these days," said Pat with a wink, "is really just a gentle breeze."

*   *   *

Hurricane Bob Hazle, having finished another week on the road selling whiskey, suffered a fatal heart attack one spring morning in 1992 while tending flowers in his backyard. He was, at sixty-one, a year younger than Glenn Yarbrough. His wife called to tell me of his death, and I remembered something he had said as we bounced between liquor stores on those back roads of Carolina: "It's been a good life. I played some ball, earned an honest living, made some good friends, had a wonderful family. I don't know that a man could ask much more than that."

Without Fear or Favor

Joan Didion believes the best way to get a feel for
what's going on in a city is to find out what's going
on in its courts. Sit there for a while and you can hear
the heartbeat of the city. You get a sense of who lives
there, what the problems are, how justice is served. I admire her patience and eye for subtlety but have found I
can't sit still for long in a courtroom unless I am there to
gather specific information. So when I land in a strange
city in search of tone and texture, I often call the police
department and ask if I can spend a night riding around
in a patrol car. I have never been turned down.

The patrol car I ended up in in Bismarck was driven by
an attractive young officer named Sue Anderson, whose
father had been the police chief over in Fargo. She gave me
one of those are-you-from-outer-space? looks when I said
I was surprised to find a policewoman working the night
shift alone, without a partner. "This is North Dakota,"
she replied, having clearly identified me as a rube from the
city. It was about 8:00 P.M., in the season that is no longer
winter but not yet spring, and we drove down Washington
Street, past the Elks Club and skirted a big, ugly shopping
mall. We circled the town, crossed it, doubled back and
poked along the Missouri River. Not a hint of trouble

anywhere. Empty cars were parked outside the bars and shops we passed, doors unlocked and motors running, their heaters operating full blast to keep the biting cold at bay. Her shift lasted twelve hours, and on this night she would receive not a single call from the dispatcher. I asked her if it was always this quiet. "Lots of times it is," she said. "Basically you'll find people are more trusting here. If I stop a car with out-of-state plates, especially Texas, I might be a little suspicious, wondering what they're doing in North Dakota in the winter, but in terms of violent crime, we're pretty fortunate."

That, in fact, was what had brought me to North Dakota. While an epidemic of murder had struck our cities from coast to coast and crime was threatening the civility—if not the survival—of urban America, North Dakota, year in and year out, was the safest place in the nation. Your chances of being the victim of a violent crime in the Peace Garden State were half again less than in the forty-ninth-ranked state, South Dakota. In a recent typical year, North Dakota had the fewest robberies, per capita, the fewest burglaries, the fewest assaults. It ranked next to last in property crime and third to last in car theft. North Dakota (population 634,000 and shrinking) in 1991 recorded nine homicides. (All nine victims were killed by acquaintances or relatives.) Washington, D.C., with nearly the same number of people, had 489. Normally North Dakota spends about one hundred dollars per person on its justice system—less than any state save Mississippi, Arkansas and West Virginia. Washington, D.C., spends nine hundred dollars. No one in North Dakota thought this particularly interesting or unusual.

"That right?" they'd say when I mentioned it, which is about what I'd expect a Nevadan to say if I told him I'd driven through the entire state and hadn't seen an ocean.

To put North Dakota's crime rate in context, consider: Americans murder 26,000 Americans a year. That's more dead than the U.S. Marines suffered on the combined battlefields of both world wars. It's the equivalent of wiping out the entire population of Montana's capital, Helena. Murder is the leading cause of death for the nation's teenagers. In Washington, D.C., one of every 440 black males is murdered each year. "Mommy," asked an eight-year-old girl in the capital, looking out her window one morning, "why are there bodies on our front lawn?" She spoke matter-of-factly, perhaps because, according to the American Psychological Association, the average child witnesses at least eight thousand TV murders by the time he or she leaves elementary school. For these children television and life are one; reality has no shock value anymore, and unless you can turn the channel, nothing is real.

The roots of violence in our past are, of course, deep and firmly planted. European writers who traveled the American West in the nineteenth century were struck by the lawlessness and drunkenness they encountered, and many wrote about the legions of sullen, taciturn men for whom a gun and a bottle of whiskey were as much a symbol of manhood as a penis. Mark Twain, writing about his early days in Virginia City, Nevada, in the 1860s, provided a telling portrait of a new, violent society where the saloon was the focus of community life:

The first twenty-six graves in the Virginia [City] cemetery were occupied by *murdered* men. So everybody said, so everybody believed, and so they will always say and believe. The reason why there was so much slaughtering done was that in a new mining district the rough element predominates, and a person is not respected until he has "killed his man." That was the very expression used.

If an unknown individual arrived, they did not inquire if he was capable, honest, industrious, but—had he killed his man? If he had not, he gravitated to his natural and proper position, that of a man of small consequence; if he had, the cordiality of his reception was graduated according to the number of his dead. It was tedious work struggling up to a position of influence with bloodless hands; but when a man came with blood of half a dozen men on his soul, his worth was recognized at once and his acquaintance sought.

In Nevada, for a time, the lawyer, the editor, the banker, the chief desperado, the chief gambler, and the saloonkeeper occupied the same level in society, and it was the highest. The cheapest and easiest way to become an influential man and be looked up to by the community at large was to stand behind a bar, wear a cluster-diamond pin, and sell whiskey. I am not sure but that the saloonkeeper held a shade higher rank than any other member of society. His opinion had weight. It was his privilege to say how the elections should go. No great movement could succeed without the countenance and direction of the saloonkeepers. It was a high favor when the chief saloonkeeper consented to serve in the legislature or the board of aldermen. Youthful ambition hardly aspired so much to the honors of the law, or the Army and Navy, as to the dignity of proprietorship in a saloon. ✍

While I was in North Dakota, I went to see Nicholas Spaeth, the attorney general. He had an eye on higher office, and I expected him to have a ready answer for the state's low crime rate; first he would tell me about the innovative crime prevention programs he had instituted, then he'd talk about superior law enforcement and throw in some statistics on the number of drug busts. Instead, this is what he said: "I'd love to take credit for the low crime rate, but I can't. The reasons are almost entirely social and economic. This is still a state with family stability, a low divorce rate, an ethnically homogeneous population. The influence of the Catholic and Lutheran churches is strong. We don't have much urbanization. There's no great diversity between rich and poor. We don't have gangs and we don't have a big drug problem. What we're talking about is a cultural thing that really has very little to do with our efforts." Spaeth's political candor was refreshing, though I suspected it might not serve him well if he ever got to Washington. But in North Dakota voters accept nothing less from their politicians. They expect their officials to be low profile and appropriately humble.

Anyone who tries to take undue credit is chopped back to size quickly because the voters are as knowledgeable as the politicians about what is going on in their sparsely populated state.

Significantly, when a mini–oil boom brought hundreds of workers into North Dakota in the late seventies, there was a blip and crime increased. Then the boom ended, the workers left and crime returned to minuscule levels. What this suggested to some criminologists was that the low crime rate in North Dakota and its sparsely populated neighbors was related to mutual respect engendered when people know one another and to peer pressure that makes antisocial behavior unacceptable. It was as though Bismarck and, say, New York City had nothing in common except a place on the same map.

Michael Meyer, chairman of criminal justice studies at the University of North Dakota, had another thought: In a rural setting, those who violate the law are considered outcasts and misfits. "Is crime less acceptable here?" he asked. "The answer is yes, definitely. In North Dakota, the community has more potential to exert controls. You're not an anonymous person and your anchor, your status, your identity in the community are affected by what you do. I don't want to carry this analogy too far, but look at what is written about Japan's low crime rate. One of the explanations often given is that there is linkage between the individual and his family, his job, his community, his identity. And a consequence of these conditions is that people have respect for each other."

North Dakota's entire prison population numbered just 550, the nation's smallest. The stone penitentiary—

built in 1885, four years before North Dakota became a state—lay at the far end of Bismarck, across the railroad tracks. There were no security gates or guards asking for my identification, and I drove in and parked near the warden's office. Inside, the new sixty-two-cell South Block would have been considered a nice motel if it had been placed on a Dakota roadside. It had a pool table and television set and soft-drink machine in the common area and tidy one-man cells. With good behavior inmates could work their way out of the old four-tier block and into the new facility. There were smoking and nonsmoking cells, and several of the prisoners I passed were sitting on their bunks, typing into laptop computers. In all the years the penitentiary had been there, no prisoner had ever been murdered; there hadn't even been a stabbing or an escape in a decade.

I had called ahead to ask if I could talk with some prisoners. No problem, the warden said. He took me into an interview room, and a moment later Richard McNair walked in. He was blond haired, thirty-three years old and as articulate as he was polite. McNair was the editor of the prison magazine and studying for a college degree in literature. He dreamed of being a writer and had found that writing helped him come to terms with his anger. "What's it like in here?" I asked. "This doesn't seem anywhere near as bad as a lot of prisons I've seen."

"It's kind of weird when you think about it," McNair began. "Here you've got five hundred guys closed in and you don't have fights and stuff. Guys don't carry knives. You don't have rapes. You see young people sent here, and once they get over the stigma of being in prison, they say, 'Hey, this isn't so bad.' I've talked to a lot of people who've been in federal prison and they say this is like a campus. I think we pretty much have rapport with the officers. The state's so small that a lot of the prisoners and officers know each other. They grew up together in the same towns."

McNair didn't fit my stereotype of a felon. He spoke softly, looked me in the eye and asked what books he should read to master the craft of writing. He wrote down my responses on a yellow notepad. I figured he had probably run afoul of the law with drugs and asked him what his crime had been. "Murder," he said. "I'm doing life."

Outside the interview room, Warden Tim Schuetzle, alone and unarmed, was making his morning rounds. "Good luck with the parole board, Jim," he said to a passing inmate. And to another, "Hi, Ambrose. How's that leg of yours?" The word on Schuetzle, who coached a youth-league hockey team at night, was that if you stayed straight, he would treat you fair. Get out of line, and the perks disappeared fast. Because the prison was underpopulated and North Dakota needed money, Schuetzle made room for forty hard-nosed federal prisoners, shipped in from tougher, overcrowded institutions across the country. (North Dakota earned forty-five dollars a day for each federal prisoner.) Most arrived with a swagger and plans to take control of the cell blocks. The warden explained the rules only once. At first misstep, recalcitrants were exiled to out-of-state prisons, and some, realizing the hell that awaited them, appeared in tears before Schuetzle's desk to beg for a second chance. They never got it.

The staff couldn't smoke inside the prison—only the inmates could—and Schuetzle and I put on overcoats and went outside for a cigarette, turning our backs to the prairie wind. "Other places have lost control because of the sheer numbers," he said. "That hasn't happened to us. Our philosophy is that we're not the punitive ones, the judges are. We try to treat the prisoners with some respect, and we find, for the most part, that they in turn treat the staff with respect. I know that sounds very liberal, leftist, goody-goody, but it seems to be working."

Schuetzle and the criminologists I talked to agreed that many factors contributed to North Dakota's low crime rate and prison population. (The pattern even extended to the state's two air force bases, where the incidents of violent crime were about 50 percent less than the national average at other Strategic Air Command bases.) Among the factors was space: The population density in North Dakota—nine people per square mile, compared with 960 in, say, Rhode Island—reduced the tensions that gnaw at city dwellers. Nineteen of every 20 youths, aged seven to eighteen, were in school. And a like-minded citizenry—95 percent white, largely of German and Scandinavian ancestry—produced less conflict than did the components of an urban melting pot. Then there were the tough winters and shortage of summer tourist attractions that kept out, in local parlance, the riffraff. Strangers passed through North Dakota on the way to somewhere else, but few stayed long.

North Dakota was so off the beaten path that Rand McNally once forgot to include it in one of its maps. The director of tourism conducted a survey in neighboring Minnesota and asked people the first thing that came to mind when North Dakota was mentioned. The predominant response was no response; almost everyone drew a blank. All this isolation and flat, empty land used to make North Dakotans defensive. Now they looked at it as part of their good fortune. It helped spare them the problems of the city, and visitors driving into the state were greeted by a tongue-in-check billboard the tourism department had put up, saying that North Dakota's "mountain removal project" was now complete. One of the ironies of North Dakota's low crime rate was that the state was armed to the teeth and a bastion of support for the National Rifle Association. The availability and number of guns in the United States—200 million, four times more than in 1950—had always seemed to me to be absurd. If guns made people safe, we should have been the safest nation on earth, but in 1991, handguns killed 8,915 people in the United States (compared with seven in the United Kingdom and eight in Canada). There were few politicians, though, with the courage to confront the NRA. Advocating gun control was considered as un-American as vetoing aid to Israel.

I fell into conversation about guns and gun control in a cafe in Bismarck. Five or six men met there every afternoon for coffee, and I introduced myself to Jim Thompson, who with his son Ryan owned the Sioux Sporting Goods store across the street on Broadway. "You want a cup?" he asked. "I'm buying." What was happening in the cities? someone asked. Had everyone gone crazy? "Tell me this, Jim," said Art Beuar, an attorney. "In all the years you've been in business, how many of the guns you've sold have been traced back to a crime?"

"Well, I've been in business just short of forty-five years," Jim Thompson said. "There were years I'd sell fifteen hundred guns. And at the outside, at the absolute tops, the answer is six." His son said, "People here are brought up properly. They have a reverence for guns and they understand what a wound is. It's unfortunate what's happening in the cities, but I don't know why that should reflect on us in the prairie. Why should someone want to take my gun away in North Dakota because someone in Los Angeles or Miami doesn't act responsibly?"

"What's a man in Los Angeles need a gun for anyway except to shoot someone?" Jim Thompson asked. "There are over twenty thousand laws on the books right now controlling guns. I don't know that we need any more. We just ought to enforce the ones we've already got."

Oddly, crime, with the exception of gang-related homicide, has actually been declining in the United States since the mid-1980s, at least in part because the general population is growing older, and the prison population has tripled since 1975. But there is one group that is statistically more apt to commit a crime today than a generation ago—the young male. Sociologists offer two possible reasons: first, the pervasive spread of the drug culture, and second, a value shift in American culture that makes people more inclined to do their own thing and less inclined to worry about their reputations in the eyes of their elders.

If something fundamental has changed in the United States, it is worrisome, because the elements that keep

crime low in North Dakota—family stability, a homogeneous population, an absence of slums, drugs and poverty—are the very attributes that are eroding in our cities.
That is North Dakota's challenge—to maintain a balance:
It wants to preserve its character as an agricultural society
that provides a stable environment, jobs and self-esteem
(offered that, why would anyone steal or rob?) and at the
same time, to strengthen its economy it needs to attract
manufacturing, which in turn will bring in outsiders and
perhaps create the problems other places already have. No
one knows if North Dakota, at the crossroads, can have it
both ways, but I can tell you this: I left my wallet and room
key in a Bismarck bar one night, and when I got back to
my motel, a message awaited me. Thirty minutes later a
stranger dropped the wallet off at the reception desk, with
every dollar accounted for.

Nowhere to Run

I can lose myself for hours poring over road maps and columns of demographic statistics that tell us who the "typical" American is. My finger has traced Route 6 a hundred times as it meanders from Provincetown, Massachusetts, to the doorstep of California's Death Valley, and my mind has absorbed all manner of mostly useless information: 14 percent of us, for example, hate liver; the average female weighs 144 pounds and will live to the age of seventy-eight; our average family income is $35,225, and our average monthly mortgage is $737. We watch television an average of twenty-eight hours and thirteen minutes a week—about one quarter of our waking hours—and have in our average homes two telephones, two TVs and a VCR (but no answering machine or gun). Only one in three of us read a book for pleasure last year.

Each year the federal government publishes a fat statistical abstract of the United States that tells us how we—the 250 million Americans who make up one twentieth of the world's population—live, work, die. Flipping through it one day, I came to a section on suicide, the third leading cause of death among people aged fifteen to twenty-four, ranking behind only homicides and accidents, and the eighth leading cause among persons of all ages. Suicide takes thirty thousand lives a year.

During the 1960s the port cities of the western seaboard—Seattle, San Francisco, Los Angeles and San Diego—had the nation's highest incidence of suicide. What they had in common was unrooted, unstable populations, the transient qualities associated with port areas and a lot of residents who had moved west in hopes of starting over, only to learn, at the westernmost shore of the American Dream, that dark shadows still pursued them. While the rest of the nation dared only whisper the word *suicide,* Los Angeles had set up the country's first twenty-four-hour suicide prevention center and was handling dozens of phone calls a day from people desperate for human contact, even with just a voice.

But as the port cities became more settled and less a mecca for restless dreamers, as communities evolved and Californians no longer asked one another, "Where are you from?" the suicide rate dropped significantly. Those stark numbers in the government abstract revealed that for the past two decades the region with the highest per capita incidence of suicide has been the Mountain States, an area where men are apt to be help-rejectors. "You're a good guy, Doc," they'll say, "but I'm going to solve this my way." That attitude can carry a person far when the breaks go with him and be dangerously destructive when they don't. Although psychiatrists are unable to explain precisely why, the seven states with the highest suicide rate are, in order: Nevada, Montana, New Mexico, Arizona, Wyoming, Idaho and Colorado—states whose characters are entwined with the rugged, sometimes violent individualism of the Old West. Just one Mountain State is not on the list: Mormon-dominated Utah, the only state that still lives by the teachings of the church. (The settled, more traditional Northeast region has the lowest suicide rate.)

I spent a week traveling the Mountain States, talking to people who had endured a suicide in the family and now called themselves "survivors." They congregated as strangers in towns across the West and were bonded by a loss so deep and so unfathomable that some could not even speak of it. I expected to find my journey distressing but instead came away moved by the courage and honesty of the survivors, each of whom had had to deal with a bewildering array of emotions: grief, confusion, shame, denial, a sense of rejection and, most painful of all, the awareness that one's love had not been powerful enough to save a life.

The support group in Colorado Springs, Colorado, was known as Heartbeat, and when the survivors arrived, twenty or twenty-five strong, at 7:00 P.M. on the first Tuesday of every month, they cleared away the tables in the conference room, placed the folding chairs in a tight circle and awaited the few words from LaRita Archibald that would open the meeting. "We are all here tonight because someone we care about very much intentionally ended their life," she said. "For each of us our grief is private and individual, but we all share the commonality of suicide."

Her son, Roger Kent Archibald, had shot himself to death in the family dining room. He was twenty-four. His college career had been derailed by a serious strain of flu; he had later searched desperately for a job, any job; and as his friends began moving into professional lives, it seemed he was being left behind. The note he wrote read: "Mom and Dad, This is not your fault. I tried. I can't make it. I guess I'm just not worth it." Mrs. Archibald and her husband, Eldon, an insurance agent, had known Kent was discouraged but had not sensed the depth of his depression. Said Mrs. Archibald: "I really believe we were good parents. I did all the things a good mother does. But I never talked with him about depression. And certainly not about suicide. I'm sure if I'd tried, I'd have said all the wrong things."

Marlene Scanlon, a registered nurse, was also at the Heartbeat meeting. Her son, Patrick, a second-year medical student, had been under stress academically and financially. "Do you realize, Mom," he said one day, "that when I get out of school, I'm going to owe more money than your house is worth?" Not long afterward, Patrick Scanlon, a chemistry major, took his life by inhaling the toxic fumes of a substance he had mixed. "How long he planned it, I have no idea," said Mrs. Scanlon, whose ex-husband also committed suicide. "My son and I were very close, and you ask yourself, 'Why couldn't he have come to me just this one time?' You search and search for answers and you finally realize there are none. You will never know the reason why."

Suicide is democratic, and there is little to distinguish one of its victims in the West from those elsewhere. Women are three times more likely than men to attempt suicide, but men are far more apt to complete the act. Whites—particularly the young and elderly—are at greater risk than blacks or other minorities. Alcohol is closely related to the act of suicide, especially when guns are used. Typically there are more suicides in wartime than in peacetime, more in shifting population centers than in stable ones, more in bad economic times than in prosperous ones.

But it may be the very qualities of the Mountain States' celebrated past that help explain their high suicide rate: isolation, hard drinking, young, mobile populations and the gun as an affirmation of manhood. Everything in the West is marked by bigness. The mountains. The sky. The land. One's own possibilities and expectations. If a man can't prosper there, be happy there, if his spirits don't soar like the mountains, then where does he belong? In this landscape of the soul, the "Western dynamics," as John Sanford, a suicidologist in Cheyenne, Wyoming, calls them, are constantly at work and in conflict. "I don't want to stereotype my fellow westerners," said Sanford, "but in general the image of the western male is a classical sexual stereotype. He's tough. He's controlled. He's physically violent if necessary. The image is built into the West's cultural heritage. These dynamics tend to give rise to a denial or inhibition of expression. A man's really limited to one feeling—anger. The anger becomes physical. And when you stop feeling until you have to explode and the explosion comes in a physical manner, that's what kills."

Crisis support, though, is often difficult to find in the long, bleak winters of Wyoming, the nation's most sparsely populated state. Colorado and Arizona are at risk with populations swollen by thousands of newcomers seeking the promises of the West. Montanans, who revere their saloons as shrines and wouldn't think of going anywhere without rifles mounted in their pickups, relish all that is manly, including the art of suffering silently. Nevada, unique because of its gambling and twenty-four-hour life-style, has, in addition to the nation's highest suicide rate, the highest divorce rate, fourth highest homicide rate and lowest church attendance. In the states with in- and out-migration patterns, the social milieu makes it more probable that when a person has a suicidal impulse, there are no restraining forces in terms of cultural heritage, sense of community or just knowing neighbors. There is, said one western psychologist, no recognizable group that can pass on its history to newcomers as can Bostonians or New Yorkers.

The Suicide Prevention Center in Reno had begun operation in the mid-sixties in a pay-phone booth donated by Nevada Bell. It now received an average of fifty calls a day and, with the financial help of United Way, occupied what had been the living room of an old house near the University of Nevada campus. It was filled with second-hand furniture: a three-legged sofa, covered with a pillow and blanket, on which someone apparently had snoozed recently; several stuffed armchairs; three or four desks, each with a phone on a long extension cord that reached over the list of community service numbers tacked on the wall. A man of about thirty was talking quietly on the phone, the receiver cradled between neck and shoulder, his feet stretched out on the desk. There was an open box of crackers and a container of milk by the phone, and I assumed this had been a long conversation.

The man's name was George, and he later told me how he had become a volunteer listener at the crisis center. Five years earlier, depressed over his battle with cancer, he had loaded his father's 10-gauge shotgun, placed the barrel in his mouth and pulled the trigger. Nothing happened. Stunned, he returned the weapon to the gun rack. Three hours later it discharged, blowing a huge hole in the ceiling. "I'm not a religious person, but that damn sure made me believe in divine intervention," he said. "I should be a statistic. I shouldn't even be here." His cancer in remission, no longer suicidal, George literally had been given the gift of life and spent much of his free time on the hot-line phone as his way of repaying a debt. He had no way of knowing if he had ever saved a life, or even eased the pain of an anonymous caller, though he suspected he had. But in his mind it kept coming back to one question: Would he have loaded the shotgun had he had a number to call and known that at the end of the line there would be someone who understood?

I don't know how much George and Roger Kent Archibald had to do with it, but shortly after moving back east, I started working as a listener on a crisis hot line near my home in Virginia. My wife, who cooked meals at a homeless shelter and tutored a neighborhood child with a learning disability, had long been urging me to get involved in a volunteer program—"Any program," she said. "Just do something that would contribute to our community." I resisted, though not without guilt, and usually cited the unpredictability of my travel schedule. The fact is, like many journalists, I was more comfortable poking into the lives of others than I was giving of my own. We gather up people's sorrows and joys but leave little of ourselves behind. When the secrets are revealed, the emotions laid bare, we close our notebooks, say thank you and are gone. Those we meet chance everything; we risk nothing.

The details of my capitulation are insignificant, but every Thursday night, from 8:00 P.M. until midnight, I now spend in a shabby room, much like the one in Reno, talking to nameless callers who share with this stranger their dark, desperate anxieties. I, too, don't know if I have ever truly helped anyone, but I know the gratification I feel when, after a long conversation, a flat, unemotional voice comes slowly to life and an implied pledge is made: This day will be lived in its entirety. I have tried to imagine what the callers look like, how they live, when their nights succumbed to the grip of loneliness. But portraits do not slip easily into focus. Only the voices are real. I often wonder if I have passed a caller on the street that very day. Are any of them my neighbors? Whose way of coping is normal—theirs or mine?

Only a generation or two ago, a person consumed by suicidal thoughts, drug abuse, the scars of rape, the loneliness of old age, the dread of some deadly disease had nowhere to turn, except perhaps his clergyman. Today America is the support-group capital of the world, and no subject is off-limits. No one need suffer alone and silently any longer. Our society has become more permissive, but that has opened closet doors and made us more tolerant of those who are different. Our lives move too fast, but that has given rise to a huge cadre of volunteers with time to listen. Our restless spirit has made us mobile, but that has made us understand that Utopia has less to do with what the destination offers us than with what we bring to the place we unpack our bags and finally call home.

A
VANISHING
WORLD

Home on the Range

The settling of the West is our oldest and most enduring legend. It transformed cowboys from tradesmen to folk heroes, turned villains into national celebrities and so shaped our self-image that the frontier became the metaphor for the values of America itself. So sacrosanct is the legend that historian Paul Hutton was accused of being unpatriotic when he wrote in *Texas Monthly* that Davy Crockett, rather than dying gallantly at the Alamo, had actually surrendered and been executed. Jimmy Stewart—a Princeton University graduate who had originally planned to be an architect—got the same nasty response in 1939 when he played a gunless, milk-drinking deputy sheriff in *Destry Rides Again.* "The idea that I came to be marshal of a town and didn't use a gun was, people said, insulting to the western and to everyone who believed in the West," Stewart recalled. "The western, after all, is really about the basic values of our country—freedom, the settling of new frontiers, the determination to push on."

Our western mythology gives us good and evil with no shades of gray. There is happiness at the end of every trail and a good saloon in every town. We extol those men who rode tall in the saddle as we never did our look-alike, act-alike astronauts; such men were loners, surviving on courage and wits, trailblazers for a nation that places greater value on physical prowess than on intellectual capacity. They were common men, and they could have been us. "Americans admire the cowboy leading the caravan alone astride his horse," Henry Kissinger said, while likening himself to exactly that during his negotiations with the Chinese and North Vietnamese in the 1970s. Those first American heroes—clever, tough, honorable, self-reliant— were the grist of folklore we adopted as a portrait of ourselves.

But from the southeastern prairies of New Mexico comes a less romanticized look at the Old West that challenges our notion of tall cowboys and knightly deeds. It comes from an overgrown cemetery in a cattle town that disappeared in the late 1890s, and, if the secrets anthropologists unearthed there are any measure, frontier life was a ghastly thing: violent, grueling, impoverished, often pitiful, and not at all filled with dashing young men of statuesque form. Seven Rivers, just north of today's Carlsbad, was on the Goodnight-Loving Trail, over which the great cattle drives followed the Pecos out of Texas en route to the rangelands of Montana and Wyoming. It was a forlorn and empty place that had several saloons and no church. In summer it steamed under furnacelike temperatures, in winter it lay under deep covers of wind-driven snow. By 1885 its population had grown to three hundred, and the *White Oaks Golden Era* newspaper reported: "Business is lively and our little settlement thrives apace."

The town prospered only briefly. Then, bypassed by the railroad, the cattle drives over, Seven Rivers died and was reclaimed by the prairies. It lay forgotten until 1988, when a federal team, headed by anthropologist Bobbie Ferguson, hurried there, just before the completion of an irrigation dam that would soon flood the flatlands along County Route 32. The scientists exhumed fifty-two skeletons from the cemetery. They studied the remains with the help of forensic experts, examined court records and newspaper clippings and, by the time the cemetery was relocated to a new site fifteen miles north, had pieced together a remarkably clear picture of the brief life of Seven Rivers and the southerners who had settled it. "I was stunned," Ferguson said. "I had always assumed all those tales about the Wild West were exaggerated. But what I think it comes down to is that these people's lives were so hard, so full of physical labor, that there just wasn't much time for tenderness or care or warmth."

Of the fifteen men between the ages of eighteen and forty-five buried in Seven Rivers, ten had died violently. There was Zach Light, a troublemaking cowhand from Texas, shot in the saloon owned by the sheriff; Light's skull bore a bullet hole just above the left eye; K. S. Keith, killed by one of the two Indian tribes in the region, Apache or Comanche, who cut off his right leg above the knee; William Johnson, his head blown off by his father-in-law's shotgun when he mentioned at the dinner table he had fought for the Union side in the Civil War; an unidentified man about thirty, who had lived more than a year with a knife blade embedded in his shoulder, and whose cause of death was listed as "buckshot in the chest area"; and John Northern, for whom the *Golden Era* had predicted "a serene and happy life, cloudless, save with rare and roseate shadows" when he took a teenage bride, Julia, just before Christmas 1885. Less than two years later he, too, was dead, at the age of twenty-seven, shot in the saloon where he worked.

Many of the men were hardly five feet tall; the tallest was five-nine. None was buried with his boots on, boots (and often even shoes) being too expensive to waste on a dead man. Of the fourteen children under the age of two, most had died of scarlet fever, diphtheria, measles, croup or other diseases that today are not even part of our concerns. John Andress, who arrived in a settlers' wagon train from Pipe Creek, Texas, lost his wife, mother-in-law and two children the same year to dysentery contracted from bad drinking water.

Surely this wasn't the stuff of B-grade westerns or pulp novels. But if life on the prairies was so miserable, how did we come to convince ourselves that that was a glamorous era of our past? How did we come to make folk heroes of cowboys—a word which in the eastern press of the 1800s was used as a pejorative for itinerants and roustabouts? Would Randolph Scott really have felt at home in such an environment? "In the West," wrote the English novelist Anthony Trollope in 1862,

> I found men gloomy and silent,—I might almost say sullen. A dozen of them will set for hours round a stove, speechless. They chew tobacco and ruminate. They are not offended if you speak to them, but they are not pleased. They answer with monosyllables. . . . They drink but are seldom drunk to the eye; they begin it early in the morning

and take it in a solemn, sullen, ugly manner, standing always at a bar. . . . They drink often and to great excess. . . .

I cannot part with the West without saying in its favor that there is a certain manliness about its men, which gives them a dignity of their own. . . . It seems to me that no race of men requires less outward assistance than these pioneers of civilization. ✒

It is an odd juxtaposition, finding dignity and manliness in a bunch of intoxicated monosyllabic misanthropes. Yet one is left with the impression that these were men who didn't wilt in the face of adversity. They got the job done and suffered, if at all, stoically. Emotion, our myths teach us, is not a masculine attribute; sensitivity is best left to women. Note the matter-of-fact tone in the 1866 journals of trail driver George Duffield, who took a herd from Texas to Iowa and appears to have accepted adversity as nothing more than an unpleasant inconvenience:

> ✒ Upset our wagon in River & lost Many of our cooking utencils . . . was on my Horse the whole night & it raining hard . . . Lost my Knife . . . There was one of our party Drowned to day (Mr. Carr) & Several narrowly escaped & I among [them] . . . Many Men in trouble. Horses *all* gave out & Men refused to do anything . . . Awful night . . . not having had a bite to eat for 60 hours . . . *Tired* . . . Indians very troublesome . . . Oh! what a night—Thunder Lightning & rain—we have fol-

lowed our Beeves *all* night as they wandered about
. . . We Hauled cattle out of the Mud with oxen
half the day . . . Dark days are these to me. Nothing but Bread & Coffee. Hands all Growling &
Swearing—everything wet & cold . . . Sick & discouraged. Have *not* got the *Blues* but am in *Hel*[*l*]
of a fix . . . My back is Blistered badly . . . I had
a sick headache bad . . . *all* our letters have been
sent to the dead letter office . . . Flies are worse
than I ever saw them . . . weather very *Hot* . . .
Indians saucy . . . one man down [with] the Boils
& one with Ague . . . Found a Human skeleton on
the Prairie today. ✍

The America that George Duffield encountered, just
before the nation's centennial, was really two countries,
one untamed, one settled. The meeting point between
wildness and civilization was the ninety-eighth meridian, a
line drawn through the eastern part of Dakota Territory,
the middle of Kansas and San Antonio, Texas. To the east
lay thirty-one states and 42 million people; to the west,
seven states and nine territories, inhabited by just 2 million
souls. But the era of free-roaming cowboys and lawless
cow towns lasted hardly more than twenty-five years, from
the end of the Civil War to the introduction of barbed
wire, and by 1890 the U.S. government declared the "frontier closed" and said the West had been settled. Except
where the cowboy "lingers in the mountains of New Mexico," wrote Owen Wister, author of *The Virginian,* "he has
been dispersed . . . as all wild animals must inevitably be
dispersed."

About that time, in 1893, a relatively obscure historian from the University of Wisconsin, Frederick Jackson Turner, delivered a paper at a conference in Chicago entitled "The Significance of the Frontier in American History." His thesis, though drawing mostly yawns and but faint praise at the time, was to become a cornerstone in defining the American character. What made Americans—even those who stayed in the East—distinctive as a people, he said, was the frontier experience. It was the West, not our European heritage, that was primarily responsible for shaping our makeup, developing our institutions and honing our democracy, he believed. "To the frontier," Turner wrote,

> ❧ the American intellect owes its striking characteristics. That coarseness and strength combined with acuteness and inquisitiveness; that practical, inventive turn of mind, quick to find expedients; that masterful grasp of material things, lacking in the artistic but powerful to effect great ends; that restless, nervous energy; that dominant individualism, working for good and for evil, and withal that buoyancy and exuberance which comes with freedom—these are the traits of the frontier, or traits called out elsewhere because of the existence of the frontier. ❧

He went on to observe that "what the Mediterranean Sea was to the Greeks, breaking the bond of custom, offering new experiences, calling out new institutions and activities . . . the ever retreating frontier has been to the United

States." He called the frontier "a gate of escape from the bondage of the past" and said that as an expansionist nation "the American energy will continually demand a wider field for its exercise." Each move westward meant a "return to primitive conditions on a continually advancing frontier line," a "continual beginning over again" in the process of national maturation.

Turner's romantic view of the West meshed well with the self-assured, brazen, nationalistic mood in America a century ago. But today many historians have launched a vigorous attack on Turner's thesis, contending that the western experience was racist, sexist and irrelevant. The protagonists of Turner's vision were all English-speaking white men guilty of conquest, exploitation and environmental destruction, the revisionists hold. The West was but a colony of eastern investors, who controlled the railroad monopoly, set the wheat and grain prices and owned many of the territorial banks and much of the rangeland. No doubt there is truth in all this, but I still prefer the story of Cowboys and Indians to that of Cowpersons and Native Americans. Strip away all our myths and we lose our capacity to imagine.

One of the myths that today's historians are challenging is that of violence, and—a few towns like Seven Rivers, Virginia City and Tombstone notwithstanding—many believe that violence in the Old West was not markedly greater than that in eastern cities. Most also agree that western cities today—Los Angeles alone recorded 206 gang-related killings one year—are far more dangerous than were western towns of a century ago. Roger McGrath, a UCLA professor, studied violence in western mining towns and concluded that one of the wildest, Bodie, California, had a robbery rate comparable with Boston's in the late 1880s. Using the FBI's crime statistics, he found that Miami's burglary rate in 1980 was twenty-five times higher than Bodie's had been a century earlier, that the theft rate in the United States as a whole is seventeen times higher today than it was in Bodie. He did not find a single instance of reported rape in the towns he studied, and juvenile offenses were seldom more serious than the use of obscene language. McGrath argues that violence in America is the consequence of the modern city, not the frontier experience. Yes, he says, there was a high homicide rate in the Old West, but the killing was usually between willing combatants. Today's crimes are carried out by cowards, who prey on the weak and unsuspecting. They are America's version of Serbian militiamen lobbing mortar rounds on civilians. The classic shoot-out on the dusty street of some frontier town has given way to ambushes and drive-by shootings on the pavement of the twentieth century.

Ironically, what we celebrate with poetic license in the Old West are the very qualities that are inherently anti-colonial: We have made heroes of outlaws who shunned the Establishment's dictates, sentimentalized the lone gunman who answers to no one, admired those with sudden wealth acquired by luck. We have reclaimed, on the now-dead frontier, virtues that often seem to escape us in the urbanized America of the 1990s. "The moral tone of the cowcamp indeed is rather high," Theodore Roosevelt wrote in 1888. "Meanness, cowardice and dishonesty are not tolerated. There is a high regard for truthfulness and keeping one's word, intense contempt for any kind of hypocrisy and a hearty dislike for a man who shirks his work."

Contrary to common perceptions, the cow camps of which Roosevelt wrote and the westward expansion itself were hardly just an Anglo-Saxon experience. One in three cowboys was black or Mexican, and the early territories had sizable populations of Jews, Hispanics, Chinese and Japanese. The two cavalry regiments with the highest reenlistment rates and among the most storied reputations, the Ninth and Tenth, were black units. The West may have been a man's world, but the first place in the country to grant women the right to vote was Wyoming, in 1869, and the first state to send a woman to Congress was Montana, in 1917. (That woman, Jeannette Rankin, was the only person to vote against declarations of war in both 1917 and 1941.) "Next thing you know they'll be outlawing liquor," said a disgusted Bat Masterson as the suffrage movement spread through the West. In 1902 he abandoned the West and moved to New York City, where he became a famous sportswriter. His contemporary, Wyatt Earp, ended up selling real estate in Los Angeles after his brief stay in Alaska. Billy the Kid's killer, Pat Garrett, received as his reward from President Theodore Roosevelt appointment to the comfortable post of customs collector in El Paso.

Well before such gambler-marshals turned middle class, the history of the West had been turned into myth. The creators of the legend were eastern authors of the "dime novel," who, from 1860 to 1890, churned out thirty-thousand-word tales of wildly imaginative content; one leading publisher said when a rival entered the field, his stable of writers had only to kill more Indians. Then newspapermen from Boston and Philadelphia ventured west and regaled their readers with embellished accounts that made heroes of ordinary people. And, as far back as 1883, Buffalo Bill's Wild West Show exploited the daring and violence of the frontier before packed audiences in Europe and on the East Coast. Fact seldom got in the way of lively fiction as America began popularizing men of dubious achievements and celebrating the violence of its past. "I am sorry to have to lie so outrageously in this yarn," William "Buffalo Bill" Cody wrote his New York publisher. "If you think the revolver and the Bowie knife are used too freely, you may cut out a fatal shot or stab wherever you deem it wise." Earp, who served only briefly as a lawman, was elevated to superstar status after Stuart Lake's best-seller, *Wyatt Earp, Frontier Marshal* was serialized in the *Saturday Evening Post.* Wild Bill Hickok became a national figure after a story in *Harper's* magazine about his gunfight with Dave Tutt in the city square of St. Joseph, Missouri. The reason for the death duel: Tutt had won Hickok's watch in a poker game and had ignored Hickok's warning that he would be killed if he ever wore the watch in public.

There's probably no western luminary who, by today's standards, didn't have some kind of sordid past, but that has not stopped us from paying homage. William "Billy the Kid" Bonney, born in the cellar of a New York City tenement, is still honored every summer in Lincoln, New Mexico, with a pageant celebrating his last escape from jail in 1881, even though he killed two deputies in the process. Texans reenact the Alamo, though rather than use the real site in San Antonio, the battle now takes place on the set in Brackettville that John Wayne used for the 1960 movie. Jesse James's home is a museum in Jackson County, Missouri. And Tombstone, Arizona, whose population has grown from four hundred to sixteen hundred since the Second World War, stages twice a month for tourists the Shoot-out at O.K. Corral—a fight that didn't become ingrained in Western history until Walter Noble Burns's book *Tombstone* was published in 1927. Seven movies followed the book. If it weren't for the gunfight, Tombstone probably would have disappeared from the maps like Seven Rivers.

Although Clint Eastwood's *Unforgiven* was a big 1992 hit, Hollywood has virtually stopped producing traditional westerns, the most prolific genre of American film—forty-eight were made in 1948, none in 1983. Still, the Old West remains as ingrained in our national psyche as religion or baseball. More than 200 million copies of Louis L'Amour's books are in print, and sales at the Cowboy Artists of America's annual show regularly top a million dollars. Gene Autry raised $25 million for his Western Heritage Museum, which opened in Los Angeles in 1989 and now rivals the city's most popular attractions.

Inherent in everything we read and see about the settling of the West is the concept of The End of the Trail, which holds the same sweet sorrow we hear in the words "Where have you gone, Joe DiMaggio?" Hollywood, in fact, has made thirty-seven westerns with the word *last* in the title (*The Last Pony Rider, Last of the Cowboys, Last Stagecoach West*), and two of its last great western productions, *Ride the High Country* with Randolph Scott and

Joel McCrea (1962) and *The Shootist* (1976) with John Wayne mourned the passing of the western era.

To what extent that era was built on myth may always be argued, but few would debate that "westering," as A. B. Guthrie called it, offered as much misery and hardship as it did Last Sunset and High Noon heroes. Still, it is reassuring to think of the frontier as always being there, one last place to test our strength and ingenuity, for if there is no Alaskan wilderness, no Montanan expanse, aren't we all doomed to huddle in tall buildings of glass and cement, restricted by conventions and sameness, the horizon nowhere in sight?

"Well," the marshal of Tombstone observed, "you could safely say the town's a lot more calm than it used to be." He reached down to pick up a discarded scrap of paper from the wooden sidewalk. Allen Street was filled with the shadows of a quiet afternoon, and believing the peace to be secure, the marshal nodded to me, as though to say, Let's go, and we headed back toward his office behind the O.K. Corral. His boots thumped on the boardwalk, and I padded along in my sneakers, liking the echoes of history I heard at every footstep. Some of the Old West's most legendary gunmen and lawmen had walked this same route a century earlier—when Tombstone looked much as it does today—but that impressed Marshal Ed Schnautz hardly at all. "Sure there's history here," he said, "but there's history everywhere. I just try to look at the town for what it is and what the people are."

Schnautz, a sixty-year-old retired Phoenix policeman, cut an impressive image in his tan Stetson, black boots and leather vest, ambling past the saloon where Bat Masterson used to deal faro. Schnautz earned $2,100 a month and figured an officer of the law shouldn't frequent bars in his jurisdiction. Marshal Virgil Earp earned $25 a month in 1881, and, with his brother, Wyatt, had financial interests in some of Tombstone's finest drinking and gambling establishments.

Back when Tombstone was the West's most lawless mining town, 110 saloons operating around the clock spread out from Allen Street, and Boot Hill cemetery held 250 corpses, none of which had been the victim of old age. Sheriff Scott White used to send out invitations to hangings—seven men were taken from his sixteen-cell jail and hanged one March day in 1884—and John Heath, who had robbed a Bisbee, Arizona, store owned by the great-uncle of former U.S. Senator Barry Goldwater, became something of a local legend by telling a mob before his lynching: "Promise me not to shoot into my body when I'm strangling and give me a decent burial. I'm ready."

Tombstone lies a couple of hours' drive southeast of Tucson, tucked among the buttes and jagged cliffs of a wide valley, and is, I thought, a marvelous place. Though touristy, it felt right and looked right. The century-old Crystal Palace, one of the West's grand saloons, still mixed its own sarsaparilla (but had raised the price for a shot of whiskey from twelve cents in Earp's time to two dollars) and had towels hanging beneath the bar so men could wipe tobacco juice from their beards when they didn't get a clear shot at the spittoon. Old men gathered to stare off silently into space on the bench in front of the *Tombstone Epitaph,* which was set by Linotype, and dogs napped in the sun outside sleepy cafes. Like the town itself, Marshal Ed Schnautz was an anachronism, slipping uneventfully toward the retirement that had eluded his early predecessors. (Tombstone's first marshal, Fred White, was killed in a gun battle on Allen Street; the second, Ben Sippy, fled Tombstone for fear of his life; the third, Virgil Earp, was wounded at the O.K. Corral and later crippled for life when shot outside the Crystal Palace.)

Schnautz and I passed the Lucky Cuss, where ninety-three-year-old Nettie Fernley—"America's oldest professional pianist"—played briefly every day at 5:15 P.M. Schnautz had worked the homicide detail in Phoenix, and I asked him what it was like stepping into a town whose two holding cells were almost always empty and the sheriff's dispatcher closed up shop at 1:00 A.M. Tombstone hadn't had a fatal shooting since two men had gotten into a drunken argument in a private residence almost two years earlier.

"If I was young, I wouldn't stay a minute," he said. "But as it is, if you're a forty-hour man, this is a good, quiet town to be in. Good people, not much trouble. Lot of times people get ticked off and they just want someone to complain to. I nod and they feel better."

The town had once dreamed of offering so much more. John Clum, the editor of the *Tombstone Epitaph,* had written in 1880: "Tombstone is a city set upon a hill, promising to vie with ancient Rome, in a fame different in character but no less in importance." His prophecy never came true, though Tombstone's population did grow to twelve thousand, making it the largest town between El Paso and San Francisco. It had an opera house, fine restaurants that served fresh oysters and quail, elegant hotels and so much violence—most notably the gunfight on October 26, 1881, when the three Earp brothers and Doc Holliday (then dying of tuberculosis) fought the Clanton gang at the O.K. Corral on Third and Fremont streets—that President Chester Arthur threatened to impose martial law.

What saved Tombstone from the fate of other western towns whose mines ran out was nothing more than its heritage of violence. Thousands of curious visitors venture onto Allen and Fremont streets every year, pausing to read historical markers that tell who got killed where, and while they may damn the lawlessness that grips their own hometowns, they commemorate what happened in Tombstone as confirmation of the daring and toughness in the American spirit. They conjure up TV images of handsome, righteous men fighting for what was theirs by inalienable right, and in doing so, they keep the myth alive.

No one ever confused Allen McCanless with T. S. Eliot, but listen to the gait of his words and you can smell the prairie winds. Listen and you hear a cowboy's soul, alone and free in the vast kingdom of western mythology:

> *My ceiling the sky, my carpet the grass,*
> *My music the lowing of herds as they pass;*
> *My books are the brooks, my sermons the stones,*
> *My parson's a wolf on a pulpit of bones . . .*

McCanless's poem, published in 1885 and once sung as a night-herding tune, is part of a little-studied oral tradition of the West that still flourishes on ranches from Montana to Texas—cowboy poetry. Though *cowboy* and *poet* may seem a contradiction in terms, no working men in America are more closely identified with writing and reciting poetry than cowboys. And none gets more quizzical looks than a cowboy who comes out of the closet and admits he is a practicing poet. "I've been writing poetry for years," said Gene Jordan, a cowboy from Bayfield, Colorado. "I kept a pen hidden under the bed all that time 'cause my wife'd say, 'Don't embarrass people with that garbage.' She's my ex-wife now."

Until recently, poetry was the cowboy's secret, a private language of the Plains that relied not on metaphor and meter but on the simple expression of shared experiences. It was full of creaking leather and the tramp of horses' hooves and the smoke of campfires many miles from all concrete. As Bruce Kiskadon (1878–1950) wrote:

> *Let people that set and talk explain*
> *just whether I'm wrong or right.*
> *My hoss is pullin' the bridle reins*
> *and I'm hittin' the trail tonight.*

Eighteen years ago, on a tour of western ranches, Utah folklorist Hal Cannon was amazed to find that poetry was still as much a part of the cowboy's life as it had been in the days of the unfenced range. This storytelling in verse represented, he thought, an important form of American folklore that deserves to be heard and preserved. "If you look at cowboy poetry as a technician, you can riddle it," he said. "It's simple meter, simple form. But people reserve poetry for the most important things they have to say. Throughout time, our best histories of different civilizations have come through poetry, because poetry is what you feel about your history and how you make the language sing. So if you look for the emotions, the pure language, the vernacular, cowboy poetry becomes very heady, wonderful stuff." Or, in the words of John Dofflemyer:

> *Few men feel these hillsides breathe*
> *or hear the heartbeat underneath,*
> *'cept those that live here day to day*
> *and nature's beasts can hardly say*
> *a thing. They, like me, tend to slip*
> *to spots just outside most men's grip . . .*

Cannon, director of the Western Folklore Center in Salt Lake City, decided to coax the poets out of the closet and in 1985 brought fifty of them to share their verse in Elko, Nevada, a cattle town whose railhead was the terminus for Texas longhorns driven north in the 1880s. They came not to mourn a vanishing era but to celebrate a life that is as free and independent as any that still exists, and Elko, with its four casinos, five brothels and countless saloons, seemed the perfect place to do just that. No one in Elko wears over-the-nose reading glasses or orders cherries in his cocktails or takes his ten-gallon hat off at the dinner table. Bartenders at Stockmen's and the century-old Commercial Hotel hand customers bottles of Budweiser, on the assumption that no one would drink beer from a glass, and at J. M. Capriola's, one of the West's finest saddlemakers, cowboys speak in hushed tones as though they had entered a church. Anyone in improper dress is suspect. When Kim Stafford, a (noncowboy) poet and essayist from Oregon, showed up at the assemblage wearing a straw Stetson, a man from Montana took him aside politely and said, "Son, we don't wear straw in the winter. Besides, that hat's got a Texas crease in it."

The cowboy poetry gathering proved a bigger success than Cannon had dared hope and soon became an annual event, attracting a couple of hundred participants and several thousand spectators. Before packing for Elko, I debated whether to wear an excellent Stetson my wife had given me for Christmas but decided against it, for fear I couldn't camouflage my urban pedigree. I'm not sure why I even cared, except that I've always thought of western attire as being akin to a military uniform: It is a mark of identity, and you shouldn't wear it unless you've earned entitlement. So I slipped into my drab khaki slacks and blue button-down shirt, knowing I wouldn't look as jaunty as those men with their tight Levi's, bandannas and shirts with snap buttons, but content in the knowledge that at least I wasn't trying to fool anyone.

For three days, I listened to men (and a few women) from places such as Stagecoach, Nevada; Eagle, Idaho; Red Owl, South Dakota; and Lometa, Texas, play out their role as the troubadours of the Plains. They didn't read their poems as much as they did "tell" them from memory. What they shared were stories, sometimes contrived, always heartfelt, poems that were about people and real happenings, about ornery broncs and long trails, about a love that is between not man and woman but man and land. Some of the poems had a raw and primitive power. Nearly all, like the late Badger Clark's "A Cowboy's Prayer," echoed with an appreciation of a life not miscast:

> *I thank you, Lord, that I am placed so well,*
> *That you have made my freedom so complete*
> *That I'm no slave of whistle, clock or bell,*
> *Nor weak-eyed prisoner of wall and street.*

Were it not for university presses from Oklahoma westward, many notable works of the West never would have been published, and in eastern literary circles cowboy poetry draws not much more than a condescending sniffle as the stuff of dime novels. *The New York Times Book Review* devoted a full page to the medium under the headline: "Whoop-ee-ti-yo, git along little doggerel," and concluded: "Cowboys don't really write poetry any better than lawyers play golf, but you can learn a good deal about lawyers by how they play golf." The public, though, is more enthusiastic. More than two hundred books of cowboy poetry (many of them thin volumes published privately and available only in tack shops and local drugstores) are in circulation, and Cannon's anthology has sold more than forty thousand copies. The self-styled poets are suddenly in demand on TV talk shows and college campuses, and a handful have even managed to hang up their spurs and devote full time to writing. In their work, one hears a melancholy salute to passing times. Leon Flick writes:

> *They say with barbed wire came the*
> *fall of the West*
> *I ain't denyin' it's true.*
> *'Cuz there's few places left, in this*
> *once empty West*
> *you can go and just buckaroo . . .*
> *For the East runs this land, and*
> *they don't understand*
> *about cows or our points of view.*
> *They don't even care if they're playin' square*
> *or care 'bout some lost buckaroo.*

Cowboy poetry—and the Elko gathering—will grow more popular, and Cannon, the folklorist, sees potential danger in that. If the medium becomes overtly commercial, it will lose its authenticity. The poets will play to their audiences, instead of to one another. Or worse, the poets will be dudes from State Street instead of hired hands from the Double Bar X. "When things get popular and you're in front of an audience, strange things start to happen," said Montana rancher Wally McRae. "You tend to read or recite funny. Our experiences come from deep emotion, and in front of an audience, you're apt to forget that and just look instead for acceptance."

As the language of the working range, cowboy poetry will survive as long as cowboys have cattle to move and stories to tell. I found an empty stool at the Stockmen's bar and ordered a whiskey, feeling as out of place as a choirboy amid the wide-brimmed hats and weathered faces that filled the saloon. I have a habit of always bringing a book with me when I eat or drink alone—for protection, I guess, against unwanted intrusions—but I tucked it inside my shirt. I took off my over-the-nose reading glasses. Two cowboys with drooping mustaches leaned against the bar to my left. They talked quietly, both staring straight ahead. The jukebox was playing Keith Whitley's "Hard Livin'."

"Did you heal up pretty good after gettin' throwed, John?"

"Yup, I did. Don't hurt nowhere anymore."

"I can't tell you about bein' crippled up. You been crippled up more 'n me."

"Only problem I got now is I can't bend over for any period a time. Can't shoe a horse even. But I can still ride pretty good."

"Did you know I got a new baby daughter, fifteen months ago?"

"You don't say."

"Yup. She's a sweet little buckaroo. Course, don't know what to do with her 'cept put her on the table as a centerpiece."

For ears like mine, tuned to the murmurings of the city, the conversations in Elko had a magical ring. They were simple, honest, unembellished. A few nights earlier I had been in a Los Angeles restaurant where young Hollywood producers and would-be producers spent the evening lying to each other about deals and money and works in progress, and I wondered what the cowboy poets would have made of all that. I was going to speak to the two men with the drooping mustaches, but frankly, I had no idea what to say. So I ordered another whiskey and, in my best western demeanor, sat there silently, staring straight ahead.

Over the Rainbow

Several years ago I spent a baseball season on the road, wandering sixteen thousand miles through America's minor leagues in a secondhand motor home. The design of my snug little vehicle was remarkable. Packed into an area hardly larger than an old finned Cadillac was a comfortable double bed, a tiny bathroom and kitchen, a dinette and enough cabinet space to accommodate all my needs. I learned a couple of things about myself during the journey: first, how content I was to have the highway as a companion for months on end; and second, how all the possessions I had surrounded myself with at home quickly became forgotten and meaningless. I gave away my TV the first month of the trip and started reading more. I don't remember missing a single so-called convenience. My life truly had become simpler and easier.

Although I pride myself on still driving the Buick convertible I bought when I returned to the United States from Vietnam in 1970, the lessons learned during my trip in the motor home were not lasting. Soon, life would have been incomplete without my VCR and ice-dispensing refrigerator. I started checking prices for a new computer. I had returned to the nineties. It occurred to me that one of the reasons Americans feel so disconnected is because we expend more effort collecting material possessions than we do nurturing human relationships. We live in a disposable decade, discarding fetuses, diapers, marriages and fast-food containers with equal abandon, and we search for economic and political solutions to questions that are intrinsically spiritual.

Yet when we think of the country being torn by greed and obsessed with consuming, we tend to forget how much of America has kept its values in place. Visit the Dawson ranch in Montana, sit in on an annual town meeting in a New England village or cruise the Mississippi, where entire towns turn out to greet the *Delta Queen* paddleboat as she steams upriver, and you see a montage of America that is more representative of the nation's soul than anything the networks offer us on the six o'clock news. We also forget, I think, what a daring experiment the American experience is and how much tinkering it has always taken. Here's what Walt Whitman had to say about the state of society in 1871, the year "Boss" Tweed and his Tammany cronies charged New York City $2,870,464.06 for the nine months' work of one plasterer:

> The depravity of the business classes of our country is not less than has been supposed, but infinitely greater. The official services of America, national, state and municipal, in all their branches and departments, except the judiciary, are saturated in corruption, bribery, falsehood, mal-administration; and the judiciary is tainted. The great cities reek with respectable as much as non-respectable robbery and scoundrelism. . . . I say

that our New World Democracy . . . is, so far, an almost complete failure. ◆

Hoboing, I always thought, was a profession Whitman would have approved of. Hobos had mastered the simple life; their values were largely untouched by greed or consumption, their wanderings unaffected by clocks and calendars. They were an odd group whose rootlessness and aimlessness had always intrigued me, and that was what brought me to Britt, Iowa (population 2,500). It was a quiet, friendly place, two hours north of Des Moines, with one commercial boulevard called Main Street and cornfields that started where Second Street ended. Buddy Holly, Richie Valens and the Big Bopper died in a plane crash about sixty cornfields east of Britt in 1959, and Britt's high-school football team won the state championship in 1973, but other than that the only thing that kept Britt on the maps was, of all things, hobos. The town, apparently out of the goodness of its heart, started courting hobos with an occasional free meal and a day's work back in 1900, when a lot of jobless people were on the rails. As time went by and riding the rails became a lost art, a certain nostalgia evolved around this strange breed of men, rootless and broke by choice, and Britt set aside one weekend each August to welcome home a lost chunk of Americana. The festival brought about twenty thousand visitors into town—"and that puts bread on our tables," the mayor told me—and Main Street was blocked off for a parade and the crowning of a hobo king and queen. For that one weekend every summer, being homeless was a badge of honor.

I flew into Des Moines and drove north in a rental car and, just before dark, managed to book the last available room (for twenty-two dollars) in a motel on Highway 18. The clerk looked at my registration card and said, "I'd have thought you had enough homeless in Los Angeles to look at and could've saved yourself the trip." Britt was only a few miles down the road, and by the time I got there, Ramblin' Rudy and Fishbones had already set up camp. So had Steam Train Maury, Gas Can Paddy, Frisco Jack, Charlie Tuna and A Man Named John. Honorable men all, no matter that they'd been chased off the rails by "cinder dicks" in a dozen towns and been turned down more times than a bed sheet when they knocked on a back door, looking for a meal. Their camp was by the tracks of the Soo Line, and they gathered some logs for a fire and started mixing up the biggest pot of mulligan stew I'd ever seen. Someone brought out a harmonica, and soon the night was thick with nostalgia for the yesterdays when they had been not a part of vanishing America, as they were today, but, in the words of John Steinbeck, "the last free men." The hobos had lived their lives—or at least the traveling part of their lives—without a plan, suspended in a timeless vacuum that carried them down the tracks of the nation's railroads for no particular reason except the need to roam. They went everywhere and nowhere, year after year, mile after rattling mile, masters of survival who sooner or later always found an open boxcar that would bring them to Britt. Accountable to only themselves, owning only what they could carry in a rolled-up blanket, they neither contributed to nor took from the world they passed through.

"People've asked me if I didn't waste my life hoboing and I tell 'em, no sir," said Gas Can Paddy, who, at seventy-one, had finally retired to a stationary life in southern Illinois. "Nowhere I'd rather be than on the rails. When I met a woman back after the war and tried to spend some time at home, I'll tell you, I had a helluva time. I just had to get out and hit the road."

Because of its hospitality, Britt had gained something of an international reputation in certain circles. Ask a swagman in Australia or a vagabond in France where the hobo capital of the world was, and just as surely as a free mission meal comes with a sermon, the answer was "Britt, Iowa." The town offered free food to any hobo who showed up for the festival and was turning its shuttered Chief movie theater into a hobo museum. And out in the cemetery on Second Street, among the graves of Britt's leading citizens, stood two tombstones, side by side, one for Mountain Dew (HE TRAVELED ON THE RAILROADS THAT HE LOVED), the other for the Hard Rock Kid. A red bandanna rested atop each, and the Hancock County Historical Society had honored Hard Rock by keeping two of his denim shirts on display, as item No. 2003. "When we were burying Hard Rock back in 'seventy-seven," said seventy-one-year-old Steam Train Maury, "a train comes through on the Milwaukee Road tracks right alongside the cemetery, and the engineer sees us and pulls that old whistle halfway down, like he knows what's happening, and keeps it there clear across the prairie, and it sounded like this: *whooooo-who-whoooo . . .*" Steam Train mimicked the wailing salute until his own voice faded away like a lost memory.

The light from the campfire flickered in the grove of pines and danced on the shiny, silent Soo Line tracks. All around me were the murmur of voices and the recollections of old men whose lives had been tougher and lonelier than they now cared to admit. They took a sort of roll call, passing on information about fellow itinerants who had died or fallen sick during the past year, asking about others who had not yet appeared. "Cardboard got in this morning," someone said. "But what about Seattle Slim and Bear Grease? Anybody seen them?"

"Bear Grease I don't know, but I heard two things about Seattle Slim, both contradictory. I heard he died back in February up around Portland and I heard he's sicker 'n a dog and won't be making Britt this year."

"If he's only sick, he'll be here. He's probably out there right now, waiting for a freight headed this way. Bet you my boots he'll make it. Seattle Slim's too ornery to stay home."

In the caste system of the road, the hobo—who aimlessly rides freights and works occasionally for a meal or a few dollars—far outranks the tramp, who travels but doesn't work, and the bum, who hangs about and devotes his energies to wine. There wasn't even a sniff of Thunderbird around the campfire in Britt, but the truth be told, most of the men who had gathered there weren't really hobos anymore. They had grown old and settled down with vans, little homes, maybe even wives. Like recovering alcoholics, they spoke of their affliction in the present tense—"I'm a hobo," never "I was a hobo"—and they would take their secrets to the grave because theirs was a profession that wasn't being passed on. But what secrets they knew!

They knew all the best hobo jungles—under the Twentieth Street bridge in Denver, along the Columbia River in Wenatchee, Washington—and they could recall every curve on the Billy Route from Seattle to Minnie Hopeless (Minneapolis) and every sally (Salvation Army) from Lousy Anna (Louisiana) to Shakeytown (Los Angeles). They knew that when you got into Chicago on the Rock Island from Denver, it was best to get off at the Blue Island icing station so you could catch the Indiana Harbor Belt line that went around the city and crossed thirty railroads, giving you a choice of destinations. Heading for the coast, you had to know that the Union Pacific branched at Borie Junction near Cheyenne, with the west line going to Denver and the right one to Pocatello, and that Cheyenne was a good place to avoid because of its "bull school" for training railroad police.

I sat for a long time with Gas Can Paddy, looking at the scrapbooks he carried in the back of his van. I held a flashlight steady as he turned the pages and rambled on with stories of this place and that. He had a Santa Claus–like beard, wore suspenders and walked with a cane. He was thoughtful and well-spoken, and I supposed if he hadn't been afflicted with the need to roam, he would have led a normal life in a normal town and wouldn't have been nearly so much fun to talk to. I asked if there was anyone around the camp still hoboing. "If Seattle Slim or Bear Grease was here I'd take you to them," he said, "but come on, I got a man for you to meet," and we walked over to a clump of bushes where the El Paso Kid (a.k.a. Joe Wells, of no permanent address) was sitting alone, smoking a cigarette on his blanket. El Paso was a wiry, fiftyish man who still rode full-time and made, I was told, a dandelion stew fit for a king. Did he think the legions of unemployed and homeless in the country might again start riding the rails and give hoboing a second life? "No way," he said. "The old days are gone. No one'd go to the front door for a meal anymore. You wouldn't even go to the back door. There's probably a Doberman pinscher in there. I've been terribly dirty in my life and I will be again, but you see how I keep myself when I can? My hair's short, my nails are clipped. There's no grime under my toenails. You get work that way. Yesterday I went out and chopped some grain for a man. Immediately I got his name and put it in my little book for the next time I'm through Britt, because there isn't that much work around for laborers now."

Hoboing began after the Civil War, when ex-soldiers looking for work hopped freights heading west, though no one knows for sure why they were called hobos. Some say the term is derived from the rail yards in Hoboken, New Jersey, or from the Latin words *homo* (man) and *bonus* (good) or from *hoe boys,* as early migrant workers were known. But whatever its derivation, hoboing for years was a good measure of the nation's economic health, and in the 1930s, on the heels of the Depression, freight cars were home to more than 100,000 Americans. Free they may have been, but most also were prisoners of the poverty, rootlessness and self-centeredness that comes with that freedom. Hobos were strangers wherever they went, no matter how many faces they recognized in the jungles along the way. Theirs was a special, isolated world reserved for those who could not or would not compete and produce in a structured society.

"I became a tramp, well, because of the life that was in me, of the wanderlust in my blood that would not let me rest," wrote Jack London in *The Road* in 1907. He credited his hobo experiences with influencing him to get an education and become a socialist. "I went on the road because I could not keep away from it, because I hadn't the price of a railroad fare in my jeans." London would have found hoboing less appealing today. The branch lines and boxcars are fewer now, making it more difficult to get where you want to go, and the doors of cars are kept shut even when the cars are empty to reduce drag and conserve diesel fuel. Security is tighter in rail yards, the number of toughs and petty criminals hanging out in jungles is higher and jumping freights is a dangerous, unforgiving pastime that claims dozens of lives a year.

Back in the seventies, when professionals in New York or Boston burned out and sought a simpler life, they moved to Maine or Vermont, learned how to garden, handle isolation and cope with winter. Few found the fulfillment they had expected. Todd "Adman" Waters did something like that too, except that he became a hobo. He left his Minneapolis advertising agency in 1974, sold everything he owned and caught a freight out of town. Waters didn't look like a hobo, though he and the men around the campfire in Britt were obviously at ease with one another. He told me he had lasted two years on the road and now, at age forty, was back in Minnie Hopeless, running a successful ad agency.

"A lot has been written about the free-wandering, free-spirited souls on the rails," he said. "But most of the people I met out there were pretty damn desperate. They weren't free at all. You're not free if you're dependent on a bottle of alcohol. Or if you're one of the mental patients us liberals put on the street because we said it wasn't right to keep them in institutions. Sure, there are still people who ride for the adventure, but a lot of the people out there today tend to be reclusive and paranoid. They're simply men who don't fit in. They've made a choice to live on the rails mainly because the other choices they had were so horrible. You go through some terrible loneliness on the road that wrestles you to the ground. You lose all sense of time. There is no such thing as three P.M. Pretty soon you're not traveling with a plan, you're just drifting. You live in an intellectual valley."

A couple hundred of Britt's townspeople walked over to the jungle the second night I was in town. They set up folding aluminum lawn chairs around the campfire, a few feet from the Soo Line tracks. In the darkening shadows, the grain elevator towered overhead, and on a nearby spur waited a boxcar with an open door, beckoning old men back into the past. Cardboard, who had ridden a freight in from Sacramento, dozed behind the cardboard shed he had erected, complaining of the flu, his can of mosquito repellent close at hand. Harmonica Mike stood up and began playing "You Are My Sunshine." East Coast Charlie, Alabama Hobo, Steam Train and the other members of the dwindling little fraternity fell quiet. Then down the track, like a ghostly visitor from yesterday, came a mournful whistle, louder by the second, and with it a blinding light cutting through the darkness, growing ever brighter and bigger, until the earth shook and the clickety-clack din of metal wheels hurtling over metal tracks filled the night. The men rushed from the campfire and pressed close to the tracks, peering at the Soo Line freight that rumbled by like an iron monster, hauling a quarter mile of covered grain hoppers. The train became a blurred silhouette, and the men stood motionless, as if expecting something, or someone, and sure enough, there crouched between cars, ready to jump, a day late but still in time for some mulligan stew, were Seattle Slim and Bear Grease.

Hood River Blackie, a hobo who took to the rails during the Second World War, at the age of fourteen, wrote some years ago: "Never has man produced a more lonely sound than the whistle of a steam locomotive. It was a sad sound that seemed to say to each of us who heard it: 'Come with me and I'll show you America. Follow me all the days of your life, and as you lie down to die, you'll pray with your last breath to follow me once again.' Whistles had that effect on a lot of us, and I've seen many a man get up and catch a train out in the night when he had no intention of leaving until morning."

A few weeks after my introduction to mulligan stew, I was traveling what *Life* magazine once called the loneliest highway in America—Nevada's Route 50, from Fallon to Ely, through skeleton towns that had prospered in the turn-of-the-century mining boom—and I heard one of those whistles. It came from a diesel, not a steam locomotive, but I knew exactly what Hood River Blackie was talking about. For a brief moment, it was 1946 again, and I was six years old, standing with my mother on the platform of Boston's Back Bay Station, waiting for the train that would take us to New York. It arrived amid clouds of hissing white steam and a wailing whistle that made my heart pound with anticipation.

My assignment in Nevada was the type I loved: I had no appointments or interviews set and—like a hobo with an expense account—no plan except to wander around and satisfy my curiosity. The state was in the midst of another gold boom in 1988, and it struck me that the hobos I had met in Iowa and the miners I encountered in Nevada presented an odd contrast. Neither understood the permanency of place or the desirability of conformity. The hobo dreamed of nothing, the miner of everything. The whistle called the itinerant into unknown worlds, as did the jingle of coins the gold digger. Both, in their own ways, were trailblazers, the first following tracks that had been laid for him, the second searching for the wealth that would build new tracks over which others could travel.

For more than half a century, from the California rush of 1848–49 to the Alaska boom of 1896–97 to Nevada's second big strike of 1902–4, gold was the inspiration of the gamblers' dream that built the West. It had brought the men who opened up the land beyond the Great Plains, and behind the miners and prospectors came the merchants, stagecoaches, saloonkeepers, craftsmen and newspapermen. Gold built San Francisco and Denver. Gold lured the emigrants from Europe, China and Australia. Gold was responsible for populating California. (Its population jumped from 14,000 to 250,000 between 1848 and 1852, and the $20 million worth of gold mined there was at that time the richest treasure ever found on earth.) Gold brought so many people into the Rockies that Colorado was carved out of Kansas in 1861 to become a separate territory.

Were it not for gold and silver, Nevada might have never become a state. Because of its mineral wealth and the federal government's need to fund the Civil War, Nevada was granted territorial status in 1861 and statehood in 1864. Nevada is the only state in which the provisions for taxing mining are written into the constitution. When the mines eventually declined and the state's population fell (only 43,000 people lived there in 1900), some lawmakers suggested that Nevada should surrender its statehood. By 1902 gold had been struck again, this time around the town of Goldfield, and Nevada boomed once more. Polish traveler Henry Sienkiewicz noted that the bonanzas produced towns with homes "three times more beautiful than the villas along Belevere Avenue in Warsaw." He went on: "I give you my word that the most prolific writer in Poland does not earn as much as any Irishman here who carries out rubbish. But should you see these people on the street with their flannel shirts, tattered hats and dirty faces, you would not consider them worth two cents." The population of Goldfield swelled to thirty thousand, making it the largest city in Nevada, and Goldfield staged a world lightweight championship with a purse of $34,000—the biggest ever offered for a boxing match. The town had fifty-three saloons and counted among its residents Virgil Earp. (Some years later James Casey, the founder of United Parcel Service, got his business start there, delivering telegrams at the age of seventeen.)

Mark Twain found more romance in the western mining towns than did Sienkiewicz and wrote of the driving, vigorous, restless, curious populations he encountered in them. "It was the *only* population of the kind that the world has ever seen gathered together," he said,

> and it is not likely that the world will ever see its like again. For observe, it was an assemblage of . . . *young* men—not simpering, dainty kid-gloved weaklings, but stalwart, muscular, dauntless young braves, brimful of push and energy, and royally endowed with every attribute that goes to make up a peerless and magnificent manhood—the very pick and choice of the world's glorious ones. No women, no children, no gray and stooping veterans—none but erect, bright-eyed, quick-moving, strong-handed young giants—the strangest population, the finest population, the most gallant host that ever trooped down the startled solitudes of an unpeopled land.

Towns died as quickly as they were born, and Nevada's miners moved on or settled down. But they left behind an estimated $24 billion in unmined gold for the simple reason that in the pick-and-shovel days you didn't mine what you couldn't see and touch; today, with new technology, miners sift through forty tons of ore to recover just one ounce of gold. The gold particles—in deposits often pinpointed by satellite—are so fine that they are not visible even under a microscope. That is the unexpected windfall Nevada is exploiting today, and it has made the United States the world's third largest gold producer, after South

Africa and the former Soviet Union. In the new recovery process, called heap leaching, hillsides are dug up and carted away by $700,000 trucks that can carry 150 tons of cargo. The ore is ground into nut-sized chunks and soaked in diluted sodium cyanide, which dissolves out the gold. The alloy is then poured into seventy-five-pound bricks and shipped by armored car to refineries to be "four-nined"—made into gold that is 99 and 99/100s percent pure. An ounce of gold can be produced for $200 in heap-leach mines, making it a profitable venture when the metal brings about $400 an ounce on the open market.

The new technology, and the cost of supplying it, has transformed gold mining from a labor-intensive operation to one that is capital-intensive. No longer can a prospector stake a claim and strike it rich, unless a big company wants to take over his mine. Like the U.S. economy itself, the gold industry has undergone a fundamental restructuring: Corporations have replaced individuals as the backbone of economic power, and brains, not muscle, are what produce fortunes. So no great gold fever has swept Nevada as it did in the Comstock strike of 1859 and the Goldfield strike of 1902. Nor has a stampede of out-of-state immigrants poured into the state. The miners who come today, unlike those bearded, brawling men of a century ago, have college educations and carry business cards that identify them as geologists or engineers. But what the boom has done is to revive dying towns and rekindle a few dreams— dreams that are more cautious than those of the gold-rush past, when people lived on hope, not reality, and boom-towns became extraordinarily careless with human life and natural resources.

I turned off Route 50 at Scott Summit, a mile and a half above sea level, and headed south on a road to nowhere that my map identified as Highway 376. The hills were full of towns like Wonder, Jacobsville and Ophir that once bustled with hotels, Wells Fargo offices, stagecoach lines to Virginia City and local newspapers, and had disappeared without a trace. Star City—population one thousand in 1868—had died so suddenly that the telegraph office and express-freight office remained in operation even after everyone, save one family, had abandoned the place. All about me was empty solitude, the houses gone, the men vanished, not even the remnant of a ruin or the whisper of a memory to break the stillness. There was only one real town, Round Mountain, on the 120-mile drive between Scott Summit and Tonopah. Echo Bay's open-pit mine there loomed out of the rocky, barren land like a fortress with earthen parapets, and in the distance I could see yellow machines as big as dinosaurs eating away the hills. I drove up a gravel road and found the mine office in a series of air-conditioned prefabs, surrounded by a chain-link fence. I asked someone in the office if I could walk up to the mine or talk to an engineer about Nevada's revived gold industry. "I'm afraid you'd need to contact company headquarters for that," the man at the reception desk said. Headquarters was located in some far-off city whose name escapes me now, and I suggested we telephone. "Sorry," he said. "Policy is all requests be submitted in writing, and corporate approval usually takes several days." So I left and went looking for the town of Round Mountain, which I found tucked in a little valley, over the next hill.

Round Mountain was sixty miles from the nearest

bank and 235 from the nearest movie theater. Its population had increased tenfold, to 750, in the past two decades, but almost everyone lived in trailer homes, and I had the feeling that if the price of gold dropped and the mine closed, the whole town would pack up overnight and be gone by morning. Even the post office was a prefab structure that could be torn apart at a moment's notice. The only signs of prosperity I saw were the new cars and pickup trucks parked outside the General Store and the Hungry Miner Cafe. During the Comstock boom, miners earned twenty-five dollars for a sixty-hour week. In Round Mountain they were taking home fourteen dollars an hour and must have been hiding it under their mattresses. "It's hard to put your roots down if there's nothing to put them into," said Treesa Lear, who was buying groceries in the General Store. Each day she tracked the price of the Echo Bay stock shares she and her husband owned. "If the mine went down, my parents would stay. They're ranchers. But my brothers would leave. I'd probably leave, too. Even in these good times, you don't feel like you're really going to live here long, so people don't invest much back into the community."

I found only one couple who were investing in the town and attached a permanency to life in Round Mountain. Greg and Suzie Scott ran a bustling roadside cafe, known as Carver's Country, on Highway 376 and had expanded, adding a video-rental library, a bar and a single gaming table, where Susie dealt blackjack Wednesday through Saturday nights. Across the road they had built a Laundromat and a do-it-yourself car wash, the latter favored by ranchers for scrubbing down their horses.

"We're doing ten times the business we were when we bought the place in 1980," Greg said. "The payroll right here in Smokey Valley, we're talking one million dollars a week, with five mines operating round the clock. What I want to do now is expand the restaurant and build a casino. They'd make nothing but money, but I can't get the banks in Tonopah to go along with us. They say if the mine goes, the town goes. Is that the kind of attitude that built this country?"

Tonopah lay sixty miles away on a deserted road, and I covered the distance in forty-five minutes. It was a real town, crowded with construction workers, truck drivers and miners, and I walked into the Mezpah Hotel to give away a few dollars at the blackjack table. A worn-looking redhead dealt me two cards. I asked her if Tonopah had gotten its start during the Goldfield boom. "Haven't a clue," she said. "You got fifteen. Want a hit?" Jack Dempsey had once been a bartender and bouncer at the Mezpah, and its restaurant was still named in his honor. It offered a single choice of wine—a chilled Almaden red—and advised on its menu that a cup of intermistal preceded the entree. "That's champagne and sherbet to cleanse the palate so you don't taste the soup or salad with dinner," the waitress explained. I guiltily snubbed out my cigarette, and she brought me a jar of Wish-Bone ranch dressing for my salad.

Having relieved myself of forty gambling dollars and the Jack Dempsey Room of a porterhouse steak, I went to see the Scotts' banker, Anthony Roman, manager of the Valley Bank, down the street from the Mezpah. He had learned his western history well and was uncomfortable with the illusion of permanence and prosperity that boom-towns exude. "The basic mining community is still a boom-or-bust economy," he said. "Round Mountain's a perfect example. I like Greg, but how do you appraise something in Round Mountain? There's nothing out there to compare it to. An apartment complex or casino may be very profitable as long as the mine is open, but then what happens? How do you know how long to finance a building for? So what's the easiest way out for a banker? To do nothing."

Such caution did not seem in keeping with Americans' propensity for risk taking or with the freewheeling banking practices that led to the savings-and-loan crisis. But perhaps it was healthier. The Valley Bank did not have to become Bank of America, and Greg and Suzie Scott could prosper with their roadside cafe and one blackjack table without becoming Harrah's. Bigger isn't always better. Nor is quicker always faster. The hobos understood this better than anyone in their dawdling, meandering journey to nowhere. And so, in a way, did the miners as they built their stakes, knowing all booms eventually end and the day would come when they would have to move on.

King Coal

Through the valleys and hollows and along the creeks and wandering country roads, the mining hamlets of Appalachia huddle in weary seclusion, as if waiting for a thankful nation once again to embrace the power of coal. This was the resource that warmed our homes, fueled the Industrial Age, powered the westward expansion. But it was never glamorous stuff. Gold was limitless dreams and the spirit of the frontier. Coal was poverty, black lung and illiteracy. Gold dazzled. Coal just got you sooty.

The coal-laden seams reach back deep into Appalachia's wooded hills and for more than a hundred years have sustained generations of men who each morning disappeared into the bowels of the earth. As the darkness sucked them up, someone out in the sunlight, by the tunnel's mouth, always called out a final customary greeting of the day: "Y'all have a safe trip, ya hear." It was a laborious life, steeped in danger and disease, but the money was good—$35,000 a year is about average for a Virginia miner today—and the work was steady. In the end the coalfields were as benevolent as the church: They took good care of decent men who were long on endurance and short on education. Over the years the miners bought the drab, company-owned homes along the banks of the creeks and fixed them up with new roofs, extra bedrooms, small gardens, sometimes screened-in porches. They raised large families, saw their women grow plump early and were proud when their boys entered the mine and were initiated into manhood. The hollows became their universe.

Certainly there was nothing in my past that would explain what drew me back to the coal camps of Appalachia so often. I had been born into a life of privilege: private schools, a summer home in Vermont, invitations to debutante balls at the country clubs around Boston. I never considered this a birthright. But my friends came from similar backgrounds, and it didn't occur to me either that we were luckier than any other family. The closest I came to being exposed to the world's misfortune was when my mother would tell me to eat all my dinner. "There are boys and girls starving in Europe who would give their eyeteeth to have a meal like this," she'd say, and guiltily I'd poke away at an egg and tuna casserole. Much to my parents' dismay, my life took an odd twist about the time I was old enough to get my driver's license, and I fell into a stage of mild rebellion, from which, I guess, I never quite recovered. In the poorer, ethnic sections of Boston—the North End, Roxbury, Southie—I found a new world that excited me. It was a tough place without privilege, populated by gamblers and saloonkeepers and off-duty cops, and I adopted it as my own. My father would have been surprised had I told him of the primitive wisdom and innate gentility I found among my new acquaintances. They were teaching me the adventure of discovery, of stepping outside the boundaries of one's own life to pay attention to another's, and during the summer of my freshman year in college, while friends sought employment that would enhance their résumés, I went to work driving a trailer truck.

Gratten Webb was sixty-four years old and built like a fire hydrant. He had quit school in the seventh grade to enter the mines, and, sure, he told the waitress, he'd take a refill on the coffee. We were in a cafe in Richlands, Virginia, and he leaned over the table to make his point confidentially: "You see those fellows behind me, by the wall? They're miners, retired. They got black lung. With their pensions, though, they're not doing bad. 'Course, you got to take into account their health is ruined. Everyone around here's got black lung. It's our gold watch. I'll tell you, when I quit school, my father didn't speak to me for a month. He said: 'Get your schooling, boy, the jobs'll always be here waiting.' Now remember, he'd quit in the third grade so he really couldn't lecture me too good on that point. Lord, after thirty-one years in the mines he'd worked himself nearly to death and could hardly walk.

"Grandad spent a life running coal too. By the time he died in nineteen 'n' thirty-six, he had a hundred and thirty-seven grandchildren and great-grandchildren. Now there's Webbs all around here. Most of 'em worked in the mines, but you know what? I got nine nephews and they've all left the area. They know there's no future in coal."

Webb said he'd show me where he used to work, and we headed in a Bronco up a narrow hollow toward Jewell Valley. The road was hilly and full of twists, and along it families sat on the steps of porches, their eyes following us. Thirty minutes later we pulled into an old company coal town. Webb took a deep breath. The deserted parking lot was clogged with weeds, and all the buildings had been abandoned. "Lord," he said, "there's nothing left."

We poked among the ruins, and Webb remembered how canary cages once hung in all the mines to test methane levels: When the birds dropped dead, gas levels were considered dangerously high. Inside the mine's red-brick bathhouse swallows swooped overhead and miners' soot-covered overalls hung on pegs where they had been placed after the last shift eight years earlier. The rows of white clapboard company homes stood windowless and empty, the church had been stripped of its pews, the movie theater had no door. The little restaurant where Webb had grabbed a last cup of coffee before heading into the dank mine each day was barren, except for a stove, and in the company store files were strewn about the floor and a sign pointing at nothing advised: QUICK CHECK OUT. 5 ITEMS OR LESS. Jewell Valley, 1992, was the coal miners' version of Bannack, Montana, 1872. I asked Webb if he still heated his home with coal. "Nope," he said. "Not for twenty-five years. Even if you wanted to, I don't think there's any place that'd delivered you a ton of coal these days anyway."

The message from Jewell Valley was a harbinger: No matter what Gratten Webb's father had told him, coal could no longer provide the jobs to support Appalachia. The miners had been left behind, and their little towns were returning to their preindustrial roots. They had labored in what had been a feudal proprietorship, belonged to a union that cared more about per ton production royalties than new safety regulations and found that getting out of debt was a life's work. More than 125,000 of them had died on the job since 1870, and when an explosion jolted the Consolidation Coal Company mine at Farmington, West Virginia, in 1968, union chieftain Tony Boyle showed up and said, in effect, it's tough, but that's how mining is. His union and the company agreed to seal the mine with the bodies of seventy-eight men still inside. It was the best way, they said, to extinguish the fire and save the salable coal.

For all they had endured, the miners were strangely accepting of misfortune, as though it was their lot in life. "I'll tell you what killed this country," said John Bartko, rocking back and forth, back and forth, on his porch. He breathed heavily, and each movement of the chair was accompanied by a squeak. "It was all those federal regulations—pollution, the environment, safety. They forced the independents out, and they were the ones who kept this economy alive during the Depression. We've been pumping mine water into the streams for a hundred years here, and I never saw any dead fish. Then overnight you can't do this and you can't do that and then you got to have a toilet in the mines. A toilet. Why, we used to have one inspector, a fellow named Patrick Friel, looking after all these mines, and now we got ten or twelve inspectors coming through here and there's no mines."

Environmental reasons are part of Appalachia's problems. So, too, are the decline in the steel industry, Washington's indifference to developing alternative energy sources and foreign markets that have grown so competi-

tive that Virginia—the nation's seventh largest producer—
sometimes uses cheaper coal imported from Colombia to
power its utility plants. But there is something more: A
man's labor doesn't count for what it used to. Just as
hand-held digital methane readers have replaced canaries,
and electric belts and carriages now do the coal hauling in
the mine that had once been done by dogs and ponies, men
have given way to machines. They are large, long things,
computer controlled, that eat through the walls of coal
and vaguely resemble mechanical aardvarks. Each does
the work of about a hundred men and never gets sick or
goes on strike.

The mine I went into outside Bluefield, West Virginia,
was burrowed straight into the hill. I was outfitted in a
helmet with a lamp, a baggy protective suit and tall boots
and was given a lesson on what to do if gas forced our
evacuation. I felt as though I were going to war. Our
tracked carriage rattled deeper and deeper into the mine,
down a slight incline and ahead toward, God, what? The
ceiling grew lower, until we had to crouch in our seats, and
the last faint light from the tunnel's entrance behind us
disappeared. In an earthen room not large enough to
stand straight in, a mile from where we had started, a
dozen men were at work, some crawling around on bellies
and elbows, others attending to the aardvark-looking machine. When I looked directly at them, I could see only
their spotlight lamps and could not distinguish any facial
features. I stood hunkered, my right hand resting on the
bolted supports overhead. The world closed in. My stomach tightened. I imagined the sound of crashing timber
beams, thought I heard rushing water, smelled for gas. I

can't remember ever wanting to get out of a place so badly.

No matter how often I return to the coal country, I know I will always be an outsider, in the mine and in Appalachia. They form a culture within a culture. In them there is none of the free-spirited adventurism I have found in the West or the smug contentment of New England. Appalachia is populated by a people who expect to stay put and plod on. Every few years a national politician wanders through at election time and makes promises and then the next election someone else will come and say the same things, but not much changes. The miners know the battle for survival is theirs alone. They are the ones who waged the coal strikes for the right to organize and break free from corporate colonialism. (During West Virginia's Kanawha Valley strike of 1912–13, miners were evicted from their homes and forced into tent encampments along the highway.) It was the miners who staged the great black-lung revolt and fought for the safety regulations that their own decadent union had long ignored. And it was the miners who refused to relinquish hope. One day, they said, America would come to its senses and would again turn to Appalachia, instead of the oil fields of Arabia, to nourish its factories and warm its homes.

"You ever see coal burn, bud?" asked John Kaschak, who'd spent four decades in the mines. "It burns warm and even and clean. Not like that gas that'll blow your house apart if your wife forgets herself and leaves the jet on. Coal lies there all day and you get home at night and the fire'll be there. All this coal just waiting. It beats me what America's thinking about."

The paradox of Appalachia's plight is that coal production and consumption (80 percent of domestic coal is used by electric utilities) are increasing nationwide. But in an era when strip mining can get the job done faster and cheaper and with less manpower, greater production no longer means more jobs. Progress, such as it was, had sealed the fate of Appalachia's coal-camp communities as surely as the interstate highway doomed the western way-station hamlets that once straddled Route 66. What will survive—if they can learn from the lessons of the Great Plains—will be the larger service-center towns. Some have already designated two cents on each ton of coal for a fund to attract new industries, and there has been talk of promoting tourism. If visitors flock to Tombstone, Arizona, why not to Jewell Valley, West Virginia? At the community colleges throughout Appalachia, new courses are being introduced to train miners for other occupations. "It's like a family breaking up," said one union official. "Miners ask me, 'Where do we go, what do we do now?' and I have to tell them, I honestly can't answer that."

Everything is changing, yet, in the mining towns of substance I had visited over the course of many years, nothing seemed different. They weren't depressed in spirit or appearance. Miners still drove to Myrtle Beach, South Carolina, for a week's vacation every summer, their cars bearing bumper stickers that saluted COAL—AMERICA'S SECURITY BLANKET. The roller skating rinks and bowling alleys were filled on Saturday, milk was delivered door to door from family dairies and the Norfolk Southern snaked through town, hauling 120 coal-laden cars toward the ports. Its whistle wailed in the night, and the people paused and felt good.

The Road Less Traveled

The highway that John Steinbeck called the mother road—U.S. Route 66 from Chicago to Los Angeles—vanished from the maps of America in 1984 when the last stretch of Interstate 40 was completed outside Williams, Arizona. But so what? Maybe the romance of Route 66 was only a myth in the first place. Certainly the desperate Okies who fled the Dust Bowl in the thirties found no romance in 66's way-station towns, with their flashing signs that said EAT and their auto courts with names like Rest Well and Westward Ho. Oklahoma City, despite what Bobby Troup's song says, never was "mighty pretty," and who would have ever heard of Winona if it hadn't rhymed with Arizona? Remember the popular 1960s TV series named for the old mother road? Most of it was filmed in Oregon and Florida. Get your kicks on Route 66? Why not on the interstate instead? It goes faster and straighter, stretching from Chicago to the Pacific Ocean without a single traffic light, five connecting superhighways that allow you to speed in air-conditioned comfort right through the franchised soul of America without having to see its people or touch its towns or feel its heartbeat or hear a single waitress call you honey.

I had first traveled Route 66 in 1959, while hitchhiking

from Boston to Los Angeles with a friend, and I don't remember it as much more than a long ribbon of blacktop that crept from one Main Street to another, linking vast tracts of empty land with clusters of all-night cafes, downtown hotels and gas stations where attendants checked your oil and washed your windshield. That is how I think of all America as looking then, though I'm sure it didn't. Neither my friend nor I had ever been west before, and we hurried toward our destination with outstretched thumbs, more intent on where we were going than on where we were. The song we heard was for the road, *any* road, and I wish now we had been more attentive to 66 itself on its—on *our,* really—2,200-mile journey, through three time zones, eight states and fifty-five towns, from the corner of Jackson Boulevard and Michigan Avenue in Chicago to the intersection of Ocean Avenue and Santa Monica Boulevard on the doorstep of Los Angeles.

Thirty years went by before I again was looking for a California-bound road out of Chicago, but by then Route 66 was gone. If nostalgia is, as I think, an appreciation of—rather than a yearning for—the past, then what I had learned in the intervening years about the fabled route west had made me nostalgic for an era when traveling was a social experience and we had time to talk to one another along the way. Route 66 had crossed the wheat prairies of the Midwest and the Mississippi River, climbed Missouri's Ozark Mountains, meandered through the Texas panhandle, followed the rutted wagon tracks across the New Mexico and Arizona deserts and found its way over the Colorado River and into California near Needles. That territory belongs to the interstate today, and all it has left behind of the old highway are small disjointed sections designated as state, not federal, routes. The longest drivable stretch runs for 137 miles, from Seligman, Arizona, to Topock on the California border. Not much of a journey, but, I thought, worth a look.

Ray and Mildred Barker's Frontier Cafe and Motel sits on the shoulder of what had been U.S. 66 in Truxton, Arizona, one of the many towns broken by the new interstate. Their only customer, a local rancher, finished his coffee and drifted out. Barker pulled down the shades and locked the door. It was 7:00 P.M., and with no rooms rented that night and no traffic on the ghost road, he didn't bother to turn on the neon vacancy sign outside. I asked him if he wanted me to get on my way. "No need to unless you're in a rush," he said, bringing over the coffeepot. Barker, a tall, lean man who cooked, served, swept, washed and tidied up, was sixty-two and had been around Truxton a good many years. He had seen China during the Second World War but hadn't much cared for it and had no real desire to do any more traveling. When 66 had started dying, he and his wife had talked about starting over someplace else. "That's going to be tough to do at our age," Barker had said. "We're probably better off just staying put, don't you think?" Mildred had agreed. Outside the wind pushed clumps of sagebrush dancing over the gravel parking lot, and in the abandoned gas station across the road a metal sign depicting a flying red horse swung to and fro on its support.

"Before the road changed," he said of I-40, which ran twenty miles south of town, "I'd say we had ten thousand vehicles a day passing here. You wanted to drive from

Chicago to L.A., you went through Truxton. Then all of a sudden, and I mean all of a sudden when they opened the bypass, we dropped to about three hundred, and that was mostly locals. We used to work two shifts with nine employees. Now it's just me and my wife, with our daughter helping out, and we close up at seven instead of ten. . . . Complaints? Not really. You may not make a lot of money, but you still eat, you have a bed, you have warmth. All in all I don't know that a man needs much more than that. I can always look around and find people a lot worse off."

His wife joined us at the counter. "You know," she said, "I've lived along Sixty-six all my life. Sayre, Oklahoma; Grants, New Mexico; and here. This highway's like family." From behind the cash register, she took out a guest register she had started in a stenographer's notebook. In it were the names of recent travelers from Switzerland, France, Holland, England—people who had paused in their journey to find America's most famous road west.

Nobody, of course, ever thought of Route 66 going east, and perhaps that is precisely why the highway captured a restless nation's imagination. It wasn't the road itself that mattered as much as what lay at the end, an El Dorado of orange groves. Sweeter water, greener fields, gentler breezes. It was, as Jack Kerouac wrote, the symbol of existential wandering and back roads culture: "A fast car, a coast to reach and a woman at the end of the road." For the dispossessed who fled Oklahoma's Dust Bowl in Steinbeck's 1939 novel, *The Grapes of Wrath,* this was the path of escape. "Refugees from dust and shrinking land,"

Steinbeck wrote, "from the desert's slow northward invasion, from the twisting winds that howl up out of Texas, from the floods that bring no richness to the land and steal what little richness is there. From all these the people are in flight, and they come into 66 from the tributary side roads, from the wagon tracks and the rutted country roads. 66 is the mother road, the road of flight."

It also was a route west that predated the arrival of cars, trains, even stagecoaches. Parts of the old highway followed the ancient Osage Indian Trail, and Père Jacques Marquette and Louis Jolliet traversed the route in exploring the upper Mississippi in 1673. During the California gold rush, army Captain Randolph B. Marcy and Lieutenant James Simpson were ordered to "make, and report, a reconnaissance" from Fort Smith, Arkansas, to Santa Fe, New Mexico, "in direct reference to the future location of a national road," and they came along what was to become Route 66 too. Eight years later, in 1857, Lieutenant Edward Beale pushed the exploration of a national road farther west, to the California border, with seventy camels imported from Arabia and Egypt. "I look forward to the day," he wrote, "when every mail route across the continent will be conducted . . . with this economical and noble brute." Then came the first telegraph lines to penetrate the southwest territories—for a long time the 66 passage was known as the Wire Road—and then the settlers in covered wagons and finally, first in Model Ts, then in sleek cruisers with radios and sweeping fins, the new generation of Californians. They motored west past Burma Shave signs and red barns whose painted sides advised, CHEW MAIL POUCH TOBACCO, and a billboard outside Albuquerque that displayed a sweating skull and the words 700 MILES DESERT . . . WATER BAGS, THERMOS JUGS, ICE.

"It was the year after the war and my wife and I were driving from Pennsylvania to California, in a 1941 Buick convertible I'd bought with the royalties from my first song, 'Daddy,' " Bobby Troup, the seventy-year-old composer and performer, recalled. "The family had music stores in Lancaster and Harrisburg that I could have gone into, but I told my mother I had to find out if I had any talent and there were only two places for a songwriter to go—New York and Los Angeles." Somewhere, back in the early miles of the journey, his wife, Cynthia, suggested he write a song about Highway 40, and Troup shrugged. "Then later, out of Chicago, when we realized we'd be following the same highway all the way to California," he said, "she whispered, kind of hesitantly because of the put-down on the first suggestion, 'Get your kicks on Route 66.' " He had two stanzas and the melody written on a road map by the time they got to Los Angeles, where Nat King Cole soon recorded the song, making it part of America's musical lexicon:

> *Won't you get hip to this timely tip*
> *When you make that California trip.*
> *Get your kicks on Route 66.*

Along Interstate 40, which vaguely follows the path of the old Route 66 in many sections, the traffic moves in a blurred whoosh today: Peterbilt and Mack semis from places like Scranton, Pennsylvania, and Archbold, Ohio;

RVs with snowbirds escaping the frozen North; salesmen (who used to be called drummers) bypassing the little towns in favor of the next city a hundred miles or more down the highway; cars moving so fast that the drivers appear faceless. Now instead of billboards advertising Ted's Root Beer and chili at the Longhorn Ranch Cafe, the road signs say, LITTERING HIGHWAY UNLAWFUL, or LOS ANGELES 467 MILES, an easy day's drive with stereo music all the way.

Back in 1785, the Weddale Stage Lines took six days to get from Boston to New York. The coaches followed the postal routes, traveling nineteen hours a day and spending the nights at inns. Passengers frequently complained that the drivers were drunk. If the nation was to communicate with itself, delivery of the mail had to be speeded up, and in 1916 President Woodrow Wilson signed the Federal Aid Road Act, enabling Congress to establish "post roads." What evolved was a network of named "highroads" that crisscrossed the continent and were identified by the colors on roadside signs: The Dixie Highway with its white-red-white markers on the route from the Great Lakes to Florida; the red-white-yellow markers of the Old Spanish Trail westward from Chicago (now largely taken over by Interstates 80 and 90); the white-yellow-white markers of the Cody-Billings Way in the Far West. The Lincoln Highway crossed the northern half of the nation; the National Old Trail headed toward California on a more southerly route. Color coding proved confusing as the number of cars increased, and in 1925 the secretary of agriculture approved a plan to assign route numbers to named roads, with odd numbers given to north-south roads and even numbers to east-west ones. The lowest even number (Route 2) went to the northernmost road, from Maine to Idaho, the highest (Route 96) to the most southern highway in Texas. The road from Chicago to Los Angeles—known at various times as the Postal Highway, the Ozark Trail and the Will Rogers Highway—got the mellifluous designation of 66 simply because that was the next number in geographic sequence. Complaining that the numbering system would rob the open road of its romance, *The New York Times* editorialized: "The traveler may shed tears as he drives the Lincoln Highway or dream dreams as he speeds over the Jefferson Highway, but how can he get a 'kick' out of 46 or 55 or 33 or 21?"

The Times eulogy was premature and probably should have been written in 1956, the year President Eisenhower signed a law creating our 42,500-mile, $27 billion network of superhighways. Mile by mile the little communities that had sprung up along the old roadways started dying like played-out mining towns. And America changed. The interstates broke down the barriers between rural and urban America and diffused the drawing power of our cities. If you lived in Terre Haute, Indiana, Indianapolis wasn't the only place to go anymore; Louisville, Cincinnati, St. Louis and Chicago were all just a few hours down the road. For the first time the average family had affordable mobility. We bought bigger cars and traveled farther, discovering national parks and elegant resorts and long-dreamed-of cities by the bay, and went places only the wealthy used to go. The interstates contributed to the democratization of the country, but along our routes of travel the approach to Portland, Maine, started to look pretty much like that to Phoenix, Arizona. We became part of a more homogenized, depersonalized culture.

Jim Scott's trailer truck hissed to a stop outside the one-chair barbershop in Seligman, Arizona. The door was open, but Angel Delgadillo, the barber, was nowhere in sight, so Scott walked into the grocery store next door, where Joe Delgadillo, the barber's brother, was passing time playing his guitar, accompanied by a friend on the fiddle. Scott pulled up a chair to await the barber's return. After a while Angel did come back, eating an ice cream cone, and said, "Come on, Mr. Scott, I've been saving a chair for you." Angel smiled and hummed as he clipped. Scott made the thousand-mile round trip from Victorville, California, to Winslow, Arizona, three times a week, and I asked him why he'd bothered to pull off the interstate and sidetrack through Seligman. "Hell, I love Sixty-six," he said. "I still come over it every now and then just to get the feel of it. I saw every mile of that interstate being built and what it's done is make things impersonal. Anyone can herd a truck up and down the freeway, but I remember when you had real respect as a trucker. We took care of each other, we sat together in the cafes. You never pulled back into a lane without blinking a thank you on your lights. And if someone was broken down along the road— man or woman, it didn't matter—you offered help. Now we don't even stop. Things have gotten so uncourteous, it's unreal. People'll throw you the birdie today and honk to make sure you see it. Far's I'm concerned, the whole damn world's changed."

If the world is the interstate, Scott was probably right.

We could hear the steady, muffled roar of traffic on I-40, two miles away, and the sound worked on sixty-year-old Angel Delgadillo, who had lived in Seligman all his life. "Listen to that," he muttered. "All those cars, thousands of them, and how do we get them off the interstate and into Seligman?" He said business had dropped 70 percent since "we got bypassed." At first I thought he was talking about open-heart surgery, but then I realized he was referring to the day the last section of the interstate had been completed. "It was like they put a gate up at the east and west ends of town," he said. "Remember how it was the day John Fitzgerald Kennedy, the president, was killed? Traffic everywhere just stopped moving all of a sudden. Well, same thing happened here when we got bypassed."

U.S. 66 used to turn off Main Street, just before Delgadillo's shop, and swing onto Railroad Avenue. "Hard to believe," he said, "but I can remember when this was a busy street. Main Street, U.S.A., is what they called it." Not much remained. The cafe his grandfather, Camilo, had built and run on Railroad Avenue was gone. So was Bud Brown's pool hall next door. And Frank Smith's convenience store. All that stood in good repair was the Harvey House hotel, next to the railroad station, and Delgadillo could remember when trainmen disembarked there from great journeys, carrying the latest editions of *Life* and the *Saturday Evening Post.* But the hotel had been boarded up since 1954, its grassy courtyard weed-dead, and now when the Southwest Chief passenger train out of Chicago moved through Seligman each night just before midnight, it was only a silvery phantom, hurtling toward Los Angeles, acknowledging the town with nothing more than a wailing salute of its whistle.

The quiet road out of Seligman took me west, winding through Hackberry, where the one-room adobe schoolhouse had an enrollment of six; past Kingman's "air cooled" Beale Hotel, where Clark Gable and Carole Lombard spent the first night of their honeymoon in 1939; over Sitgreaves Pass, with its roadside ruins of old cars, service stations, even towns; and into Oatman, a one-time mining community where wild burros turned loose by prospectors years ago still roamed the main street. Back in Williams (named for a trapper who had been killed by Indians in 1849) the town had just raised several thousand dollars through a bake sale and charity dance to help the young cancer-stricken cook at Rod's Steak House, and I remembered what Steinbeck's Ma Joad had said about people who lived in places like these: "I'm learnin' one thing good. Learnin' it all the time, ever' day. If you're in trouble or hurt or need—go to poor people. They're the only one's that'll help—the only ones."

The requiem for a highway was being carved in buckled cement, but a funny thing had started to happen. Though the black and white shields that marked U.S. Route 66 were gone, travelers were trickling off the interstate in search of the past. "Hardly a day goes by that someone doesn't flag me or one of the other officers down and say, 'Hey, is this the old Sixty-six?' " the marshal in Williams said. The mother road had become a period piece. The *Route 66* series was enjoying a new life on cable TV, a Route 66 Association, founded by a hypnotherapist, sprang up in California, and in Kingman, Arizona, a saloon and restaurant known as the Route 66 Distillery tapped into a gold mine with its memorabilia from the 1940s and '50s: road signs, gas pumps, water bags, posters and a Wurlitzer jukebox with 78 RPM records. Over one corner booth was a black and white promotional picture of the two free-spirited bachelors, Martin Milner (in real life, married with four children at the time) and George Maharis, who traveled the highway in a 1955 Corvette as Tod Stiles and Buz Murdock in the popular television series. The show worked so well, Milner told me, because "it captured the desire in people—or least their imagined desire—to pick up and move and know wanderlust and be free spirits."

Sensing that all this nostalgia translated into tourist dollars, Arizona had designated Route 66 a historic state highway. The little towns along the route were planning festivals to call attention to their heritage, and double-six route shields with arrows pointing inland were being placed along Interstate 40 to remind travelers there was an alternative to speeding west at 65 mph.

> *If you ever plan to motor West*
> *Travel my way, take the highway*
> *that's the best.*
> *Get your kicks on Route 66.*

I drove over to Topock, near the California line. Two hundred people who lived along the road of flight and had formed the Historical Route 66 Association of Arizona were gathered at the VFW there. The hall was filled with rows of folding chairs and a considerable amount of excitement. After years of thinking their towns had fallen terminally ill, people were now talking about new beginnings and revived Main Streets and making things as they were. The past, they hoped, was but a prologue. Billie Jo Trammell, the association treasurer, said their balance stood at $1,155, including interest of $7.14; the owner of the 66 Distillery gave details of a meeting he had had with state transportation officials; and Angel Delgadillo, who had driven over from Seligman, outlined plans for a celebration of street dances and barbecues, to which Bobby Troup and Will Rogers, Jr., had been invited. Delgadillo called me aside after the meeting. He was exhilarated and talking fast. "You see," he said, "this is community. It's democracy. It's what happens when people get together to work things out for themselves. This isn't the federal government doing this. It isn't the state government. It's just us, the people on Sixty-six, and I'll tell you this old route's going to boom again." I hoped he was right, though I suspected just surviving was still an admirable goal.

The Joad family of Steinbeck's fiction had forty dollars left when they drove past the "shattered stone debris" of Oatman and slipped through Topock. They crossed the river bridge that stands on the western edge of town—though now it is used only to support a pipeline—and on the other side entered California. But as for so many others before and after the Joads, there really was no El Dorado. The dream had been only a dream. Behind them lay the terrible white-rocked cliffs of Arizona, ahead the scorching, empty desert. It was not at all like the pictures Tom Joad had seen. "Wait till we get to California. You'll see nice country then," Pa Joad said. "Jesus Christ, Pa!" Tom said. "This here *is* California."

LESSONS OF
HISTORY

✍ ✍ ✍

The Last of the Nez Percé

To those of us who grew up as children of the fifties, history was a scamless thing: America was powerful, righteous, faultless, and that was that. Our institutions and politicians were there to serve us, nobody questioned the motives or veracity of the media, our heroes were as unsullied as Pat Boone's white bucks. It wasn't until I found out that *The $64,000 Question* had been rigged that the thought of challenging what we accept at face value even crossed my mind. Had someone in those days made a movie about Nez Percé Indians being slaughtered by the U.S. Army in a Montana valley, I doubt anyone would have gone to see it. Certainly I had never heard about a group of Alaskans being sent off by the U.S. government to internment camps during the Second World War or about fourteen German soldiers being executed at Fort Leavenworth after the war. Concern for the nation's minorities wasn't much on our minds either, because most of us who were white and middle class had no contact with them.

Fortunately history is always being fiddled with in an effort to get it right. We reconsider it and revise it and rewrite it, and somewhere in the process, as a nation and as individuals, we learn, more often than not, from our mistakes. That is one mark of maturity. During the years I lived in Africa, I was often saddened by how history kept repeating itself there because the continent's leaders treated history as if there were nothing to be learned from it. Famines, political instability and the suppression of dissent had become institutionalized. Questioning voices were silenced, and the aggrieved were pampered with neither compensation nor recognition.

Although revisionists who see just evil in Columbus's journey to the New World and only racism in the settling of the West may have been carried away in their eagerness to dismiss all history, I imagine most Americans agreed with General Philip Sheridan when, in 1869 after being introduced to a chief named Old Toch-a-way and told the man was a "good Indian," he said: "The only good Indian I ever saw was a dead Indian." It took more than a century, but today, thanks in part to revisionist movies such as *Dances with Wolves,* the word *Indian* summons thoughts of dignity, valor and those who suffered hardship with a nobility of purpose.

It seems odd that we carry so much guilt over what we have done wrong and express so little satisfaction about what we have done right. The nineties, in fact, had started off in a particularly somber fashion, with "I Hate Everything About You" reaching the top of the record charts, a suicide manual becoming a best-seller and a movie about serial killers, *The Silence of the Lambs,* sweeping the Oscar awards. I checked the card catalog at my local library under the heading "America" and came up with a dazzling array of titles, one after the other, that seemed more appropriate to some failed Third World dictatorship than to a country that had spent $900 billion on public assistance programs since 1984, created 40 million new jobs since 1968 and welcomed nearly 9 million immigrants in the 1980s alone. There was *America the Raped, America the Poisoned, Vanishing America, America the Violent, America Under Siege, America: What Went Wrong?* It occurred to me scanning the titles that our penchant for directing an endless stream of criticism at ourselves is one of our best corrective mechanisms and is, in many ways, an expression of idealism. We expect more of ourselves than the people of most nations, and we still cling to the belief that aspirations and realities can be shaped into a union of realized values. Idealism, as we know it, is what unscrambles past injustices and enables us to hear the voices of those who want to set history straight.

Along the North Fork of Montana's Big Hole River, Wilford Halfmoon stopped to listen. And there it was again, just beyond the wind, the sound of battle, a faint rumbling that came up from the pines and, growing louder, dizzied his head with whirling visions. Ever since his parents first brought him to the riverbanks as a child, Halfmoon had walked the skirmish lines of the Big Hole National Battlefield, drawn again and again back to the place where his people—the Nez Percé—were massacred in their final days of freedom more than a century ago and his great-grandfather, Five Wounds, was mortally wounded in a suicide charge against Colonel John Gibbon's soldiers. Eighty or so Indians, many of them women, children and old men, were killed in the battle, and over the years Halfmoon had come to think of himself as their guardian, protecting the hallowed grounds that to the Nez Percé are tantamount to Arlington National Cemetery. Once when he camped by the river's bend where the tepees had stood, he awoke to the muffled echo of soldiers' footsteps splashing across the creek and the wails of mourning women. Then the silence of the valley returned, but he did not sleep again that night. "It is difficult to comprehend," Halfmoon said. "Why should someone be killed just for being an Indian?"

The Nez Percé—the name came from the French words for "pierced nose," which the tribe never had—had been a wealthy, culturally advanced people when Halfmoon's great-grandfather was a young man. Its tepees were made of canvas, not hide, and its treasury was stocked with gold earned from selling horses and cattle to Idaho settlers. The tribe had befriended Meriwether Lewis and William Clark in the Bitterroots in 1805, saving their expedition from disaster, and had dealt amicably with the early white pioneers who pushed westward in wagon trains. But by 1877, with the hills yielding a bounty of gold and migration increasing, the newcomers had declared the land was theirs and the second American Civil War—a war between Native Americans and the forces of the U.S. government—had been launched by Washington to secure the West. Custer had been defeated at Little Bighorn only the year before, and white America was not in a conciliatory mood. Of the 3 million Indians who were in North America when the British first arrived, even so staunch an opponent of imperialism and racism as Mark Twain said, "I would gladly eat the whole race if I had the chance."

"A great many lies have been told about us," one of

the Nez Percé chiefs, Ollicot, said in the 1870s. "They say we want to fight, which is not true. I have a wife and children, cattle and horses. I have eyes and a heart and I can see and understand that if we fight, we will have to leave all this land and go to the mountains." The Nez Percé defied the government and, refusing subjugation on a reservation, left Idaho in June 1877 for Canada, a trail of retreat that stretched sixteen hundred miles. "I . . . was made not to suffer the bondage of government," a Nez Percé warrior, Shot-in-the-Head, said. "I would be as the coyote and the wolf . . . seeking to die in the wild forest alone . . . to be eaten by the wolf's fang or the vulture's beak, instead of the slow dying of bondage."

Followed by U.S. soldiers, Chief Joseph and his five bands of Nez Percé skirmished with their pursuers at White Bird Canyon and the Clearwater River and reached Montana's buffalo country in early August, thinking the war was behind them. They set up camp along the North Fork, where Halfmoon now walked among the ghosts of his ancestors. There were about 800 Nez Percé with Chief Joseph, including 125 warriors, and so confident were they of their security that their war chief, Looking Glass, did not bother to send out sentries or scout the back trail. Had he done so, he would have known that Colonel Gibbon, a Civil War hero of the Battle of Gettysburg, was marching from Fort Shaw with 146 soldiers and 34 civilian volunteers and closing in on the Big Hole Valley. "We came to the place in the afternoon, towards evening," said White Bird. "We stayed that night and the next day. Evening came on again and it was after sundown—not too late—lots of children were playing. It was below the camp towards the creek that . . . boys played the stick or bone game. They were noisy, having lots of fun."

The soldiers of the U.S. Seventh Infantry struck on August 9, at 4:00 A.M., while the camp slept. "We . . . said it was a shame to kill these people," Corporal Charles Loynes later recalled, "but we were soldiers and had to do as told." After taking heavy initial casualties, the Nez Percé regrouped and forced the soldiers into defensive positions. "Two brave women must have run for shelter," said Red Wolf, "but seeing so many women and children falling, got guns, maybe from dead soldiers, and helped drive the enemies from the camp."

Two days later Chief Joseph and his surviving people slipped away in subfreezing weather to continue their trek toward northern Montana's Bear Paw Mountains and Canada. In the valley behind lay forty soldiers and about eighty Indians. No one doubted the valor of either side—seven enlisted men were awarded the Congressional Medal of Honor as a result of the battle, and all officers earned battlefield promotions—but *The New York Times* later editorialized that the four-month Nez Percé War "on our part, was in its origin and motive nothing short of a gigantic blunder and a crime."

All this had never left Wilford Halfmoon's mind alone, and on the anniversary of the battle, he would go down to the river at dawn and chant and beat his drum and sometimes cry. He remembered, too, being in Lewiston, Idaho, one day as a teenager when someone walked by his mother on the street and said, "Hey, squaw. Where's your tomahawk?" The incident had stayed with him as his earliest realization that he was "different" from others in Lewiston. "I got real radical," he said. "Braids. Long hair. I could condemn the U.S. government with the best. I knew who stole our land. I knew what Christianity did to my people. For whatever reason, shortly after my mother was insulted, I stopped being ashamed and started being proud of who I was." The son of a Second World War veteran and himself a former army medic, Halfmoon had graduated from Washington State University and seen his life take a remarkable twist. He had gone to work for the U.S. government, as a park ranger, and badgered the agency to assign him to the Big Hole National Battlefield. There, at the age of thirty-nine, he had become a sort of one-man custodian for the Nez Percé culture, leading groups of visitors through the battlefield and explaining the heritage of a tribe that had numbered six thousand in his great-grandfather's time and, after the Indian wars, fifteen hundred.

"What interests me most is the interpretation of history and that means understanding both sides. So I try to be fair. I am respectful of the soldiers when I tell people what happened here because they died for their nation, too. A few of the people who come think there are no good Indians, but that's rare now. Most are very open-minded. They ask questions and they want to know about the other side, the Nez Percé side."

Big Hole had become one of the West's most romanticized battlefields, and I had gone there, in the summer of 1991, to talk to National Park Service rangers who were surveying the valley with metal detectors, lasers and computers, just as they had done at the Custer battlefield two years earlier. The exercise was being paid for by singer

Hank Williams, Jr., who owned a ranch nearby. I caught up with the archaeologists at lunchtime on the eighth or ninth day of their monthlong survey. There were a few rangers among them, but most were volunteer hobbyists who owned their metal detectors, had paid their own expenses to Montana and were involved in the treasure hunt of their lives, a hunt for the information that would, they hoped, enable historians to piece together the final unknown details of the army's surprise attack. The heat was intense, and we sat in the shade of some willow trees at the foot of the hill, eating roast beef sandwiches and drinking Kool-Aid out of thermos bottles.

Derek Batten offered me a brownie. He said he had participated in the Custer survey and had flown back for this one from his home in England. "It cost me a bloody fortune to get here, and you know what? I wouldn't have missed it for the world," he said. "I spent my youth in the movie houses watching westerns, so for me this is like touching history." He thought for a moment and said, "What a grand country you've got! All this big beautiful land and look at that sky. My goodness, how lucky you people are to have a place like this."

Batten and the others spent eight hours a day, six days a week, scouring the bald hillsides that ring the Big Hole and plodding through the clusters of willows and ponderosa pines at the foot of the Bitterroot Range, metal detectors beeping at every hint of buried evidence. Each find—an 1841 Mississippi rifle, a trowel bayonet, a stone and earthen oven, buttons from an infantryman's blouse, brass suspender clips, a skillet handle, thousands of spent cartridges—was like a speck of paint that eventually would become a portrait. By studying the placement of the cartridges, the archaeologists hoped to determine the lines of skirmish and retreat. The markings of a firing pin on a casing—each mark as distinctive as a fingerprint—would enable them to trace the movement of individual rifles, and thus that of the men who used them. One unspent round they found, cut in half, probably indicated that a soldier had removed its powder to sear the wound of a comrade. Several other bullets unearthed by a ravine, their tips mushroomed by impact, may have been the ones that struck Five Wounds; scientists would search them in their laboratory for particles of flesh.

Halfmoon had reservations about participating in the survey when the idea was first broached to him. "I may be backing the wrong horse," he told his supervisor. He wondered if it was appropriate to disturb the spirits of his people. He also worried—unnecessarily as it turned out—that the surveyors would not respect the sanctity of the battlefield, and on many afternoons he slipped silently up the hillside trail behind them and crouched in the sagebrush to watch their progress from unseen lookouts. "Part of me just wanted to let things be," he said, "and the other part said, There are things to be learned here. Let's see what secrets history is hiding."

Halfmoon tugged at my sleeve. "Let me show you something," he said. We walked along a forested trail to a clearing where wooden symbols—blue hats for the soldiers, feathers for the Indians—marked where each man had fallen. He led me to a monument that had been erected six years after the battle. "This used to get me mad," he said. It was inscribed "To the soldiers and citizens who fought a superior force of Nez Percé." Before the battle, he said, Five Wounds and his friend, Rainbow, had made a suicide pact and agreed that if one was to be killed, the other would die on the same day. Rainbow had been the first to fall.

Wilford Halfmoon picked up an imaginary rifle as though to aim it. He was trying to figure out precisely where his great-grandfather had been shot, and he decided that right here, by the shallow pit two soldiers had desperately dug with their trowel bayonets, was probably where the fatal bullets had been fired. Five Wounds would have had to have charged up a steep ravine, and it seemed he must have realized he was facing certain death. Halfmoon sighted, tightened his trigger finger and in his mind's eye could see his great-grandfather fall.

That night in Wisdom, a nearby town anchored by the Antlers Saloon and a general store, Doug Scott, the ranger directing the archaeological project, sat in his motel room, entering data on his laptop computer that showed the location of cartridge casings found earlier in the day. The screen filled with numbered dots that swept along the ravine where Five Wounds had died, then thinned out by a wooded slope. "Everything is speculation until we study and analyze the information, but what we believe is happening," he said, his finger tracing a maze of dots, "is that this concentration represents a skirmish line. We've got another nice line here where the soldiers dropped back to set up a new position. Then we lose the line. What I'm betting is that the guys were moving back toward the woods, then they just broke."

Some of the people represented by those computer

dots—the Nez Percé who survived Big Hole—trekked up the mountainous spine of Montana and in the first days of autumn reached the Bear Paws on the doorstep of Canada. Federal troops caught up with them there. In four days of fighting the Indians' pony herd was driven off, casualties mounted and food supplies were exhausted except for dried meat. The war had lasted eleven weeks, and in that time the Nez Percé had engaged ten separate U.S. commands in thirteen battles, winning or fighting to a standoff all except the last one. It was, said General William Sherman, "one of the most extraordinary Indian wars of which there is any record." But now the trail of retreat had been closed, and, rejecting the counsel of his warriors, Chief Joseph agreed to surrender the Nez Percé nation.

Just before nightfall on October 5, 1877, with snow falling across the high prairies, he rode out across a dry riverbed, wearing a blanket and moccasin leggings, his rifle across the pommel of his saddle. He was thirty-seven years old. He dismounted in front of six U.S. officers and an interpreter, handed his weapon to Colonel Nelson Miles and said: "I am tired of fighting. Our chiefs are killed. Looking Glass is dead. The old men are all killed. . . . It is cold and we have no blankets. The little children are freezing to death. . . . I want time to look for my children and see how many of them I can find. Maybe I shall find them among the dead. Hear me, my chiefs, I am tired; my heart is sick and sad. From where the sun now stands, I will fight no more forever."

Chief Joseph and his 417 followers were taken as prisoners to Fort Leavenworth. "We are a doomed people," he said. Before long settlers filled the Big Hole Valley and families held Fourth of July picnics on the Indian burial grounds. A sawmill and blacksmith shop went up there. It took many years, but today the Nez Percé are back in northwestern Idaho, their former homeland, living on a reservation. Their language will probably be lost in another generation or two, elders say. Wilford Halfmoon, his wife and daughter are the only Nez Percés left in the Big Hole Valley. "I can't blame anyone for what happened," Halfmoon said. "The people who did it are gone. They came from a different time, a different age."

Fourteen Forgotten Men

There were no women or children buried in the little hilltop cemetery at Fort Leavenworth, Kansas, overlooking the Missouri River, only military convicts, about 240 of them, all men, their bodies unclaimed, their souls forever tainted by some dishonorable deed that had made this godforsaken place their final outpost. Unlike the pristine national cemetery half a mile away, few visitors stopped at the convicts' burial grounds, and for many years not a flower was laid on the unblessed ground. The small tombstones bore nothing more than a name and a date of death, and that, twelve years ago, is what caught the attention of army Sergeant Ken Knox, a corrections officer at the Disciplinary Barracks at Fort Leavenworth, while he was bicycling around the post one Sunday afternoon with his wife. "Come here. Look at this," he called to Dianne. They leaned their bikes against the fence and went through the gate.

Off to one side, separated from the other graves, were fourteen tombstones, each with a German name. Seven were inscribed with the same date, August 25, 1945. Knox's first thought was that the men there must have died in a bus accident, but what he had stumbled onto were the forgotten graves of the only foreign prisoners of war ever executed in the United States, and the more Knox thought about it, the more troubled he became over the circumstances of their hanging. Gradually his curiosity became an obsession. He started delving through archives and libraries and newspaper clippings and, although he had no credentials as a researcher, he gained access to presidential papers at the Truman Library in Independence, Missouri, for the simple reason that he wouldn't go away.

"I'm not contesting their guilt, only the injustice," Knox told anyone who asked. "These guys just don't belong in that cemetery. They were honorable military men and, right or wrong, if Germany had won the war, they'd have been given a medal. They ought to be reinterred in Germany, in a place of respect. That's all I'm trying to accomplish. Besides, they were executed after the war was over, and that raises a lot of questions over whether they were the victims of a society's desire for revenge against all Germans."

For two years Knox looked down on the prison court-yard from his second-floor office, and it got so he could imagine Walter Beyer and Otto Stengel and the dozen other German sailors and soldiers, handcuffed, each escorted by an eight-man guard, walking to the makeshift gallows the fort had set up in the elevator shaft of an old warehouse. He could almost hear the Episcopal chaplain, John Sagar, reciting Psalm 130, the litany for the dying: "Out of the deep I have called unto thee, Lord, hear my voice . . ."

The condemned men—one of whom was a grocer in civilian life, one a pattern cutter, another an engineer—were among 400,000 Germans held prisoner during the Second World War at five hundred camps in the United States, scattered from Houlton, Maine, to Douglas, Wyoming. They worked in the wheat fields of Kansas, stuffed olives with Spanish peppers in Texas, repaired army vehicles in Virginia, sewed American army uniforms in Maryland, picked peas in upstate New York. "Put them in Death Valley," suggested one townsman in a letter to the director of the Prisoners of War Division, "chuck in a side of beef and let them starve to death." By the end of the war, aided by prison tailors who made them civilian clothes and artists who provided them with forged documents, Germans were escaping the camps at the rate of one hundred a month, often melting into American society.

U.S. intelligence officers worked diligently to recruit "snitches" among the newly arrived prisoners, putting unsuspecting inmates in bugged two-man cells occupied by moles, and the information they gathered proved invaluable to the Allied war effort. One snitch, Johannes Kunze, passed on details of the camouflaging of Hamburg intended to mislead British bomber pilots—the roof of the train station had been painted to resemble a highway, the lake had been covered over—and others identified Nazi camp ringleaders and shared secrets about German U-boat strategy.

At 10:00 P.M. on November 4, 1943, one of the German prisoners at Camp Gruber in Tankowa, Oklahoma, Walter Beyer, a thirty-year-old first sergeant captured in North Africa, ordered his company to assemble in the mess hall. Johannes Kunze was one of the last to enter. White-faced and perspiring, he took a seat at a table by the

door. Beyer held up two notes in identical handwriting—
one unsigned, containing a brief description of Hamburg's
camouflaging, the other a letter, signed by Kunze, to his
wife in Leipzig. "Comrades," said Beyer, whose wife and
two-year-son, Edgar, lived in Hamburg, "I am sorry and
it hurts me in my soul to be forced to tell you some sad
news, and the case is so grave that I am not in a position
to pass judgment myself. Bad as it may seem, we have a
traitor in our midst."

Beyer had hardly finished before someone shouted,
"That's him! Don't let him get out!" and a score of men
pounced on Kunze, who struggled wildly to escape the
fists and feet of his tormentors. He died a short while later
of a fractured skull and cerebral hemorrhaging. Beyer,
court testimony later revealed, did not participate in the
beating.

During the next five months, three other German
snitches were murdered in unrelated incidents at POW
camps in Florence, Arizona, Camp Chaffee, Arkansas,
and Aiken, South Carolina. After lengthy investigations—
one of the suspects, Otto Stengel, confessed only after
being forced to wear a gas mask stuffed with onions and
garlic—the fourteen Germans were convicted in four separate courts-martial and sent off to Fort Leavenworth to be
hanged. Each contended that he had acted as any consci-
entious soldier would have. "I am no murderer," the grocer, Sergeant Erich Gauss, told the court. "I merely fought
for the honor of my fatherland and for respect as a soldier,
and I believe that every decent German soldier would do
likewise." The Germans' defense was based on the argument that their victims were traitors and that prisoners of

war were obligated to prevent treason against their mother-
land. To defend Beyer and the four others accused of
killing Kunze, the U.S. government assigned, part-time,
Lieutenant Colonel Alfred Petsch; he described himself as
a country lawyer and farmer and told a review board that
he had "practically no experience in matters of this sort."
The prosecutor was one of the army's most respected lawyers, Lieutenant Colonel Leon Jaworski, who later would
gain fame as the Watergate special prosecutor.

Ken Knox had pieced all this together from four thousand documents he had collected, many of them under the
Freedom of Information Act. He had written 159 pages of
a book, and evening after evening he sat at his Atari
computer in his Sacramento, California, home, sifting
through testimony and declassified army memos, wondering if he had overlooked some clue that would prove the
injustice of the Germans' deaths. His life had become a
crusade for a cause that no one cared much about. "I can't
explain why this thing has become so important to me, I
really can't," Knox said one day as we sat in his living
room, surrounded by piles of documents and trial tran-
scripts and correspondence. "I'm not an obsessive person.
I don't get all involved in causes, but this has been like an
ulcer. I keep thinking of the families in Germany who've
been told their father or grandfather died as a criminal,
when this wasn't the case at all. We'd consider Americans
who did what they did heroes."

Knox, the son of a decorated aviator in the Korean
War, had served in peacetime Korea and warring Vietnam
and, having just retired from a twenty-two-year military
career, was now working as a sandblaster and had gotten

my attention through sheer persistence. For months he had been calling newspapers and television stations in California, trying to elicit interest in the story he had uncovered. "I'm reaching my limit," Knox would say. "I really need someone with more education and experience than I've got to get this done." The editors he talked to always professed empathy and would make vague promises to send someone over to talk to him. But no one ever called Knox back or knocked on his door.

Then one day, making a random phone call to the *Los Angeles Times,* having been shunted from one desk to another, put on hold, asked to wait and told no one was available to talk to him, Knox was finally connected to an editor who knew the smell of a good story. They talked for two hours. The editor phoned me in Washington, D.C., the next day and said, "There's this former army sergeant in Sacramento who's on to something that might be interesting. He says he's been trying for a couple of years to get someone to listen but no one will." One of journalism's greatest rewards is being able, from time to time, to give a voice to worthy people who think they will never be heard, and Ken Knox was dumbstruck when I called. "The gentleman I talked to at your paper said someone would be in touch, but I really didn't think it would ever happen," he said.

Knox took two days off work and turned his home into a sort of research laboratory for me. Documents a foot high stretched across the dining-room table and spilled onto several adjoining tables. Chronologies, old photographs and profiles of the fourteen German prisoners were laid out in proper order. "Ten years of frustration, accomplishing nothing," he said. "I was ready to give up. Then, boom, I find someone who wants to listen. This is one of the best days of my life." He put on a pot of coffee. I plugged in my laptop computer and started typing.

The fourteen Germans lingered on Death Row in Fort Leavenworth for a year. During that time 15 of the 90,000 Americans being held prisoner on German soil were also sentenced to death—surely a quid pro quo deal, Knox thought—and Washington and Berlin began negotiating through Swiss intermediaries on a prisoner exchange. Both sides agreed not to execute anyone until the negotiations were complete. "No death sentence imposed on German prisoners of war in this country will be carried out," said a classified message from the assistant chief of staff to Fort Leavenworth authorities on April 28, 1945, "and . . . no steps will be taken to obtain confirmation by the President of any death sentences not yet confirmed, until further order from the personnel division." Nine days later, the war in Europe ended with the German surrender at Reims, France. The fifteen Americans sentenced to death were returned to the Allied command, and President Harry S Truman signed the Germans' death warrants, despite the recommendation of a review board that the sentences be commuted to life imprisonment.

Just past midnight on July 10, after a meal of stew, steamed rice and cake, the first batch of five German prisoners, all former members of Rommel's famed Afrika Korps, were taken from their cells in Fort Leavenworth's solitary confinement wing, known as The Castle. They moved in formation across the long, open yard Sergeant

Ken Knox would spend so many hours looking at years later in bright moonlight, accompanied by a Catholic priest and an Episcopalian chaplain. The door to the warehouse that held the gallows opened, and they entered. All wore, at their request, military uniforms. Sergeant Walter Beyer was the first to approach the American soldiers who waited by the noose.

"The prisoner appeared none too robust and his cheeks were drawn," *The Kansas City Star* reported the next day.

> ❧ A black stubble, matching his hair, indicated that he had not shaved for at least twelve hours. His eyes were those of a trapped beast. They moved nervously from right to left. But he never turned his head or moved his chin from its jutting position. . . .
>
> A noncommissioned officer standing beside him removed Beyer's cap and placed a black hood over his head. There was a brittle command 'Right face, forward march,' and the Nazi pivoted on his right heel in rhythm with the bodyguard of soldiers that brought him into the building and stepped off the remaining thirty feet to the gallows. His bearing was military to the last. ❧

Beyer's wife knew something was very wrong early that spring of 1945 because of "a sudden, terrible sadness" in her husband's letters. But it was a year before she learned that he was dead and several more before she learned the circumstances of his death. By then she could not afford a trip to the United States to claim the body. "I can still remember the moment Mother found out my father was dead," Beyer's only child, fifty-one-year-old Edgar, recalled in a telephone conversation from Hamburg, where he was now the assistant manager of a bank. "I was five years old. She was cooking beans in the backyard when it came, a simple, open postcard. She read it and started to shake. She let out a wail that I will never forget. It must have lasted five to ten minutes. I thought she was going to die."

The postcard was cryptic: It was dated August 2, 1946, and gave no details except for the fact and date of death. Eventually it was followed by a death certificate and a note from the Red Cross saying no further information was available. For more than twenty years Mrs. Beyer shared her secret with no one, and it was not until Edgar Beyer was about to marry that she sat him down and told him his father had been executed and was buried in a criminal's grave. "It was a complete shock," Beyer said. "I couldn't believe it."

In 1981 an aunt gave Edgar Beyer the equivalent of $4,000 for a trip to the United States on the proviso that he visit all the family's relatives—Walter Beyer's brother had immigrated to the United States in 1922, settled in Mississippi and married an American—as well as his father's grave. He flew alone from New Orleans to Kansas City, drove to Fort Leavenworth and met an army officer who told him where the convicts' cemetery was. The gate was locked, so he climbed the chain-link fence and found his father's grave, the first one in the row of fourteen. There was no one else around: Beyer stood by it for a long time. He had not seen his father since Christmas Day, 1941.

From time to time, German and American military authorities had suggested that the prisoners' remains should be returned to Germany for burial in a war cemetery. But while Germany was divided, the West German Embassy in Washington preferred that the matter not get raised at all, fearing East Germany would use it to cause a rift in the Washington-Bonn alliance, and none of the victims' families had tried to claim the bodies. Even Edgar Beyer wasn't sure repatriation was a good idea. "I'd need time to think about that," he said.

I flew out to Kansas City and drove over to Fort Leavenworth in a rental car. It was a Sunday afternoon, November 18, a day the Germans call *Volkstrauertag,* People's Remembrance Day. A cold autumn wind whipped across the cemetery on Hancock Hill, murmuring through the leafless trees. From the road down the way five German soldiers wearing gray jackets, leather gloves and maroon berets approached the row of fourteen tombstones, marching in military unison. They carried a wreath of carnations.

Colonel Michael Hueber, a twenty-seven-year veteran of the German Army and the son of a Second World War paratrooper, came first, remembering on this day of memories the Allied air strike on his home in Kreuznach that had killed his mother, his grandparents, an aunt and a nephew. Abreast of him, arms swinging crisply at their sides, strode the other four soldiers, who, like Hueber, were temporarily attached to the U.S. Army's Command

General Staff college at the fort. They placed the wreath between the tombstones of Private Rudolf Sraub, the thirty-nine-year-old pattern cutter, and Private Helmut Fisher, a twenty-two-year-old high-school dropout. "We stand here," Hueber said, head bowed, "in front of the graves of young soldiers who died in meeting their given missions. They were just soldiers like you and me. They died harder than their colleagues in combat because they knew that in the end they would die. They were honorable men, and today the people of Germany, finally free after sixty years of dictatorship, pay them their respects." Then with a salute, the Germans were gone, their steps rustling through the ground cover of dead leaves, and in the coming darkness the wreath and the fourteen headstones were hardly visible at all.

Not much changed for Ken Knox for quite a while. He spent his evenings writing letters and sifting through documents, and every once in a while a friend would ask, "What are you doing with your Germans today, Ken?" Then, sometime in 1992, after the reunification of Germany, mysterious things began to happen. Red roses appeared, one at a time, on each of the Germans' graves, over the course of several weeks, and inexplicably one morning their marble headstones stood clean and polished. The German War Graves Commission heard about Knox's work and sent a man to Fort Leavenworth to photograph the graves and make a report on the circumstances of the deaths. An organization of German paratrooper veterans devoted twenty-nine pages of its yearbook to the fourteen Germans, and a Hollywood producer started sniffing out the possibility of making a TV movie. After twelve years Knox had found an audience, and people were finally saying the Germans deserved better than a criminals' grave. Knox now knew it was only a matter of time before he could lay his lonely obsession to rest. I told him to be careful if Hollywood got the movie rights because it was apt to change the story all around. Knox sounded surprised that anyone would want to do that. "That wouldn't do," he said. "I mean, how do you improve on history? What happened happened, and that's the history we have to live with."

Twilight of the Aleuts

Had I been asked a few years ago who the Aleuts were, I would have been hard pressed to answer, other than to place them somewhere up in the frozen North, probably in an igloo. The arctic part would have been right, but not the igloo, and as I was going through a thick file about the Aleuts on the plane to Alaska, I kept thinking that something about the people, something about their tragic role in the Second World War, would jog my memory, and I'd say, "Oh sure, now I remember." But nothing clicked. I knew more about the Copts of Egypt and the Maori of New Zealand than I did about these fellow Americans. My ignorance gnawed at me as I read on. Like most journalists I have a short attention span and devote insufficient energy to assigning history a role in today's events. Yet my profession is forgiving and offers many opportunities to make amends. One of them came from the Aleuts. Their history, I found, was full of lessons: on our insensitivity toward those who are different, on the inadvisability of suffering stoically, on the dangers of censorship.

The Aleuts were a shy, quiet people who migrated to the islands from the Alaskan mainland four thousand years ago. They traditionally hunted seals, sea otters and whales, fished for salmon, lived in seaside villages of related families and could paddle their sleek kayaks known as *bidarkas* for eighteen or twenty hours at a stretch. Men greeted each dawn as the Creator's daily miracle, and pregnant women bared their bellies to the rays of the sun to gain strength for their infants. The sick and the unruly were immersed in the ice-cold waters of the sea, whose healing and cleansing power was said to be great. When Russian fur traders came to the Aleutians in the mid–eighteenth century, nearly every island was populated and the Aleuts numbered an estimated 25,000. The Russians—whose names many Aleuts still bear—conquered, enslaved and frequently massacred the islands' natives. Flu and smallpox epidemics in 1848 and 1918 further reduced their numbers. "It is only a matter of time," John Muir said, "before they vanish from the earth." By the Second World War, the Aleuts' population had dwindled to about 1,400.

I had lunch with an Aleut—the first I had ever met—a couple of hours after my plane landed in Anchorage, and as usual, another stereotype collapsed. My host, in a coat and tie, was a successful businessman and an articulate protector of the Aleut culture, which he considered endangered. "For forty-five years," he said, "we've been trying to tell our story, and no one's wanted to listen." His words echoed with the same frustration I had heard in the voices of Wilford Halfmoon and Sergeant Ken Knox. What the Aleuts had been trying to tell was the story of a forgotten U.S. military campaign on American soil and of a people who sailed off from their island homes to a life of misfortune.

"Here's what I mean," the businessman said. He

passed a military history book across the table, and I skimmed it quickly. Not a mention of the bloody Aleutian campaign or the plight of the Aleuts. Japan had coveted the Aleutians as a bridge to the U.S. mainland, and, hoping to divert the U.S. Navy's attention from Midway, its bombers attacked Dutch Harbor, the islands' main commercial center, during two days in early June 1942, killing seventy-seven American servicemen. On June 6, Japan invaded the island of Kiska, capturing eleven Americans manning a weather station. Attu, the westernmost island, just 650 miles from Japan, fell the next day, and the forty-two Aleuts living there were taken prisoner. For the next eleven months the outer reaches of Alaska would remain under Japanese occupation.

The Aleutians are our most remote outpost—seventy treeless, volcanic islands that curl out of the Alaska Peninsula, separating the Bering Sea and the Pacific Ocean. At their most distant tip, New York is five time zones and more than five thousand miles away. The Devil Wind buffets the islands with incessant fury, and the weather is so intolerable that planes often can't get in for days at a time. Only on the Aleutians, Bob Hope said during the Second World War, could a man "walk in mud up to his knees bucking a snowstorm that blew sand in his face, while being pelted by hail in the rear on a sunny day."

My flight from Anchorage carried only a handful of passengers and took two hours. I hitchhiked the mile from the airport to Dutch Harbor, which seemed reminiscent of a Wyoming town, circa 1880. It had a population of two hundred and a single windswept dirt street with some storefronts and an inn. The inn's bar was packed with

local white fishermen—mainly descendants of New Englanders and Scandinavians—just off the high seas. Most
appeared drunk. It was not yet lunchtime, so I wandered
off in search of John and Eva Tcheripanoff, whose names
I had been given in Anchorage. I passed an oil storage
tank, its skin wrinkled and warped from the Japanese
attack, and a Russian Orthodox church—most Aleuts
practice the faith of their first colonial masters—and
found the Tcheripanoffs' tidy home tucked in an inlet. The
wind blowing off the harbor was so stiff that I had to bend
into it to maintain an upright position. The Tcheripanoffs,
who looked older than their sixty-odd years, were watching television when I knocked. We sat together on the sofa,
Tcheripanoff's arm around his wife's shoulder, and talked
about the war. Mrs. Tcheripanoff clicked her remote control device to mute the TV. On the table next to her was
a basket her mother had made of seal gut.

"After the attack, the government sent a boat and
said we were being evacuated," Tcheripanoff recalled.
"Course, you could stay behind if you wanted. Henry
Swanson stayed behind. But most of us wanted to get
away from the war. They didn't seem to know where to
take us, though, and the place we ended up, in Ward Cove,
was pretty terrible, with everybody being sick all the time
and a lot of people dying. Outside of meeting my wife here,
Eva, not much good happened at Ward Cove."

And Mrs. Tcheripanoff said, "I can still remember me,
my auntie and my auntie's mother going into that camp
for the first time. There were trees there and we had never
seen trees before. That scared many of us. It was a terrible

thing, but I do not blame anyone for what happened. Crazy things happen in war."

Unlike the 120,000 Japanese-Americans who were interned during the war as a perceived threat to U.S. security ("A Jap is a Jap; it makes no difference if the Jap is a citizen or not," said the West Coast military commander, Lieutenant General John DeWitt), the 881 Aleuts evacuated from the Aleutians and the tiny Pribilof Islands to the north were moved for their own protection. But that's where the altruism ended.

The Aleuts were jammed into damp, drafty, unheated canneries and herring salters on Ward Cove and Funter Bay along the southeastern Alaska coast, men and women sharing the same, unpartitioned space. The floors of the empty buildings were crumbling with dry rot, the windows were broken, the doors were off their hinges. Women slept with their children, three and four to a cot. Candles were used for light. The outhouses overflowed, the waste was dumped from the slop chute into the bay. On the shores of the polluted bay, the Aleuts foraged for clams and fish. Then bootleggers found the Aleuts, and alcoholism soared; venereal disease, contracted with whites in nearby towns, spread like an epidemic. A group of doctors sent to inspect the camps run by the Department of the Interior called the quarters "unfit for a pig" and said the Aleuts were virtual "prisoners of the government." Ten percent of the Aleuts died during their internment; half would never return to their homeland. Tuberculosis, whooping cough, measles and mumps were the usual causes of death, though the cause of one man's death was listed merely as "pain."

"I have seen tough places during my days in Alaska, but nothing to equal the situation at Funter," the state's attorney general, Henry Roden, wrote acting Governor Ernest Gruening on September 20, 1943. "I have not the language at my command which can adequately describe what I saw." And the U.S. surgeon general received one report from a physician that predicted it was "only a matter of time before some publication, such as *Life* magazine, will get ahold of this story." But the Aleuts' internment didn't elicit much sympathy in Alaska, which in the forties was a territory where signs posted outside bars and restaurants advised: NO NATIVES ALLOWED. Ward Bowar, chief of the Alaska Fisheries Division, wrote the governor in 1943, saying, "It may well be that the natives . . . have been coddled too much and the time has come to bring home to them forcefully the need to look after themselves in more decent ways. . . . If they do not respond to ordinary instructions and suggestions along this line, more drastic measures will be necessary." Harry McCain, the acting mayor of Ketchikan, told Governor Gruening that in order to prevent his town from being "infected with their diseased condition," the Aleuts should be relocated. McCain suggested Hyder, "a dead town with less than thirty people." He noted, "It is my feeling the residents there would welcome them because of the trade they would bring."

News of the Japanese invasion and the Aleuts' internment initially was kept from the public for morale and security reasons. In the process the U.S. military managed to conceal serious blunders in its handling of the Aleutian campaign. Then early one evening in May 1943, nearly a year after the invasion, Walter Winchell opened his broadcast with "To Mr. and Mrs. America and all the ships at sea . . . Keep your eyes on the Aleutian Islands." Just after midnight a week later, the U.S. Thirty-second Infantry Regiment landed secretly on the northern beaches of Attu (an island that today is a national wildlife refuge, unpopulated except for thirty American Coast Guardsmen). With the arrival of the Fourth Infantry, the American forces on the Aleutians swelled to more than sixteen thousand men, and slowly the fierce resistance of the Japanese, outnumbered eight to one, crumbled. At 8:00 P.M. on May 29, the surviving Japanese met in front of the hospital to discuss their final strategy. A Japanese medical officer wrote in his diary that night:

> The last assault is to be carried out. All the patients in the hospital were made to commit suicide. Only thirty-three are still living and I am grateful to die here. I have no regrets. Banzai to the Emperor. I am grateful that I have kept the peace of my soul. . . . Goodbye, Farke, my beloved wife, who loved me to the last, until we meet again. Grant you God speed Miseka, who just became four years old and will grow up unhindered. I feel sorry for you Fakiko, born February of this year. You will never see your father. Well, be good, Matsae, my brother. Goodbye.

The nineteen-day battle for Attu took the lives of 550 Americans and 2,600 Japanese, some of whom blew themselves up with grenades rather than surrender. Only the fight for Iwo Jima claimed a higher percentage of casualties among the combatants in the Pacific war. In keeping with the general blackout of news from the Aleutians, pictures of the Japanese bodies, stretched out across the tundra between Massacre Bay and Chichagof Harbor did not run in *Life* until April 1944, almost a year after the battle.

With the island back in American hands, the Aleuts were allowed to return to their villages in 1944 and '45, though Attu and a few other islands were never resettled. "When I finally did get back home, I had lost everything," John Tcheripanoff said. "The outboard motor was gone, the house had been wrecked. I said, 'What kind of people have been living here?' I couldn't believe it when they said it was American soldiers." All across the eleven-hundred-mile-long string of islands, the Aleuts found similar scenes of destruction. U.S. soldiers had used the onion-shaped domes of the Aleuts' Russian Orthodox churches for target practice. The religious icons were gone, and almost every house had been looted or burned. As surely as thousand-year-old villages had disappeared from the map under a rain of American and Japanese bombs, the Aleuts' culture itself had been dealt a blow from which it would never recover. Young people drifted off to the towns and cities, where they intermarried, took jobs that needed no knowledge of the sea and lost their fluency in Aleut, a language akin to Eskimo. By the 1990s full-blooded Aleuts were few and only two thousand of the nation's twelve thousand Aleuts remained in the land that bore their name.

"I'd have to say the war changed us as a people,"

Henry Swanson said. Swanson was ninety-two years old, as spindly as a fishing pole. His suspenders seemed to hold his whole body together. He took me into his backyard, where slabs of fish dried under a soft sun that gave no discernible heat. "We were used to living off the land 'cause there was nothing here. We dried our fish for the winter, just like I'm doing. What you see here will get me through the winter, maybe longer. We had hunting parties for seals that supplied the whole town with meat. After the war, all that ceased. I suppose it was because the people had been exposed to different ways—to money, to modern things. Our leadership was gone, our community was broken up by the camp experience. How did they think we could live locked in canneries with no boats or fishing nets or guns? Now the herring have disappeared and instead of hunting for seal, when someone wants meat they go to the store and buy beef for three or four dollars a pound."

Although the Roosevelt administration allocated $10,000 to compensate the Aleuts—the equivalent of $7.14 per person—it took more than forty years for the government to admit culpability. That admission came in 1989, in a promise by Congress to pay $27 million reparations, including $12,000 for each survivor of the wartime camps. The National Park Service also proposed establishing a park dedicated to the "Forgotten War" and an Aleut cultural center that would, among other things, chronicle the wartime suffering of Alaska's smallest native group.

If we are to find any solace in all this, it is in knowing that what happened to the Aleuts almost certainly could never happen in America again. At the first hint of a cannery inhabited by humans, the American Civil Liberties Union and Amnesty International would be stalking the compound. The media—more aggressive and powerful than what we knew a generation ago—would descend in droves. Congressional investigators would roll into town. Small consolation to the Aleuts perhaps, but nonetheless confirmation that the disenfranchised and the oppressed have a voice in today's society that they never had half a century before.

My plane out of the Aleutians was canceled by a howling gale, and I waited out the storm with the boisterous fishermen at the inn's bar in Dutch Harbor. "What'll it be, bud?" the bartender asked. I ordered a beer and remembered a drink I had had with Doug Scott, the ranger in charge of the Nez Percé archaeological survey, at the Antlers Saloon in Montana. I had asked him what he hoped to accomplish by rewriting history. Indeed, why bother fiddling with history at all? "No one record is entirely right and none is entirely wrong," he said. "Each is just part of the puzzle, a way to understand the past and a way to examine why cultures come in conflict with each other. On the broadest level, from studying the past we can learn something about how human behavior and socialization evolves. And if we learn enough, hopefully we can teach others so they don't make the same mistakes again."

Putting People First

For many years Westport was Kansas City's finest high school, a citadel of learning that measured up favorably to the exclusive eastern preparatory schools and that, in 1929, boasted of having more Rhodes scholars among its alumni than any high school in America. Built with cattle money at the turn of the century, Westport stood on a small hill, anchoring an all-white neighborhood known as Hyde Park. The country club there didn't accept Jews or anyone for that matter without WASP credentials, and from their grand, understated homes young men marched off each fall to the nation's top universities. To live in Hyde Park, surrounded by wrought-iron fences and acres of lush foliage, to attend school there, was tantamount to carrying a passport for success.

As with many of the nation's inner-city neighborhoods, the 1960s brought wrenching change to Hyde Park. Middle-class whites started leaving for suburbia, in Kansas, just across the Missouri River, and blacks, then Hispanics and Asians, arrived to take their place. Hyde Park became poor and Westport run-down, and as decay chewed away at communities in transition throughout Kansas City, white civic leaders redrew school boundaries, sometimes monthly, a block at a time, to make sure that minorities moving into an area were assigned to schools already predominantly black. Kansas City had, in effect, written off the inner-city schools with an explicit message that their students were inferior. The school district transferred the physics teacher from a largely black school to one that was still all white and replaced him with an instructor who taught principles of sanitation, a vocational course for janitors. After 1969—the last year the education system had more whites than blacks—voters turned down nineteen consecutive school levies and bond measures. Before long Westport's plaster walls started to crack and its athletic budget dried up. The dropout rate reached 50 percent, achievement scores in reading and science fell to the lowest levels in the district, crime and drug use soared. Westport had become the home of a lost generation. It was where you went to fail.

Then one day in April 1988, a balding, slight man named Ewing Marion Kauffman returned to the high school he had graduated from fifty-four years earlier. He mounted the stage of the auditorium and peered out over his reading glasses at the assembled Westport freshmen. Few had ever heard of Mr. K, as people in Kansas City called him, and one of the students, Arnold King, remembers thinking, Geez, this guy's so old and fragile. What's he doing here? Kauffman, born on a farm, raised by his divorced mother, who took in boarders to support the family, had formed his own drug company in 1950, packaging vitamin pills in the basement of his mother's rented home on Sixty-eighth Street by night and selling them by day. Marion Laboratories eventually made him one of the wealthiest men in Kansas City, though even now he remained something of an outsider to the handful of old-time moneyed families who ran the city. Kauffman represented new money and a break from tradition, and they considered his refusal to subsidize the arts miserly and his philanthropic concerns for the underclass frivolous.

The faces that looked up at Kauffman from the assembly hall that day were 87 percent black, brown and yellow. The world, he told them, steps aside for any person with an education, and to prove his point he made an extraordinary offer: If they graduated on time, had good discipline, remained drug-free and didn't get pregnant, he would pay for their college educations—tuition, room, board, books, the cost of two trips home a year—under a program he was setting up called Project Choice. The applause that greeted his offer was surprisingly reserved, and one of the teachers later speculated the students so accepted the prospect of failure they couldn't grasp the magnitude of the opportunity.

I flew out to Kansas City four years later, on the day of reckoning for the class of '92. The freshmen Kauffman had addressed in the auditorium were now seniors who had made the choices that would determine the direction of their lives. Before leaving I had checked the *Los Angeles Times'* library and found that hardly a word had been written in the national press about Project Choice. If I had been researching Charles Keating or Ivan Boesky or one of the men who came to symbolize the greed and corruption of a self-indulgent society, I could have traveled with a trunkful of news clippings. But on Ewing Kauffman, the philanthropist, I drew a near blank.

Kansas City is a maze of beltways and parkways and rail yards that loop around a handsome downtown skyline, and I found Westport High School only after taking several wrong turns and backtracking twice. The Hyde Park neighborhood was an odd mix of crummy-looking homes that had been turned into apartments and residences that were being gentrified, and on a hill above the community sat Westport, red-bricked and still rather stately. I paused outside to read on a stone memorial the names of twelve former students who had died in the Second World War. Malcolm X once said, "Sitting at the table doesn't make you a diner unless you eat some of what's on that plate," and it didn't take long to figure out that the students at Westport had a lot less on their plate than I had had on mine at their age. Four security guards patrolled the corridors—an inconceivable occurrence in the fifties—and on a bulletin board was a notice offering a $50,000 reward for information leading to the arrest of two suspects in the shooting of an FBI agent. The walls needed paint and the classrooms, refurbishing.

Despite the opportunity Kauffman had provided, Westport was still a dysfunctional school. Its annual athletic budget was $2,000, and there was a shortage of textbooks. Many of the teachers had burned out, and, at a time when students cried out for positive role models, only four of the school's ninety-seven instructors were black males. Computers, software and teaching aids were in short supply. The principal, Charlotte Carr, admitted all this and said that opportunity alone had not been enough to release students from the bondage of failure. Project Choice had resulted in gains, but no miracles, and was only the first step in healing the scars of sociological and economic neglect. "You'd think all the kids would jump at this chance, but that hasn't happened," she said. "As a group, their aspirations aren't very high, and a lot don't believe they can really go to college, succeed in college, even with the opportunity they've got. Education was forgotten in Kansas City for twenty years, and that legacy can't be undone overnight."

On the dark side, one of three Westport students skipped school on any given day, and 35 percent of the students were failing two or more subjects. Proficiency test scores, though improving, remained below the district and national averages in reading comprehension, math and science. Thirty girls had become pregnant, and two members of the class of '92 had been killed in street violence. Fourteen-year-old David Wilburn was sitting outside Miss Carr's office, having been disciplined for fighting. He had a high IQ and failing grades, and I asked him what the trouble was. "It's really hard to just come to school and get an education," he said. "First, you have to earn respect; you have to fight back or you get messed with. Second, you find out skipping school's easier than going to school. Things are different than when our parents were kids. We've got a lot more pressures and parents don't understand that."

Burdensome pressures to be sure. For forty years surveys have found that white Americans increasingly favor equal treatment for blacks, yet when we recite all the chilling statistics—one in five black males will spend part of his life behind bars, three times more black children than white children are born into poverty, two thirds of black children are raised by a single parent—we criticize and forget that the black experience in America has been unique. Blacks were not free to join the flight to suburbia in the sixties. They did not have the small-business skills and cohesive family units that have contributed to the success of new Asian minorities. They could not open their schoolbooks and find any mention of blacks whose contributions helped shape our history, our literature, our arts, our social consciences. It does not take much sociological imagination to understand the consequences of leaving a group behind, trapped in decaying cities while all around them others—including large numbers of blacks—prosper in a materialistic world. The disunity of America is a condition we can ill afford, and that was one of the reasons I thought Project Choice so important and the achievements of Westport's class of '92 so remarkable.

Forget the miracles. Something significant was happening. Random drug testing—which Kauffman and Kansas City's first black mayor, Emanuel Cleaver, joined the students in taking—consistently turned up negative in 98 percent of the teenagers. Among Kansas City's ten high schools, Westport's "crime index" had fallen to the third lowest. The dropout rate was cut in half, and of the 143 freshmen who had listened to an old man's offer—and challenge—four years earlier, 115 were on hand June 2, 1992, to accept their diplomas and hear Kauffman say, "We were born with the freedom to pursue an education and a worthwhile occupation. With your high school graduation, you now have the power to choose what you will make of your lives. I urge you to choose well." Eighty-one of the graduates were headed for college, five for vocational schools. Kauffman's bill for the first semester was going to be $300,000, for the entire project, $7.2 million.

Ida Johnson, the mother of one of the graduates, had thanked Kauffman in her prayers every night for four years. "This is a dream come true," she said. Despite the neighborhood distractions of gunfire in the night and corners filled with drug dealers, her son, Prentice, had made steadily better grades and won first place in a school essay-writing contest. His thesis was that blacks in the inner city have to get along with themselves before they can hope to solve their relations with others. Prentice had been accepted at four colleges. "Project Choice took a load off my shoulders," he said. "It taught me no one could stop me but myself."

The man Kauffman had picked to direct Project Choice was Thomas Rhone, a former high school principal and corporate executive. He said there had been many misconceptions about the program. First, its involvement with the students wasn't limited to paying college bills; its staff provided guidance, parental counseling, week-long seminars at various university campuses and a range of other services throughout the students' four years of high school. And second, its success or failure could not be judged by how many students went on to college. "What this really is," he said, "is a dropout prevention program. Everyone's talking college, college, college, but we know not all these kids will be college students, and Mr. K says, 'Hold it. What about the kids who want to be auto mechanics, want to own a small business or go into cosmetics or drive an eighteen-wheeler?' If we can keep them in school, they can get to a vocational or technical school and have those careers and become productive citizens. Mr. K's philosophy is that it's cheaper to right the system now than to pay the cost of our failures later."

Rhone had played professional basketball with the New York Knicks and, having practically grown up in Boston Garden watching the Celtics, I tried to steer the conversation in that direction. He resisted. "I really hope your article doesn't identify me as a former pro basketball player," he said. "That gets into the whole stereotype of the black male only making it through sports, and what we're trying to teach these kids is that they have to develop other skills to succeed today. Playing basketball is the least significant thing I've done with my life, and if you just dropped the reference, I'd appreciate it." I agreed, and I only mention his sports career here because in the context of sharing his remarks, rather than just hanging an identifying label onto his name, I realize he had raised a sensitive issue that I had never given much thought to.

"I'm having a lot more fun giving my money away than I ever had making it," Ewing Kauffman said to me, a smile wrinkling his face from ear to ear. He was seventy-five years old and looked like someone Norman Rockwell would have painted carving the turkey at a family Thanksgiving. Unlike many people of wealth and power I've talked to, he asked questions and never referred to himself in the third person. He oversaw Project Choice—and the foundation that bore his name—from the suburban office where we now sat, dispensing his millions for a variety of educational and social programs. In the adjoining office, his wife distributed her millions for the arts and culture. He refused to attach his name to buildings (having rejected suggestions that Kansas City's baseball park be named Kauffman Stadium, though he owned the major league team that played there), and he wouldn't hear of spending a dime for bricks and mortar. "I'd rather put my money in people," he told those who inquired.

I asked him if he had missed out on anything in life, having been so busy working and making money that he hadn't even picked up a golf club until he was fifty. He lit one of the three pipes on his desk with a match and took a puff. "Well, you know, it's funny," he said, "but yes, I never had the chance to bicycle. I was too poor growing up to own one, and now that I'm rich enough to afford a hundred of them, I'm too old to ride." I was trying to figure out why Kauffman had become so involved with society's forgotten tenants. He wasn't a religious man, and he wasn't a starry-eyed liberal. But the answer wasn't complicated. Though white, he had been one of them, and he was still rather in awe of all the doors an education can open. His own humble roots had made him an equal-opportunity pragmatist.

His mother had graduated from college in 1890, fluent in German and Latin. "You can imagine her vocabulary," he said. "There never was a word she couldn't break down." Kauffman had dropped out of school after two years of college to support her. He often read a book a day, having taught himself to speed-read during a childhood illness, and was so successful in his first job as a salesman for a drug company that he earned more money than the president. "That's what I really am at heart—a salesman," he said. "In that I don't have to tip my hat to anyone." When the president cut his commissions and trimmed his territory, he went into business for himself in his mother's basement after convincing seven friends to invest $1,000 each. Fifteen years later each investment was worth $750,000.

Before merging his company with Merrell Dow Pharmaceuticals in 1989, Kauffman ran Marion Laboratories like an extension of his family. Workers were referred to as associates, not employees, and every associate, from the lowliest janitor on up, shared in annual bonuses and stock options. Three hundred of them became millionaires. Kauffman regularly surprised workers with hospital visits when they were sick and with phone calls to their homes to extend anniversary or birthday greetings. "I've always had the conviction," he said, "that if you [as a businessman] treat people like you'd like to be treated, one, you'll be happy; two, it's the best way to live your life; and three, you'll make more money."

Kauffman knew he was trying to unshuffle a stacked deck at Westport. Missouri had been the nation's northernmost state to require separate schools for blacks and whites by state constitutional mandate, and Kansas City's schools had become so inferior and racially imbalanced that attorney Arthur Benson had filed a lawsuit in 1985, on behalf of black and white schoolchildren, to restructure the entire system. As a result a U.S. district court ruled—and the Supreme Court upheld in 1990—that Missouri and Kansas City had to tear down their "literally rotted" schools and construct (at a cost of $1.2 billion) the best facilities possible to eliminate the vestiges of segregation. The decision had made Benson either an unsung hero or a wacky do-gooder, depending on to whom you talked. Ultimately Benson hoped his plan would help create superior schools that white parents would send their children to by choice, thus reestablishing a racial balance in the classroom that would be reflective of Kansas City itself. (Kansas City is 67 percent white; its schools are 75 percent black.)

Before leaving Kansas City, I drove out to a tough part of town, past Trost Avenue, which unofficially separates the city into a black eastern district and a white western one. The homes were decrepit. The glances I received on the street where I parked were neither hostile nor welcoming and served merely to remind me I was an outsider. Brenda Alberti, a single parent, came to the door, broom in hand. She was a hard taskmaster who counseled her sons to stay away from girls and drugs and not skip classes. "I got seven children," she said, "and ain't none of them ever going to drop out of school." When her children misbehaved, she relied on advice her father had taught her. "Don't ever tell them they're bad. Just tell them they been mischievous. You tell them they're bad, they start believing it and that's no way to build your children up and make them feel good about themselves."

Mrs. Alberti's oldest son, sixteen-year-old Jermine, was president of Westport's student council and got home from school a few minutes after I had arrived. He was a bright-eyed young man who exuded a sense of being comfortable with himself. He wore jeans and a white T-shirt emblazoned with the word SLICK. He told me he had always intended to be the first in his family to get a college education. "But what Project Choice has done is let me set my goals higher than I could afford—a better university, a better career," he said. He had given up the idea of studying law and now looked toward a career in education, because, he said, he wanted to give something back to the community.

"This is a tough generation to grow up in," he said. "You can't even watch a movie on TV without hearing cuss words and seeing someone shoot someone. Even the cartoons have violence. There's drug language all over TV. And now there's cable and you get forty channels of this stuff. My mother tries to get me not to watch TV. I'm at an age, though, when I don't want to listen. I think I know more than my mother knows. We're all like that. But my generation hasn't been lost yet. We could still win. Maybe what it boils down to, what Project Choice is all about, is that even if you can't change everyone, you can change the ones who want to change."

He was right. Ewing Kauffman wasn't going to right the educational system, but he had made a difference. He had given young people in the barren landscape of the inner city an understanding of the power of attainable dreams. Although Jermine Alberti probably wouldn't have seen it quite this way, what Project Choice was really about was him—an escape from the ghetto, a chance to become a contributing member of society, the opportunity of hearing someone say, "You can do it." Project Choice might not have transformed Westport High into an Exeter of the Midwest, but if its safety net scooped up a few Jermine Albertis, the investment could turn out to be the best one Kauffman had made since he started packaging vitamins in his mother's basement.

Joker in the Deck

G rowing up in the fifties, as I did, seems marvelously uncomplicated compared with what the kids at Westport High faced, and I'm not sure I would have handled the nineties as a teenager very well. The Westport students were as exposed to as I had been protected from society's afflictions. They figured they had only one chance to succeed, while I had assumed any failure was manageable and was, in effect, only a building block that set you off in some new direction. I had been handed what they struggled to secure, and looking back to my own schooldays, I am reminded how the history we create for ourselves dogs us for a lifetime and never quite quits defining who we are. A personal story from another era helps make my point.

Ever since I left Phillips Exeter Academy in New Hampshire, suddenly and involuntarily, during my senior year in 1958, I have contributed to the school's alumni fund. But for a good part of that time, I used Exeter's annual plea for support merely to round off my checkbook to the nearest dollar. Thus if my account had, say, $725.18 in it, Exeter received a check for eighteen cents. And each spring an asterisk appeared by my name in the school's annual list of donors, identifying me as an alumnus who had given every year since graduation.

This came to mind after my trip to Kansas City while I browsed Exeter's directory of the all-boys class of 1958, published for one of our reunions several years ago. I skimmed through it, trying without much luck to match names and faces. The memories stirred neither nostalgia for the friends-turned-strangers nor affection for the school itself, perhaps because my accomplishments there had been dubious—frivolous, really, by Exeter's standards—and my vision of the campus had long been one of a place wrapped in New England winters, of dark brick buildings and drab dormitories, of white-haired Latin teachers, severe and humorless in ill-fitting three-piece suits. Exeter ("Oh, mother, stern yet tender . . . ," the school song went) was achievement oriented and, as I recall, generally insensitive to individual emotional needs. It gave you the tools to compete and excel but offered little of relevance on how to master the rest of life. Nonconformity and aimless fun were discouraged or punished, and on those counts alone, I was an outsider, for while my friends were sharpening their intellects, I was honing my skills as a sixteen-year-old bookie.

In the smoky cellar "butt room" of Peabody Hall, I ran poker and blackjack games, handled bets on major league baseball games and shot craps with a lot of kids who didn't know the difference between snake eyes and a natural. I knew the odds on drawing to an inside straight, understood the folly of splitting face cards and the wisdom of always backing Warren Spahn, except when he pitched against the Dodgers. I seldom lost. In a good month I took in a hundred dollars or so, which in those days was tantamount to being a prep-school millionaire. More important, gambling became my mark of identity. It reinforced the idea that we all must be good at something. I no longer shone, as I had at home, in scholarship or athletics, but with a deck of cards in my hands, I had few peers. Somewhere along the line I picked up the nickname The Joker, and my roommate, Warren Hoge, a New Yorker who understood the value of good times, became known as Big Julie, in honor, I believe, of the subway crapshooter in the movie *Guys and Dolls*. Our room was covered with posters of Frank Sinatra, of Fremont Street in downtown Las Vegas, of Hollywood starlets whose names escape me now, and we both knew the words to Frankie Laine's hit pop song of the day, "Moonlight Gambler." I kept my IOUs and my dice and cards in a small locked box on the top shelf of our bedroom closet.

The faculty ran Exeter like a POW camp and devoted an obsessive amount of energy to uncovering our secrets and keeping our spirits in check, so my extracurricular activities did not go unnoticed for long. On occasion teachers would conduct Eliot Ness–style raids on our room, bursting in unannounced in hopes of breaking up a game, an offense punishable by expulsion. But the janitor, a gentleman named Louie Keech, who rolled his own cigarettes and had taken a liking to Big Julie and me, always managed to hear of the pending raids and would give warning. When the door was flung open, we would be studying quietly at our desks and, feeling quite smug, would watch the enemy slink away, muttering apologies.

"Lamb, you lead a charmed life," one of my pals,

Benno Schmidt, used to say. I remember Ben as a stocky little guy with an ear-to-ear grin, a porcupine crew cut and a love for the New York Rangers hockey team. He was too smart to play cards with me, but his manner was mischievous and irreverent and that alone made him a member of the inner circle. I told him that if his grades improved, I'd hire him on one day as a bodyguard so he could amount to something.

The closest I ever came at Exeter to gaining scholastic recognition was in Mr. Broderick's American history class. I had operated there on the premise that one good joke was worth ten meaningless dates, and one day when I took my seat at the dark oak table around which students and teachers sat in Exeter classrooms, there was an egg in front of my place. It was balanced on a Life Saver and bore an inscription: "The Francis L. Broderick Memorial Egg is awarded once a decade to the student in History 3 who, though at a disadvantage mentally, works with unremitting lassitude and in the end gets nowhere." I was the recipient, and I was delighted. Had I been smarter I would have understood that the legend I had created was now controlling me. Mr. Broderick's sense of humor notwithstanding, faculty members considered me a liability, and my janitorial source said they were determined to outwit me, having decided The Joker and Phillips Exeter Academy were on a collision course.

On the night before Christmas vacation of my senior year, I returned to my room unexpectedly while the rest of the students were watching a movie in the gymnasium. I opened the door and went limp with fear. There on their hands and knees were two Latin teachers, a balding, six-foot-five giant named Galt and his crew-cut sidekick, Macomber. The former was peering under my bed, lifting the spread with two fingers as a cartoon figure would a woman's skirt; the latter pawed frantically through my desk drawers. At the sound of my key in the lock they looked up, speechless, wide-eyed. I had beaten them again; I was clean. My IOUs were secure in the little brown box, the pint of vodka I had brought back from Boston after Thanksgiving was in the bushes outside. There wasn't much either the hunter or the hunted could say to overcome the awkwardness of the encounter, and so, having forgotten why I had returned to my room in the first place, I backed unsurely out the door, shutting it quietly behind me.

My best friend, John Sherman, had quit Exeter before the start of the year, having decided he was too young for prison. (Before leaving he had written in my yearbook, "Davy, I haven't quite figured out your philosophy yet, but it's for damn sure you've got this school beat. . . . See you at Harvard.") Like myself, he had been a rebel, resentful of the loss of freedom and the abundance of mindless restrictions that were inherent to life in the academy. ("Lights out in there! It's ten o'clock.") As far as I could tell, John's only shortcoming was that he rooted for the Brooklyn Dodgers, not the Milwaukee Braves, and we used to argue over the merits of the teams from Exeter to New York City where, with fake IDs I had doctored up, we shared occasional vacation weekends, tanking up on gin and tonics at a Fifty-fourth Street saloon called the Las Vegas Club. We would put in a call to Warren, who lived nearby, and before the ice cubes in our drinks had even started to melt, he'd arrive in a taxi, three dates in tow.

Warren and I returned to Exeter on the train from Boston at the end of Christmas vacation, just one semester short of graduation and freedom. Galt, the Latin teacher, greeted us at the door of Peabody Hall. His face was crossed by a wisp of a smirk, and since that was the closest I had ever seen him come to smiling, my stomach took a nervous leap. The dean, he said, wanted to see us immediately. Dean Kesler did not normally work at 8:00 on Sunday nights, and I knew this was serious. Twenty minutes later I was fidgeting outside his office, waiting for the summons to attend my own execution. The door opened, and one of my gambling colleagues, John "Aces High" Stein, walked out, his own inquisition over. His face was ashen, and he whispered out of the side of his mouth as he passed by, not breaking stride, "He knows everything. He's got your box with the IOUs." Indeed he did. He had led a war party of faculty raiders into Warren's and my room over the Christmas holiday, scooped up the box and taken it to a locksmith to be opened. Today I suppose you could sue the dean for burglary, but in that era students learned early that they had no rights, no privacy, no recourse.

Dean Kesler was of medium height, broadshouldered, with a square jaw and thinning, slicked-back hair. My mouth went so dry when he beckoned me into the big stuffed chair in front of his desk that I couldn't swallow. "We know," he said flatly. "I know," I said, trying to steady my voice. Kesler paced back and forth, reading a list of my misdeeds from a yellow pad, and appeared to be enjoying himself. Every now and then, he paused to look at me and grimace. He'd shake his head in mock disbelief and carry on. If I had been a murderer, I could have pleaded for mercy. But Exeter tolerated no violation of its unwritten code that there were no rules at the academy until you broke one. Exeter, I was reminded, was not educating young men so they could go off to Harvard or Yale and become gamblers.

Two days after my interrogation by Dean Kesler, the faculty met and voted—unanimously, Louie Keech told me as he sat by the furnace, rolling a cigarette—to expel The Joker, Big Julie and Aces High. I was too terrified to tell my father what had happened, just five months before graduation, so I telephoned his secretary and asked her to relay the news. In retrospect, I think what most worried me at that point was the reaction of my father, an uncompromising man who believed in abiding by the rules and finishing what one started. The thought of leaving Exeter, though, seemed a pleasant adventure, a reprieve from endless, tiresome regulations (just having a radio in your room was cause, I seem to remember, for dismissal), bed checks, tea dances with partners held at arm's length, coats-and-ties-to-class, morning chapel sessions and Sunday church. (The student church monitor was on my payroll and always marked me present, though I didn't attend a service for two years.)

My father arrived at the campus in his black Buick sedan on a Saturday morning to collect me and my two suitcases. He met briefly with Dean Kesler and, I was relieved to learn, took an immediate dislike to him. "The Germans are always difficult," he said. Dad was indignant that Kesler advocated the use of secret-police tactics to gather evidence, and this helped sap the anger I had feared he would vent on me. Still, the ninety-minute drive back home to Boston was a long and silent one.

Being home was great fun. High school ended at 1:30 each afternoon, enabling me to get to Suffolk Downs in time for the third race. I became a client of Nate's, a bookie who sold newspapers in Brookline Village. I thought little about Exeter and even less about what I was going to do with my life. John Sherman and I met one snowy weekend in New York and gave Warren Hoge a call. An hour later the three of us were at the bar of the Las Vegas Club, trying to cozy up to the girls Warren had brought along. Life couldn't have been better. Not one of us doubted that whatever we wanted to do or be was within our grasp. Exeter had been only a side step. "I don't think my mother has forgiven you," Warren told me. "She says you're a bad influence."

Undoubtedly Mrs. Hoge was right. But I did take some satisfaction when in May, five months after my expulsion, my former Exeter classmates put me at the top of three categories in the senior class poll: "Most Likely to Succeed," "Done Exeter for Most" and "Operator." In looking at that poll in my scrapbook recently, I noticed several arcane divisions that I would have difficulty defining today: "Nego," "Poso," "Sarc," "Un-Co," "Thumper" and "Hacker." Someone named Elijah Lovejoy headed the "Nothing" category.

College took me to the University of Maine and the army to Okinawa. Later I wandered west, pulled inexorably to Las Vegas. It was probably my good fortune that I ended up with a job not in the Sands or the Desert Inn but on the *Las Vegas Review-Journal,* as a reporter. My golden luck on the tables faded quickly; in Vegas I was just another stiff ground down by the house odds. Other newspaper jobs and other cities—Oakland, San Francisco, Saigon, Denver, Los Angeles, New York, Sydney, Washington, Nairobi, Boston, Cairo—and several wars followed. Life no longer seemed a laughing matter. Doing well and staying happy was damn hard work.

It is ironic now to examine the reunion directory and see what has become of my former classmates. Most did precisely what Exeter expected of them: They went to an Ivy League university, stayed in the East, married, raised children, got jobs as CEOs, educators and government policymakers and did well. But it is interesting to note how the Exonian atmosphere that stifled me also seemed to have invigorated others, how a handful from the class of '58 became the nonconformists as adults that I had been as a youth. One former classmate from whom I never remember winning a dime is an astronomy professor and has written a book, *Playing Blackjack in Atlantic City.* Several are writers, two are actors. One is vice president of New York's Off-Track Betting Corporation, another operates bicycle tours in Vermont, a third is a farmer, a fourth a self-employed vintner in France. "I was going under with alcohol," wrote a resident of Cambridge, Massachusetts. "Been working on it since, a day at a time." He said that he and his male lover had been living together for five years, adding, "It's been a wonderful time learning what it is to be who we really are." Five members of the class of '58 are listed on the last page of the directory under "In Memoriam." I remember one of them quite well: Thinking of him, I see only the face of a blond, crew-cut teenager, and I cannot imagine what he would have looked like as an adult or how he could have been dead for all these years.

I am still in touch with the small band of friends I made at Exeter, and although we took divergent paths, we do not seem to have suffered greatly for our transgressions. Benno Schmidt became the twentieth president of Yale University. John Stein, a Washington, D.C., attorney, runs a nonprofit organization that aids the victims of crime. John Sherman presides over his country inn in Paris, Virginia, the purveyor of fine food and generous martinis. Warren Hoge is assistant managing editor of *The New York Times* and no longer goes by the name Big Julie. His mother wrote me a letter not long ago that began: "Dear David, Yes, I have finally forgiven you."

Not until the spring of 1981, after an absence of twenty-three years, did I return to Exeter. I was then a Nieman fellow at Harvard, on a year's sabbatical from the *Los Angeles Times* to study Third World politics, and driving one April day from Portland, Maine, to Boston, I noticed a sign on the interstate that said, EXETER 13 MILES. I took the turn. The New Hampshire countryside was soft and green, awakening from winter in a burst of flowers. I passed through small villages and came upon the town of Exeter. At the far end, near the river, was Phillips Exeter Academy. Its red-brick buildings were covered with ivy, and the bell tower of the Administration Office soared above the clusters of elms and maples. Not a stone or a walkway seemed to have been changed. The campus looked lovely in the glow of spring; I had to admit that.

The convertible top of my 1970 Buick was down. I parked by the quadrangle, watching a group of students sitting with open books under a maple tree, wondering if they thought of Exeter as a stockade, as had I, or if perhaps the great intellectual gifts the academy offered had given them a freedom I had never understood. The sunshine was filled with many ghosts, and the pains and joys of growing up came flooding back. In my rearview mirror I saw Donald Dunbar approach as though out of a mirage, two math books under his arm. He had been my favorite teacher, a warm and decent man, and, most important, a hard-core Milwaukee Braves fan. I recognized him first and called out. He walked over to the car, hand extended. "Look what the wind blew in," he said with a laugh. He had once seemed so much older than I; now he felt like my contemporary. Don—it being no longer necessary to address him as Mr. Dunbar—was headed for the weekly faculty meeting and insisted I join him.

The room where the faculty met had columns and paneled walls and heavy drapes, and I had only dared imagine as a student what a foreboding place it must be. Funny, even after all these years, I felt I had no right entering, that I was on one side, they on another. But contrary to my memories, the men (and, now, women too) seated on the rows of folding chairs looked reassuringly human. Graciously skipping the details, Don introduced me merely as a member of the '58 class and mentioned a few of my travels as a foreign correspondent. Several heads, now covered with gray hair or little hair, turned toward my seat in the back of the room. The first face I recognized was that of my English teacher, Mr. Heath, who had once returned one of my better compositions with the red-penciled comment: "Inane!" "Hey, Lamb," he said, as though he had seen me only yesterday, "I thought you'd be at the dog track today."

Later I was asked if I would talk to a journalism class of seniors, and I eagerly accepted. I started with a brief anecdote about being expelled and said the more experiences a writer has, particularly when he is young, the more material he has to call upon in his professional life. There wasn't much response; the students just kept scribbling notes. It was a good group, though, bright, wholesome, inquisitive, and the mixture—girls, boys, minorities—had, I was sure, made Exeter healthier and more representative than the WASPish, heavyhearted place I had known.

Don asked me to stay for dinner, but I said I had to get back to Boston. At the edge of town, I stopped at a small restaurant I had passed often as a student. I ordered a double martini and the special, scallops. It had been a pleasant day, and I lingered over dinner, reading the sports page of *The Boston Globe* and wondering if my life would have turned out differently had I played by the rules, instead of the odds, at Exeter. I smiled, remembering the question John Stein had asked when we met in Washington years after leaving the academy. "Now tell me the truth," he had said. "Did you cheat at blackjack?"

My thirty-fifth reunion is coming up next spring, but I doubt that I shall attend. Perhaps it is just as well, now that I am a more generous contributor to the alumni fund, to leave my discoveries of the past with that brief encounter on a warm April day. It has been a long time since I've done any serious gambling, and if I returned to the reunion, I would be chagrined to admit I had forgotten everything Exeter had taught me: I'm not even sure anymore whether three of a kind beats a straight or whether it's the other way around.

Acknowledgments

I'm fortunate that my best editor is my best friend—
and both happen to be my wife, Sandy Northrop. Her
ability to rein in my verbosity and shake loose some
buried thoughts was invaluable in writing this book. Without her love and support, it would have been a lonely
journey.

My editors at the *Los Angeles Times*—Shelby Coffey,
George Cotliar, and Mike Miller—have given me extraordinary freedom to search out an America that few others
write about. I am indebted to them, as I am to Tim Rutten,
who had endless story ideas that are incorporated in these
pages, and Stan Burroway, who wrestled with my prose,
and always with good humor.

Ed Cray first suggested I write this book and helped
give it form. Irwin Rosten worked with the final manu-
script, flagging errors and offering suggestions that were
incorporated into the text. At Times Books, my editors
Peter Osnos and Steve Wasserman turned a kernel of an
idea into a book and became literary partners I trusted
and valued. My literary agent, Carl Brandt, also was a
source of greatly appreciated encouragement. John and
Roma Sherman found me a room in their home with a
view of the Virginia hills and a nightly table at their Ashby

Inn down the road. It was the finest writer's refuge I could imagine. Thanks, friends.

To the people all over America who shared their thoughts and kindness and hospitality, I say thank you. And to that old gang of mine who shared the days growing up in Boston—Bob MacPhail, Ray Brown, Peter Norstrand, Tom Hawkridge, Helen and Meritt Streider—I say, Don't forget all we learned at the saloon called Danny's. The drummer there had one ear, the alcoholic trombonist cried between sets, the bartender kept a loaded .38 behind the bottles of whiskey. And life was a hell of a fun adventure.

ABOUT THE AUTHOR

DAVID LAMB has traveled the world as a correspondent for the *Los Angeles Times* and United Press International, and has lived in Egypt, Kenya, Australia, Vietnam and a dozen American cities. He is the author of three highly acclaimed previous books and is an eight-time Pulitzer Prize nominee. He currently covers the United States from the *Times*'s Washington, D.C., bureau.